THE CODE ECONOMY

THE CODE
ECONOMY

A FORTY-THOUSAND-YEAR HISTORY

PHILIP E. AUERSWALD

OXFORD
UNIVERSITY PRESS

OXFORD
UNIVERSITY PRESS

Oxford University Press is a department of the University of Oxford. It furthers
the University's objective of excellence in research, scholarship, and education
by publishing worldwide. Oxford is a registered trade mark of Oxford University
Press in the UK and certain other countries.

Published in the United States of America by Oxford University Press
198 Madison Avenue, New York, NY 10016, United States of America.

Library of Congress Cataloging-in-Publication Data
Names: Auerswald, Philip E., author.
Title: The code economy : a forty-thousand-year history / Philip E. Auerswald.
Description: New York, NY : Oxford University Press, [2017]
Identifiers: LCCN 2016017260 | ISBN 9780190226763 (hardcover) | ISBN 9780190226787 (epub)
Subjects: LCSH: Information technology—Economic aspects. | Economics.
Classification: LCC HC79.I55 A896 2017 | DDC 303.48/3309—dc23 LC record available
at https://lccn.loc.gov/2016017260

1 3 5 7 9 8 6 4 2
Printed by Edwards Brothers Malloy, United States of America

CONTENTS

INTRODUCTION

Technology = Recipes

The ingredients for bread were always the same: flour, yeast, water, and salt. But the difficulty was that there were ten thousand ways of combining these simple elements. Every little detail was important, we learned: the freshness of the yeast, the type of flour, the time of rising, the way one kneaded the dough, the amount of heat and moisture in the oven, even the weather.

—Julia Child, *My Life in France*, 2006

THE CODE ECONOMY describes the evolution of human productive activity from simplicity to complexity over the span of more than 40,000 years. I call this evolutionary process the advance of code.

Our modern conception of code—programs run on digital computers—is just the latest incarnation; code is in fact much older. How, one might ask, have we humans managed to get where we are today despite our abundant failings, including wars, famines, and a demonstrably meager capacity for society-wide planning and coordination? We have survived, and thrived, by developing productive activities that evolve into regular routines and standardized platforms—which is to say we have survived, and thrived, by creating and advancing code.

How is this process evolutionary? In the economy, raw materials are like diatoms, amoebas, or plankton in the biological food chain, whereas standardized platforms are like complex multicellular organisms. As code advances, higher-level technologies feed on more fundamental technologies in much the same way more complex organisms feed on simpler organisms in the food chain. Platforms provide essential structures for the code economy: The infrastructure that underlies a city is a standardized platform. Written language is a standardized platform. The Internet is a standardized platform.

Human civilization has thus advanced through the creation and improvement of code, which is built on layers of platforms that accumulate like the pipes and tunnels that lie below a great city.

THE MICROECONOMICS YOU learned in college was generally limited to the "what" of production: what goes in and what comes out. This book is about the "how": how inputs are combined to yield outputs. In other words, it is about how ideas become things.

Here's an example.

You are baking chocolate chip cookies. You have arrayed before you the required ingredients: 1 cup of butter, 1 cup of white sugar, 1 cup of brown sugar, 2 eggs, 1 teaspoon of baking soda, 2 teaspoons of hot water, 1/2 teaspoon of salt, and (importantly) 2 cups of chocolate chips. These items, 30 minutes of your own labor, and access to the oven, bowls, and other durable equipment you employ constitute the inputs into your production process. The work will yield 24 servings of two cookies each, which constitute your output.

From the perspective of standard microeconomic theory, we have fully described the production of chocolate chip cookies: capital, labor, and raw material inputs combine to yield an output. However, as is obvious to even the least experienced baker, simply listing ingredients and stating the output does not constitute a complete recipe. Something important is missing: the directions—*how* you make the cookies.

The "how" goes by many names: recipes, processes, routines, algorithms, and programs, among others. While I will employ each of these names at different points in this book, I use the word "code" throughout to refer to the how of production.

The essential idea is that the "what" of output cannot exist without the "how" by which it is produced. In other words, production is not possible without process. These processes evolve according to both their own logic and the path of human decision-making. This has always been true: the economy has always been at least as much about the evolution of code as about the choice of inputs and the consumption of output. Code economics is as old as the first recipe and the earliest systematically produced tool, and it is as integral to the unfolding of human history as every king, queen, general, prime minister, and president combined.

We cannot understand the dynamics of the economy—its past or its future—without understanding code.

THE WORD "CODE" derives from the Latin *codex,* meaning "a system of laws." Today code is used in various distinct contexts—computer code, genetic code, cryptologic code (i.e., ciphers such as Morse code), ethical code, building code, and so forth—each of which has a common feature: it contains instructions that require a process in order to reach its intended end. Computer code requires the action of a compiler, energy, and (usually) inputs in order to become a useful program. Genetic code requires expression through the selective action of enzymes to produce proteins or RNA, ultimately producing a unique phenotype. Cryptologic code requires decryption in order to be converted into a usable message. Ethical codes, legal codes, and building codes all require processes of interpretation in order to be converted into action.

Code can include instructions we follow consciously and purposively, and those we follow unconsciously and intuitively. Code can be understood tacitly, it can be written, or it can be embedded in hardware.[1] Code can be stored, transmitted, received, and modified. Code captures the algorithmic nature of instructions as well as their evolutionary character.

As you read this book, you will see that code as I intend it incorporates elements of computer code, genetic code, cryptologic code, and other forms as well. But you will also see that it stands alone as its own concept—the instructions and algorithms that guide production in the economy—for which no adequate word yet exists.

To convey the intuitive meaning of the concept I intend to communicate with the word "code," as well as its breadth, I use two specific and carefully selected words interchangeably with code: recipe and technology.

My motivation for using "recipe" is evident from the chocolate chip cookie example I gave above. However, I do not intend the culinary recipe to be only a metaphor for the how of production; the recipe is, rather, the most literal and direct example of code as I use the word. There has been code in production since the first time a human being prepared food. Indeed, if we restrict "production" to mean the preparation of food for consumption, we can start by imagining every single meal consumed by the roughly one hundred billion people who have lived since we human beings cooked our first meal about 400,000 years ago: approximately four quadrillion prepared meals have been consumed throughout human history. Each of those meals was in fact (not in theory) associated with some method by which the meal was produced—which is to say, the code for producing that meal. For most of the first 400,000 years that humans prepared meals we were not a numerous species and the code we used to prepare meals was relatively rudimentary. Therefore, the early volumes of an imaginary "Global Compendium of All Recipes" dedicated to prehistory would be quite slim. However, in the past two millennia, and particularly in the past two hundred years, both the size of the human population and the complexity of our culinary preparations have taken off. As a result, the size of the volumes in our "Global Compendium" would have grown exponentially.

Let's now go beyond the preparation of meals to consider the code involved in every good or service we humans have ever produced, for our own use or for exchange, from the earliest obsidian spear point to the most recent smartphone. When I talk about the evolution of code, I am referring to the contents of the global compendium containing all of those production recipes. They are numerous.

This brings me to the second word I use interchangeably with code: technology. If we have technological gizmos in mind, then the leap from recipes to technology seems big. However, the leap seems smaller if we consider the Greek origin of the word "technology." The first half derives from *techné* (τέχνη), which signifies "art, craft, or trade." The second half derives from the word *logos* (λόγος), which signifies an "ordered account" or "reasoned discourse."[2] Thus technology literally means "an ordered account of art, craft, or trade"—in other words, broadly speaking, a recipe.

Substantial anthropological research suggests that culinary recipes were the earliest and among the most transformative technologies employed by humans. We have understood for some time that cooking accelerated human evolution by substantially increasing the nutrients absorbed in the stomach and small intestine.[3] However, recent research suggests that human ancestors were using recipes to prepare food to dramatic effect as early as two million years ago—even before we learned to control fire and began cooking, which occurred about 400,000 years ago. Simply slicing meats and pounding tubers (such as yams), as was done by our earliest ancestors, turns out to yield digestive advantages that are comparable to those realized by cooking.[4] Cooked or raw, increased nutrient intake enabled us to evolve smaller teeth and chewing muscles and even a smaller gut than our ancestors or primate cousins. These evolutionary adaptations in turn supported the development of humans' larger, energy-hungry brain.

The first recipes—code at work—literally made humans what we are today.

FAST FORWARD TO the present, where much of the latest research seems to suggest that the advance of code is no longer a boon to human well-being but, rather, a threat.

In the past two decades in particular, a proliferation of published works has warned of the deeply adverse social impact we can expect from the continued advance of code. Futurist Jeremy Rifkin's 1995 book, *The End of Work: The Decline of the Global Labor Force and the Dawn of the Post-Market Era,* set forth one position in what might be termed "The Great Man-vs-Machine Debate." Rifkin argues that we should be deeply concerned about the prospect of a world without jobs, as machines empowered by code continue their advance. "We are entering into a new period in history—one in which machines increasingly replace human beings in the process of making and moving goods and providing services," he cautions.[5] "A near-workerless world is fast approaching."[6] Others who have advanced more nuanced forms of the same basic argument include Erik Brynjolfsson and Andrew McAfee, Tyler Cowen, and Martin Ford. From an economic standpoint, their argument is straightforward:

1. The power of code is growing at an exponential rate.
2. Code nearly perfectly substitutes for human capabilities.
3. Therefore the (relative) power of human capabilities is shrinking at an exponential rate.

If Rifkin and others are correct, we should be deeply worried about the impending adverse consequences of the advance of code.

In sharp contrast, Ray Kurzweil argues in his 2005 bestseller, *The Singularity Is Near: When Humans Transcend Biology,* that the exponentially increasing power of code—particularly, although not exclusively, digital computing—will trigger an epochal discontinuity in the human experience. From an economic standpoint, Kurzweil's argument is comparably direct:

1. The power of code is growing at an exponential rate.
2. Code nearly perfectly complements human capabilities.
3. Therefore the (absolute) power of human capabilities is growing at an exponential rate.

Like many others, Kurzweil argues that "only technology can provide the scale to overcome the challenges with which human society has struggled for generations."[7] However, he goes further, tracing the arc of code-enabled progress into the immediate future to sketch the outlines of what he calls "The Singularity," which "will result from the merger of the vast knowledge embedded in our brains with the vastly greater capacity, speed, and knowledge-sharing ability of our technology, [enabling] our human-machine civilization to transcend the human brain's limitations of a mere hundred trillion extremely slow connections."[8] When it comes to algorithmically empowered robots taking our jobs, Kurzweil's prescription is simple: if you can't beat 'em, join 'em—maybe even literally, in cyborg fashion.

The Great Man-vs-Machine Debate is not new, of course. Over the past four centuries it has engaged some of the greatest minds in the history of ideas: Gottfried Wilhelm Leibniz, David Ricardo, Ada Lovelace, John Maynard Keynes, Norbert Weiner, and Herbert Simon are notable among them. (I will offer more about these pioneers of code economics—none of them, with the possible exception of Keynes, household names today—as the book proceeds.) However, over the past hundred years at least, the dynamics of the debate have settled into a fairly straightforward rhythm: One side cites historical evidence to demonstrate that technology-enabled disruptions in the past have always ended up boosting both employment and output so we have little to fear about the future. The other side counters with some variant of "This time it is different," and thus deep concern about the adverse consequences of the advance of code is warranted.

As the Great Man-vs-Machine Debate raged in the 1930s, it involved not just Keynes but other greats of the economics profession, including Joseph Schumpeter, John Hicks, and Paul Douglas. It surged again in the 1950s and 1960s, prompting scores of congressional hearings and the appointment of multiple presidential commissions. And it is raging again today, prompted by a combination of macroeconomic circumstances (concern over the stagnation of wages in particular, which goes back decades) and new scholarship.[9] Each time the debate has recurred, the same intellectual contest has taken place: "History proves we'll be fine" versus "This time is different."

So which is it to be for humanity? Kurzweil's bright Singularity or Rifkin's dystopian World without Work? Without pretending to be able to predict the future but extrapolating from trends that go back for centuries, if not millennia, I argue in this book that a third line of argument is possible:

1. The power of code is growing at an exponential rate.
2. Code only partially substitutes for human capabilities.
3. Therefore the (relative) power of human capabilities is shrinking at an exponential rate in those categories of work that can be performed by computers, but not in others.

In other words, where Kurzweil talks about an impending code-induced Singularity, the reality looks much more like one code-induced bifurcation—the division of labor between humans and machines—after another.

The answer to the question, "Is there anything that humans can do better than digital computers?" turns out to be fairly simple: humans are better at being human.

THE THREE MAIN ideas of the book are as follows:

1. Creating and improving code is a key part of what we human beings do. It's how we invent the future by building on the past.

2. The evolution of the economy is driven by the advance of code. Understanding this advance is therefore fundamental to economics, and to much of human history.

3. When we create and advance code we don't just invent new toys, we produce new forms of meaning, new experiences, and new ways of making our way in the world.

In advancing these three ideas, I am seeking to address an imbalance in the way economics is broadly understood and taught. Economics as conveyed in undergraduate courses and popular accounts tends to focus on choice and consumption, to the neglect of code and production.[10] Choice and consumption are of course important dimensions of economic experience, but so are code and production. After all, we humans are producers at least as much as we are consumers.

The book is organized as follows. In Part One, "The Advance of Code," I describe the origin of code, beginning with the production of obsidian axes and continuing through the development of writing, the emergence of culinary recipes, and the evolution of cities. I then set up the discussion relating to the Great Man-vs-Machine Debate that appears later in the book by describing how the "job," as it is currently understood, is a recent historical creation—one that rests on layers of institutions that have taken millennia to accumulate. I conclude Part One by describing the history of digital computing as the latest chapter in the evolution of code, emphasizing the profound impact it has had, and is having, on the structure of institutions and thus on the definition of jobs.

In Part Two, "Code Economics," I shift to describing the deep but today largely ignored history of inquiry in the field of economics that is focused on code and production. I convey this history via the three core mechanisms for the advance of code: learning, evolution, and the layering of complexity through the development of platforms. This story begins with economists' first attempts to understand the net impact mechanization had on human society during the Industrial Revolution. As the processes of production and the structure of the economy both became more complex in the early twentieth century, social scientists began to study how firms learn and develop. This inquiry developed into the fields of operations research and management science. Still later, economists came to appreciate how the encoding of widely agreed upon practices into standardized platforms supports the evolution of economic activity from simplicity toward complexity.

In Part Three, "The Human Advantage," I explore the relationship between the advance of code and the human experience. This part of the book directly addresses the contention that the continued advance of code will adversely impact human well-being—either overall or by exacerbating social inequality. Referring to a historical record spanning centuries, I argue that the advance of code has consistently tended to humanize work and, in so doing, to generate broadly shared benefits.

Of course, that the advance of code will continue to generate broadly shared benefits is hardly assured. There are things we can and must do to ensure that the future impacts of the advance of code are as advantageous as they have been in the past. The good news is that we've been adapting to, and benefiting from, the advance of code for more than 40,000 years. By understanding the momentum of history we can use it in our favor.

PART ONE

THE ADVANCE OF CODE

I

Jobs

Divide and Coordinate

There is scarcely anything of greater moment in the economy of a nation than the proper division of labor.

—Alexander Hamilton, *Report on the Subject of Manufactures*, 1791

LIFE WAS SIMPLER in the Stone Age.

Consider production. By examining the characteristics of archeological finds such as stone tools, skeletal remains, and other physical artifacts,[1] anthropologists are able to trace the increasing complexity of the tasks performed by humans over the millennia of our existence. The earliest hominins had about the same short-term memory as a modern-day chimpanzee, which is to say that they could keep track of only two operations at a time.[2] Fortunately for us humans, we got better. From the first use of found objects as tools roughly 2.5 million years ago (please refer to the opening sequence of *2001: A Space Odyssey*), humans progressed to creating tools and then to deliberately improving those tools for specific purposes. Our methods for creating tools gradually became more sophisticated, until we were using the tools we created to produce other tools in a repetitive and predictable manner. These processes for creating stone tools were among humanity's first production algorithms—that is, the earliest code (see figure 1.1).[3] They appeared almost simultaneously in human communities in most parts of the world around 40,000 BCE.[4]

"Humans, too, probably began using stones to hammer," economist James Bessen writes in his book *Learning by Doing: The Real Connection between Innovation, Wages, and Wealth*, "but by the Neolithic period,

Dimension 0: the point

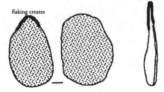

flaking creates

First Dimension: the line

The flaking sequence

Second Dimension: the surface

The flaking sequence

Third Dimension: the volume

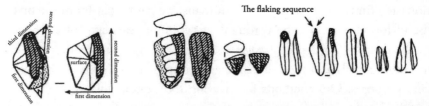

The flaking sequence

FIGURE 1.1 Demands on Short-Term Working Memory in the Production of an Obsidian Axe. This figure and accompanying caption from Read and van der Leeuw (2015) relate the code employed in the production of an obsidian axe to the cognitive capacity required to execute that code: "Short-term memory refers to the ability to hold a small amount of information in an active, available state for a short period of time. The size of short-term memory affects the number of different sources, kinds, or bits of information that can be held and processed together simultaneously in working memory when carrying out a particular train of thought or course of action. We can relate the concepts invoked in the production of stone tools to the number

they had developed scores of different stone tools—axes, adzes, chisels, arrowheads, burins, and other types—each optimized to solve a specific problem. Moreover, they made these tools using optimized production techniques—stone knapping techniques that archaeology graduate students have a hard time mastering after a semester of trial and error . . . What really distinguished the early humans from other species was not conceiving technology ideas, but perfecting those ideas to deal with the complex natural environment."[5]

By the Neolithic period, humans had developed the ability to keep seven or eight operations in mind simultaneously.[6] Believe it or not, that's pretty much as far as we got in terms of individual cognitive capacity. As a rule, humans today can do no better than our Neolithic ancestors.[7] However, whereas individual human cognitive ability seems to have plateaued roughly around 40,000 BCE, the progress of human social development began to accelerate dramatically. Why?

We invented society.

Rather than continue to evolve our capacity to perform tasks individually, we humans began to develop something that turned out to be even more powerful: our capacity to solve tasks in groups.[8] As biologist E. O. Wilson put it in his recent book, *The Social Conquest of Earth*:

> During this critical period of human prehistory, 60,000 to 50,000 years ago, the growth of cultures . . . was slow, then faster and still faster and yet again faster, in the manner of chemical and

---

of dimensions involved and thereby to the size of short-term working memory (STWM) required for the production of the kind of stone tools that exemplify each stage in hominin evolution. For humans to attain the capacity to conceive of a three-dimensional object (a pebble or stone tool) in three dimensions takes around 2 million years. (a) Taking a flake off at the tip of the pebble is an action in 0 dimensions, and takes short-term working memory 3; (b) successively taking off several adjacent flakes creates a (1-dimensional) line, and requires STWM 4; (c) stretching the line until it meets itself defines a surface by drawing a line around it and represents STWM 4.5; distinguishing between that line and the surface it encloses implies fully working in two dimensions, and requires STWM 5; (d) preparing two sides in order to remove the flakes from the third side testifies to a three-dimensional conceptualization of the pebble, and requires STWM 7."

Source: Read and van der Leeuw (2015), van der Leeuw (2000).

Reprinted with permission of the author.

biological autocatalysis. The reason is that the adoption of any one innovation made adoption of certain others possible, which then, if useful, were more likely to spread. Bands and communities of bands with better combinations of cultural innovations became more productive and better equipped for competition and war. Their rivals either copied them or else were displaced and their territories taken. Thus group selection drove the evolution of culture.[9]

Clan groups—and, over time, clusters of clan groups—used initial advances in code as building blocks that they combined into further advances in code.

By about 10,000 BCE, humans had formed the first villages, which anthropologist Sander van der Leeuw characterizes as "aggregate clusters that solved the most frequently encountered of life's challenges."[10] Villages were the precursors of modern-day business firms in that they were durable associations built around routines.[11] As the influential nineteenth-century economist Herbert Spencer noted over a hundred and fifty years ago, the advance of code at the village level through the creation of new technological combinations set into motion the evolution from simplicity to complexity that has resulted in the modern economy (see Text Box 1.1).

It was in the village, then, that code began to evolve.

GRANTED, IF ASSESSED in terms of the lived experience of most human beings, the evolution of code got off to a slow start. As Thomas Hobbes put it in his 1689 masterwork, *Leviathan,* life for most of history until that point was not only "nasty, brutish, and short," but also, and more to the point, "men lived on Gross Experience. There was no method; that is to say, no sowing nor planting of knowledge by itself, apart from the weeds and common plants of error and conjecture."[12]

The first recorded use of the word "job" in the sense of work done for pay is reported by the *Oxford English Dictionary* to have occurred in 1557, a little more than a century before Hobbes wrote *Leviathan.* In *Documents Relating to the Revels at Court in the Time of King Edward VI and Queen Mary,* Albert Feuillerat employs the phrase "jobbe of work" to signify a piece of work.[13] This usage likely stems from the word "gobbe," which (then as today) signifies a mass or a lump.

Text Box 1.1 **Herbert Spencer and the Progression from Simplicity to Complexity**

From the time Charles Darwin's *The Origin of Species* (1859) was published until at least the start of World War I, and possibly beyond, the theory of evolution was the Great Idea that drove intellectual discourse. The social theorist of greatest fame during that era was not Adam Smith or David Ricardo but Herbert Spencer, the first code economist.[14]

Spencer was a towering intellectual figure whose fame rose as quickly as it fell. Among his claims to celebrity is having coined the expression "survival of the fittest." His project was nothing less than a unified theory of the physical and natural sciences. His thesis, developed in a hugely influential 1857 essay titled "Progress: Its Law and Cause," was simple: "Whether it be in the development of the Earth, in the development of Life upon its surface, in the development of Society, of Government, of Manufactures, of Commerce, of Language, Literature, Science, Art, this same evolution of the simple into the complex, through successive differentiations, holds throughout" (p. 3).

According to Herbert Spencer, what set in motion the process of differentiation that led to the complexity of a modern economy was the uneven distribution of talents within the populations of the earliest villages:

> Where there grows up a fixed and multiplying community, these differentiations [among people] become permanent, and increase with each generation. A larger population, involving a greater demand for every commodity, intensifies the functional activity of each specialized person or class; and this renders the specialization more definite where it already exists, and establishes it where it is nascent. (p. 52)

Rather than putting unmanageable pressure on a finite resource base, as the Reverend Thomas Malthus had famously argued, growing populations in prospering villages prompted increased specialization, which in term prompted a greater capacity to produce.

As prehistoric villages developed further, Spencer reasoned, a new phenomenon arose: competition among producers. Competition prompted workers to seek new methods and materials actively. The creation of particularly successful new methods resulted in the advent of new occupations:

> Competing workers, ever aiming to produce improved articles, occasionally discover better processes or raw materials. In weapons and cutting tools, the substitution of bronze for stone entails upon him who first makes it a great increase of demand—so great an increase that he presently finds all his time occupied in making the bronze for the articles he sells, and is obliged to depute the fashioning of these to others: and, eventually, the making of bronze, thus gradually differentiated from a pre-existing occupation, becomes an occupation by itself. (p. 52)

The creation of one new occupation prompted a sequence of further differentiations in the economy:

> But now mark the ramified changes which follow this change. Bronze soon replaces stone, not only in the articles it was first used for, but in many others—in arms, tools, and utensils of various kinds; and so affects the manufacture of these things. Further, it affects the processes which these utensils subserve, and the resulting products—modifies buildings, carvings, dress, personal decorations. Yet again, it sets going sundry manufactures which were before impossible, from lack of a material fit for the requisite tools. And all these changes react on the people—increase their manipulative skill, their intelligence, their comfort—refine their habits and tastes. (p. 53)

Advancing directly from prehistory to the technological innovations of the mid-nineteenth century (that is, the time of his writing), Spencer went on to detail exhaustively the cascading sequence of economic differentiations induced by the introduction of the railway.

With each introduction of a fundamentally new technology and its associated occupations, the outcome as he saw it was the same:

> The social organism has been rendered more heterogeneous in virtue of the many new occupations introduced, and the many old ones further specialized; prices in every place have been altered; each trader has, more or less, modified his way of doing business; and almost every person has been affected in his actions, thoughts, emotions. (p. 55)

Etymologically speaking, then, the "job" was originally a lump.

The advent of the "jobbe" as a lump of work was to the evolution of modern society something like what the first single-celled organism was to the evolution of life. The "jobbe" contrasted with the obligation to perform labor continuously and without clearly defined roles—slavery, serfdom, indentured servitude, or even apprenticeship—as had been the norm through human history.

In the medieval European world, work was an obligation subject to enforcement by feudal lords; jobs and unemployment as we understand them today did not yet exist. As the great Austrian economist Joseph Schumpeter notes in his vast *History of Economic Analysis*, "In principle, medieval society provided a berth for everyone whom it recognized as a member: its structural design excluded unemployment and destitution . . . In normal times unemployment was quantitatively unimportant and confined to individuals who had broken loose from their environment or had been cast off by it and who in consequence had become beggars, vagrants, and highwaymen." As a result, "mass unemployment, definitely unconnected with any personal shortcomings of the unemployed, was unknown to the Middle Ages except as a consequence of social catastrophes such as devastation by wars, feuds, and plagues."[15]

When, in the aftermath of the bubonic plague, labor suddenly was in short supply, European monarchs responded by placing restrictions on the mobility of workers. The Ordinance of Labourers, issued by King Edward III of England on June 18, 1349, included the following mandate: "Every man or woman, free or unfree, aged sixty years or younger and without land or a craft sufficient for self-support, must serve whoever required his labour. Furthermore, the wages of servants, labourers, and artisans must be no higher than had been customary in a given locality in 1346 or common years thereabouts."[16] Parliament subsequently passed the Statute of Laborers, which was intended to address the ongoing "malice of servants, who were idle and refused to serve after the pestilence." Whereas the Ordinance had set only vague limits on wages, the Statute went further, specifying specific rates for a range of occupations on the basis of piecework or a day's work. While intended to constrain workers' ability to negotiate higher pay with their baronial employers, these statutes in effect affirmed the existence of a labor market. In its way, then, the Black Death helped to institutionalize wage work.

While medieval workers were subject to the whims of monarchical authority when it came to the imposition of wage controls, in another sense they had a great deal more autonomy than most workers today. Although they may have belonged to guilds that set guidelines for the "how" of production, the medieval baker, blacksmith, and milliner were masters of their own trade. The guilds acted at a distance, so although medieval artisans may have been circumscribed by tradition and culture, they did not have to conform to any manual or set of standard operating procedures, follow prescribed recipes, or endure having anything like a "boss" looking over their shoulders at work.

THE JOB AS we know it today is a relatively recent product of the coevolution of code and work, which in turn began when humans perfected specialization.

Plato wrote in *The Republic* circa 360 BCE, "All things are produced more plentifully and easily and of a better quality when one man does one thing which is natural to him and does it at the right time, and leaves other things." Human workers therefore initially specialized in trades, which were defined at the individual level and naturally evolved into institutions defined around specific social needs: bakeries, smithies, taverns, and the like. Change was so slow in early society relative to the human lifespan that people came to be named for their occupations: Baker, Barker, Cooper, Cramer, Eisenhower (which means "iron worker"), Shoemaker, Smith, Tyler, Wagner, Wright, and many more.

All these occupations became family names that have been passed on through the generations as enduring markers of past societal stasis.

These institutions became more complex over the centuries as "labor" was broken down into more specific tasks.[17] Famously using a pin factory as an example, Adam Smith opens *The Wealth of Nations* by highlighting the benefits of specialization by task: "The greatest improvement in the productive powers of labour, and the greater part of the skill, dexterity, and judgment with which it is any where directed, or applied, seem to have been the effects of the division of labour."[18] Fifteen years later, Alexander Hamilton stressed the importance of the division of labor in the *Report on Manufacturers,* which was a major salvo in his debate with Thomas Jefferson over the relative value of manufacturing versus agriculture to the economic future of the newly founded United States of America. As quoted at the start of this chapter, Hamilton wrote that "there is scarcely anything of greater moment in the economy of a nation than the proper division of labor."[19]

In the past two hundred years, the complexity of human economic organization has increased by orders of magnitude. Death rates began to fall rapidly in the middle of the nineteenth century, due to a combination of increased agricultural output, improved hygiene, and the beginning of better medical practices—all different dimensions of the advance of code. Accordingly, the population grew. As newly invented machines and improved practices (again, read "code") reduced the need for manual labor in agriculture, urbanization rapidly intensified and humanity's cognitive surplus increased. Greater numbers of people living in greater density than ever before accelerated the advance of code.[20]

By the twentieth century, the continued advance of code necessitated the creation of government bureaucracies and large corporations that employed vast numbers of people. These organizations executed code of sufficient complexity that it was beyond the capacity of any single individual to master. To structure work within such large, complex organizations, humans began to define occupations in terms of specific task-defined roles rather than by artisanal trades, as had been the case throughout human history. We came to call these task-defined roles "jobs." Jobs were very different from the trades, in that they were designed to optimize institutional operations rather than to perpetuate and advance inherited, mostly unwritten production practices. In this way, the artisans, serfs, and merchants who defined the medieval agrarian economy were replaced by an industrial economic order dominated by workers who executed the subroutines of complex algorithms performed by large corporate entities. Thus the "Organization Man" came into existence.

Two broad categories of epochal change occurred as a result of the evolution of the economy from simplicity to complexity, which I refer to as the advance of code.

One is that our capabilities grew, individually and collectively. For instance, we can now fly. (I am encoding these very words while moving far above the clouds at a speed many times faster than the fastest chariot, employing a highly evolved abacus known as a computer, whose history and operation I will describe later in the book. This is an impressive achievement.) We can carry on conversations with people anywhere around the world. By consuming small quantities of a serum made from mold we can defeat microscopic "armies" that attack our bodies. We can use eggs to make a delicious sauce known as mayonnaise (see chapter seven). But that's not all.

The second epochal change related to the advance of code is that we have, to an increasing degree, ceded to other people—and to code itself—authority and autonomy, which for millennia we had kept unto ourselves and our immediate tribal groups as uncodified cultural norms. We now obey written laws and rules. We follow instructions. We respect elected officials (in our actions if not always our thoughts) and the elected officials respect electoral processes (in their thoughts if not always their actions). We do our jobs. We no longer have our own wells or, in most cases, our own gardens. Most of us (myself included) have forgotten how to hunt. We depend for our survival on an ever-growing array of services provided by others, who in turn are ceding an increasing amount of their authority to code.[21]

We are at once increasingly empowered and increasingly disempowered, increasingly vulnerable and increasingly omnipotent—all due to the advance of code.

The effects of the advance of code reflect this duality. In the aggregate, the advance of code over the millennia has had some astonishingly positive consequences: Our largest villages sustain far more people today than were alive on the entire planet 40,000 years ago. We call these largest villages "cities." Babies born today nearly anywhere in the world can expect to live twice as long as babies born in the same places only two hundred years ago. At any time and in almost any place, we have access to vast libraries of accumulated knowledge and powers of computation many orders of magnitude greater than those possessed by the totality of humanity a century ago—and all are literally accessible in the palms of our hands.

The advance of code has also had negative consequences. Perhaps most significant is that we fall well short of fully expressing our humanity through code. When code overrides morality—"I was just following orders"—terrible consequences can result. Furthermore, the operation of code does not necessarily, or in all places, lead to more equitable outcomes than its predecessor in the organization of human society—brute force. In the code economy, those who author, store, and enforce code by definition have more power than those who execute code; those who execute code in turn generally fare better than those who are excluded from code. For this reason, people who have the opportunity and the capacity to keep up with the advance of code have a greater opportunity to create and contribute to society than those who do not.[22]

For better and for worse, humanity and code are coevolving. What we call "the economy" necessarily encompasses both.

While Hobbes may have underestimated the power of oral traditions to store and convey code, it is true that human societies did not develop methods to create and assess code systematically until the Age of Enlightenment in Europe. Long after the advent of villages, human communities remained relatively small and sparsely distributed, which meant there were few people around to try out new ways of doing things and few opportunities to share those new methods. And although writing was invented more than five thousand years ago, a majority of the world's people have been literate only for the past century.

As a consequence, code advanced slowly. For 14,000 years after the first villages formed, the human lifespan barely budged and the global population grew at a glacial pace: from the first century BCE to the late eighteenth century, both economic and population growth rates were well below 0.1 percent per year.

Perhaps counterintuitively, these millennia of relative stasis in the human experience produced many of humanity's greatest creations: writing, decimal numbers, algebra, water mills, the astrolabe, eyeglasses, mechanical clocks, the printing press, multimasted ships, and bills of exchange, to name but a few. Each of these advances in technology was accompanied by an advance in code, the evolution of which progressively expanded human capabilities. These advances also set the stage for the rapid improvement in the human condition that we have seen over the past two centuries.

In the next chapter I focus on two human creations that arguably have advanced human development more than any others: writing and cities.

2

Code

"This Is the Procedure"

Civilization advances by extending the number of operations we can perform without thinking about them.
— Alfred North Whitehead, *An Introduction to Mathematics*, 1911

WRITING AND CITIES are, inarguably, two of humanity's most powerful creations. Both have helped drive improvements in human well-
being over the span of millennia. The innovation that is writing goes
well beyond any implement used in the encoding process—be it the
chisel, the stylus, the printing press, or the digital computer—much
as the innovation that is the city goes well beyond the buildings and
roads that constitute its physical aspects. Writing, which is itself a
form of code, enables humans to communicate code. Cities grow as
code evolves.

Sumerians' medium of choice for "storing" writing preceded the pa-
pyrus scroll used in Egypt and the paper used in Europe: they used
tablets made of stone and clay. Since the discovery of Sumerian pic-
tographic and cuneiform writing more than a century ago on the ancient Mesopotamian plain (present-day Iraq), major excavations have
unearthed over a quarter-million tablets and tablet fragments (see
figure 2.1). Scholarly research has focused largely on the estimated
1 percent of these tablets that contain literary content. Far less attention
has been paid to the overwhelming majority of tablets that relate primarily to economic activities, such as receipts, sales contracts, worker

FIGURE 2.1 The Oldest Known Recipe Book. This tablet from the Old Babylonian period (ca. 1750 BCE) includes twenty-five recipes for stews; twenty-one are meat stews, and four are vegetable stews.

© The Near East Collection, Yale University (YBC 4644). See http://www.library. yale.edu/neareast/exhibitions/cuisine.html. Reprinted with permission of Yale University.

lists, wages, and natural resource and lexical lists.[1] If the ratio of literary to economic tablets found accurately reflects those actually produced, then the tablets as a whole suggest that the Sumerians created not only the world's first organized system of writing but also the world's first large-scale database technology.

The development of writing as a database technology reflects many patterns we find in later technologies. For one thing, it provides evidence of both discontinuous and incremental learning. Between 3200 BCE and 1500 BCE, for example, writing technology improved along every dimension. Markings initially carved in stone and on small rocks known as *bullae* were later etched on clay tablets. Accordingly, the chisel used to inscribe on stone was replaced by the reed stylus. The clay tablets, which initially were sun dried, were later baked in kilns to improve their strength. Kiln technology also changed dramatically, from primitive baking structures to high-temperature ovens. During the same period, the method of encoding tablets evolved to enable more efficient data entry. From approximately 3000 BCE to 2000 BCE, pictographs gave way to curvilinear symbols known as proto-cuneiform, and then to straight-edged cuneiform symbols.

As technology evolved, human work evolved with it. Over time, the labor involved in writing on tablets became differentiated by skill level. Early references to scribes name only the *Dub-sar* ("one who writes"); later references also refer to an accomplished subset of scribes known as *Dub-sar-mah* ("excellent writer"), and still later to an elite group known as the *Dub-sar-lugal* ("king of writers"). There is evidence that, toward the end of this period, some scribes specialized in literary writing while the remainder continued to record economic data. Scribal organizations grew from small "tablet houses" to large proto-universities that by 1700 BCE were producing various forms of literature and treatises that ranged from divination to deductive reasoning (the first forms of science) to legal codes.[2]

Perhaps the most profound innovation in Sumerian writing, however, was the cognitive leap that took place from a simple mnemonic—the accounting device pictograms were first used for—into abstract syllabograms, which are phonetic representations of the spoken language. Syllabograms made it possible to produce a more complicated message and thus to relate a greater amount of information. For example, the etched symbol of a cow changed to a cuneiform symbol representing a cow, which later was transformed into a sound, such as "ah-b" that no longer literally meant "cow" but became a phonetic term that could be combined with another phonetic term through a series of established rules.[3] This breakthrough is one of the more intellectually profound advancements in the Sumerian "information system," which was subsequently copied by other Mesopotamian peoples such as the Akkadians and the Babylonians, and by other cultures throughout time.[4]

As a result of these cumulative innovations, the density of information stored on each tablet increased even as the cost of producing tablets decreased, which is an early example of an organizational learning curve—a phenomenon to which I will return in detail in chapter seven.

Creating tablets was itself a production technology—a particularly powerful one, as it enabled humans to encode other production technologies. One of the earliest known tablets (3700 BCE), for example, contains a recipe for beer. Others appearing later (1700–1500 BCE) contain algorithms for an array of algebraic operations. As mathematician Donald Knuth described in a 1972 paper on Babylonian algorithms, each operation in these algorithms closes with the phrase, "This is the procedure" (hence the subtitle of this chapter).[5] In this sense, the earliest writing clearly embodied the dual nature of code as both artifact and algorithm.

With the creation of writing, humanity experienced its first information revolution.

IT IS NOT surprising that writing originated in one of humanity's first great cities, the Mesopotamian city of Uruk, which was the largest settlement on earth at the end of the fourth millennium BCE.[6] It also is not surprising that Uruk, located on a now-dry ancient channel of the Euphrates River, was situated in a region that enjoyed exceptional agricultural abundance. The interesting question is, did agricultural abundance enable Mesopotamians to advance the algorithmic frontier, or was it the other way around? This is the question that Jane Jacobs posed in her 1969 book, *The Economy of Cities*.

Jane Jacobs was a journalist and urban activist who dedicated her career to understanding and promoting conditions of urban vibrancy. A longtime resident of New York City's Greenwich Village, she was an outspoken critic of contemporary "urban renewal."[7] In 1968, Jacobs was arrested during a public hearing on plans to construct an expressway through lower Manhattan, including Washington Square Park. The plan did not go forward, but Jacobs found the battle so draining that she and her family relocated to Toronto. She lived there for the rest of her life, continuing her advocacy for the organic development of cities in her chosen new home.

Jacobs not only challenged conventional views on contemporary urban development in her writing and speaking, she also upended conventional thinking about the origins and growth of cities throughout history. She wrote in *The Economy of Cities* that "current theory in many fields assumes that cities are based upon a rural agricultural base."[8] She asserted that viewing cities simply as very big villages sustained by agriculture is a grave error, arguing that cities are the source, not the recipient, of agricultural abundance. Jacobs focused on the primacy of urban knowledge in agricultural productivity, as embodied in both practical ideas and physical products:

> It can readily be seen in the world today that agriculture is not even tolerably productive unless it incorporates many goods and services produced in cities and transplanted from cities ... Fertilizers, machines, electric power, refrigeration equipment, the results of plant and animal research, and a host of other tangible goods and services developed in cities.[9]

The three-field crop-rotation system that was central to Europe's sharp increase in productivity during the twelfth century "centered around cities," as did the cultivation of fodder crops and the practice of fitting them into the fallow year in the crop rotation. These innovations were developed in and around cities and then exported to rural areas.

Going back further in history, Jacobs conjectured extensively on the origins of Çatalhöyük, the earliest known city, which is located on the Konya Plain in modern-day Turkey: "Our remote ancestors did not expand their economies much by simply doing more of what they had already been doing: piling up more wild seeds and nuts, slaughtering more wild cattle and geese, making more spearheads, necklaces, burins, and fires. They expanded their economies by adding new work. So do we."[10] The creation of new work was and still is a powerful driver of economic development: every time new work—a new production recipe—is created, it in turn creates new possibilities for the division of labor. According to Jacobs, the interaction between the creation of new recipes and the division of labor required to perform them is the endogenous driver behind the development of cities in the long term.

IN THE PAST quarter-century, Jacobs' view of the development of cities has received support from research undertaken by leading economists, including urbanists Edward Glaeser and Richard Florida, and Nobel Laureate macroeconomist Robert Lucas. However, the research that has reinforced the core theme of Jacobs's work most intriguingly—that the growth of cities is a fundamentally algorithmic and organic process— has been done not by economists but by an interdisciplinary team of research scientists linked to the Santa Fe Institute in New Mexico: Luís Bettencourt, José Lobo, Dirk Helbing, Christian Kühnert, and Geoffrey West. I'll call them the Santa Fe team.[11]

The Santa Fe team takes a deterministic approach to modeling the growth of cities that is counterintuitive—if not downright alarming— to anyone who believes that free will and human agency play a central role in determining social outcomes. And yet their model corresponds remarkably closely to the data for a large number of cities over time.

Their inquiry is motivated by a provocative question:

Cities as consumers of energy and resources and producers of arti- facts, information, and waste have often been compared with bio- logical entities . . . Recent analogies include cities as "living systems," or "organisms," and notions of urban "ecosystems" and urban "me- tabolism." Are these terms just qualitative metaphors, or is there quantitative and predictive substance in the implication that social organizations are extensions of biology, satisfying similar principles and constraints?[12]

To answer this question, the Santa Fe team referred to a well-known result in the biological sciences that pertains to the inverse relationship between the body mass of an organism and the rate of its metabolic processes. The basic idea is that bigger organisms have slower metabo- lisms and thus can subsist on less food per gram of body mass. For ex- ample, if a mouse were the size of an elephant but maintained a mouse's metabolic rate it would need to consume roughly 20 times as many calories as an elephant actually does in order to survive.[13] Elephants and

other large mammals (including humans) are able to survive at our relatively large size because of the internal branching structures common to
both large and small mammals that supply nutrients and remove waste
efficiently, such as the veins that comprise the circulatory system and
the bronchi that comprise lungs.

The Santa Fe team found that cities are like biological organisms
when it comes to "metabolic" urban processes that are analogous to
nutrient supply and waste removal—transportation, for example, has a
branching structure much like veins or bronchi—but that cities differ
fundamentally from biological organisms when it comes to indicators
reflecting the creation and transmission of code. Measuring the size of
cities based on population and on the urban "metabolism" using metrics such as wages, GDP, electric power and gasoline consumption, and
total road surface, the team found a systematic relationship between
city size and indicators of the supply of "nutrients" and waste removal;
they found further that these relationships hold across many orders of
magnitude. However, while metabolic indicators do not keep pace with
the size of cities as they grow, indicators relating to the creation and
transmission of code increase at a greater rate than city size. The Santa
Fe team thus concluded that "there are two different scaling behaviors
[in cities]: material economies of scale, characteristic of infrastructure
networks, vs. social interactions, responsible for innovation and wealth
creation."[14] In short, the creation of ideas accelerates with city growth,
whereas the cost of new infrastructure is minimized (see table 2.1).

This intriguing macro-level departure from the inverse relationships
that hold for organisms ends up raising more questions about the evolution of cities than it answers: What mechanism enables larger cities to
produce disproportionately more innovation and wealth than smaller
cities? How do the macroeconomic measurables used in the Santa Fe
team's study relate to the microeconomic, work-creates-work dynamics that Jane Jacobs emphasized? Nevertheless, the commonality in the
arguments made by Jacobs and the Santa Fe team is clear: processes of
economic development in the long run are not led by land or natural
resources; they are not led by infrastructure and capital; they are—
unavoidably and irreducibly—led by ideas put into practice within the
economy. Put another way, in the long run, the processes of economic
development are led by code.

TABLE 2.1 Scaling Exponents for Urban Indicators versus City Size

Y	β	95% CI	Adj-R^2	Observations	Country, Year
New patents	1.27	[1.25,1.29]	0.72	331	U.S. 2001
Inventors	1.25	[1.22,1.27]	0.76	331	U.S. 2001
Private R&D employment	1.34	[1.29,1.39]	0.92	266	U.S. 2002
"Supercreative" employment	1.15	[1.11,1.18]	0.89	287	U.S. 2003
R&D establishments	1.19	[1.14,1.22]	0.77	287	U.S. 1997
R&D employment	1.26	[1.18,1.43]	0.93	295	China 2002
Total wages	1.12	[1.09,1.13]	0.96	361	U.S. 2002
Total bank deposits	1.08	[1.03,1.11]	0.91	267	U.S. 1996
GDP	1.15	[1.06,1.23]	0.96	295	China 2002
GDP	1.26	[1.09,1.46]	0.64	196	EU 1999–2003
GDP	1.13	[1.03,1.11]	0.94	37	Germany 2003
Total electrical consumption	1.07	[1.03,1.11]	0.88	392	Germany 2002
New AIDS cases	1.23	[1.18,1.29]	0.76	93	U.S. 2002–2003
Serious crimes	1.16	[1.11,1.18]	0.89	287	U.S. 2003
Total housing	1.00	[0.99,1.01]	0.98	331	U.S. 2001
Total employment	1.01	[0.99,1.02]	0.98	331	U.S. 2001
Household electrical consumption	1.00	[0.94,1.06]	0.88	377	Germany 2002

Indicator	β	CI	Adj-R²	N	
Household electrical consumption	1.05	[0.89,1.22]	0.91	295	China 2002
Household water consumption	1.01	[0.89,1.11]	0.96	295	China 2002
Gasoline stations	0.77	[0.74,0.81]	0.93	318	U.S. 2001
Gasoline sales	0.79	[0.73,0.80]	0.94	318	U.S. 2001
Length of electrical cables	0.87	[0.82,0.92]	0.75	38	Germany 2002
Road surface	0.83	[0.74,0.92]	0.87	29	Germany 2002

CI = confidence interval; Adj-R^2 = adjusted R^2, GDP = gross domestic product

This table provides scaling exponents (the parameter β in column 2) for a number of urban indicators as a function of city size. Values of β greater than 1 signify that the indicator in question increases *more than* proportionately with city size; values of β close to 1 signify that the indicator increases proportionately with city size; values of β less than 1 signify that the indicator in question increases *less than* proportionately with city size. Knowledge production indicators (the top six rows) all increase more than proportionately with city size, while transportation and electrical infrastructure indicators (the bottom four rows) increase less than proportionately.

Source: Bettencourt et al., 2007

CODE NEEDS A platform and it needs an operating system. A city provides both. In a city, however, code does not just run; in some literal, measurable sense it lives. In chapter nine I will elaborate on what it means for a city to be alive and clarify how platforms enable the creation and evolution of code over time. For now it is enough for me to refer back to the quotation from mathematician and philosopher Alfred North Whitehead that opens this chapter: "Civilization advances by extending the number of operations we can perform without thinking about them."[15] Whitehead makes a fundamental and important point: biological evolution and social evolution proceed according to this rule. Easier, or at least more fundamental, problems are solved first. The solutions to easier problems become encoded as hardware—roads, sewers, the power grid—that in turn provides the context for solving later and more complex problems.

Layers of history define a great city, which can be seen as a dense accretion of solved problems. We build, in some cases literally, on the ingenuity of our ancestors, systematically forgetting that we have done so as we proceed. Neolithic humans living in villages, for example, solved the problem of making stones into effective hunting tools, whereas twenty-first-century humans convey traffic data by programming an app on a mobile phone. Clearly, many layers of solved problems sit between the obsidian axe and the iPhone app. Each generation of solved problems provides a platform upon which future generations of solved problems are built.

Yet for all the positives of such a process, encoding as a platform invariably and unavoidably also results in a loss of information. Furthermore, the emergence of a platform decreases autonomy along some dimension. Plato felt this was true even of writing: "I cannot help feeling, Phaedrus, [says Socrates,] that writing is unfortunately like painting; for the creations of the painter have the attitude of life, and yet if you ask them a question they preserve a solemn silence . . . You would imagine that they had intelligence, but if you want to know anything and put a question to one of them, the speaker always gives one unvarying answer."[16] Two thousand years later, communications theorist Marshall McLuhan echoed this point: "The alphabet is a technology of visual fragmentation and specialism [that leads to] a desert of classified data."[17] The dimensions of loss McLuhan notes with regard to the advance of code through writing are directly related to the loss humans experienced as we moved first from wilderness to the village and then from the village to the city. "By their dependence on the spoken word for information, people were drawn together into a tribal mesh . . . Audile-tactile tribal man partook of the collective unconscious, lived in a magical integral world patterned by myth and ritual, its values divine."[18] The advance of code through the invention of writing intrinsically involved new constraints and a loss of information at the same time it increased human capacities and cognitive freedom. These dual effects are inherent in the advance of code.

In the past 350 years, a new alphabet has come into existence. It consists of only two letters: "0" and "1." That alphabet—binary digital code—is today leading a wave of change that has implications as fundamental to the human experience as the advent of writing.

When did this alphabet—from which the platforms of humanity's future are being constructed—originate? Ironically, its origins trace to a year that some at the time believed would mark humanity's cataclysmic end: 1666.

It is with that story that I start the next chapter.

3

Machines

"The Universal Character"

One could carry out the description of a machine, no matter how complicated, in characters which would be merely the letters of the alphabet,
and so provide the mind with a method of knowing the machine and all
its parts . . . The human race will have a new kind of instrument which will
increase the power of the mind much more than optical lenses strengthen
the eyes.

—Gottfried Wilhelm Leibniz, in a note to Christiaan Huygens, 1679

IN 1666, THE city of London was consumed by a great fire. The fire
began on Sunday, September 3, in a baker's house on Pudding Lane. By
the time it was done, it had consumed half the city, including St. Paul's
Cathedral, the Royal Exchange, and the Old Bailey. Coinciding as it
did with the portentous date of 1666 in an era of intense sectarian strife
that was rife with biblical significance, the fire was interpreted by many
Londoners as having apocalyptic significance. Historical accounts suggest that Puritan minister Thomas Vincent was expressing the senti-
ments of many Londoners when he proclaimed from the pulpit that
"London, so famous for wisdom and dexterity, can now find neither
brains nor hands to prevent its ruin. The hand of God was in it; the
Decree was come forth: London must now fall."[1]

London's fall was not permanent, of course. Like a great forest,
the city not only recovered from its fire but emerged far stronger.
It turned out that the physical infrastructure thought to comprise
the city was not it at all. The real city lay beneath the surface in the

practices, relationships, and capabilities that defined its "wisdom and dexterity."

Although events in London ultimately belied the apocalyptic claims of Thomas Vincent and his Puritan brethren, 1666 did turn out to be a portentous year for humanity for reasons that could not have been anticipated.

That same year, a German natural philosopher by the name of Gottfried Leibniz published an essay titled "De arte combinatoria" ("On the Art of Combination"). Leibniz based the essay on his doctoral dissertation, which he wrote at the age of 20. In "De arte combinatoria," Leibniz set forth a method for reducing all logic to exact statements using binary expressions, which he dubbed the *Characteristica Universalis,* or Universal Character:[2]

> "De arte combinatoria" aims to create a general method in which all the truths of reason would be reduced to a kind of calculation. At the same time, this would be reduced to a sort of universal language or script, but infinitely different from all those projected hitherto, for the symbols and even words in it would direct the reason, and errors, except for those of fact, would be mere mistakes in calculation. It would be very difficult to form or invent this language or characteristic, but very easy to understand it without any dictionaries.[3]

In the Universal Character, any concept can be expressed as a combination of a small number of basic concepts, in somewhat the same way words are combinations of letters. Statements can be composed of combinations of concepts, thereby generating a combinatoric "logic of invention"—a language for differentiation and recombination in the realm of ideas.

"De arte combinatoria" presented a theory of information based on binary code in which Leibniz described, for the first time in recorded history, the fundamental idea that would become digital computation.

IN THE MID-SIXTEENTH century, as a gradual but pervasive revolution in agricultural methods took place, the medieval social order gradually gave way to an age of unprecedented prosperity and population growth. By the late eighteenth century, as the "jobbe of work" performed for compensation grew more specialized, the organizational environments in which those tasks were performed had become significantly more structured and complex. To improve efficiency, workers gradually gave up authority. Among the leaders of this change was a statistician named Gaspard Clair François Marie Riche de Prony, who was tasked with mapping a vast, fertile plain ringed by mountains that lay at the western end of the European continent: France.

De Prony was in a tight spot. Within a few years of the storming of the Bastille, as the Revolution raged on in France, de Prony received his challenging assignment to prepare a detailed map of France that would facilitate the accurate measurement of property as the basis for taxation. The magnitude of this task would stretch the limits of existing computational techniques. At that time, before the advent of any type of calculating machine, the only way to reduce the burden of computational work systematically was to create mathematical tables that specified the values of commonly used functions, such as the sine, cosine, and logarithm. Thus de Prony initiated the most ambitious effort anyone had undertaken to date to create a full set of mathematical tables, his goal being to ease administrative computation.[4] The challenge was figuring out how to perform the huge number of calculations required to create the necessary tables.

As the supply of mathematicians trained to calculate the desired values using then-standard techniques was not nearly adequate for the task, de Prony came up with the idea of breaking down the required computation into discrete and repetitive tasks that less skilled human computers could manage. To staff the project he had another inspired idea: he would employ out-of-work hairdressers.

Picture Marie Antoinette and you will be reminded of the (literal) heights to which the craft of hairstyling rose during the reign of Louis XVI. The elaborate coiffures of courtesans at Versailles were among the most evident and reviled symbols of the French monarchy's self-indulgence in its final days. Following the French Revolution, to appear in public with such a hairstyle was to risk the loss not only of the hair but also of the head to which the hair was attached. Consequently, sculptured hairstyles went out of fashion quickly, and with them the jobs of the highly skilled coiffeurs and wigmakers who created them. It was in this minor misfortune that Gaspard de Prony saw opportunity.

Reflecting on the project following its completion, de Prony cited Adam Smith's *Wealth of Nations* as his inspiration:

> I came across the chapter where the author treats the division of labor citing, as an example of the great advantages of this method, the manufacture of pins. I conceived all of a sudden the idea of applying the same method to the immense work with which I had been burdened, and to manufacture logarithms as one manufactures pins.[5]

What de Prony accomplished—beyond creating one of the largest sets of mathematical tables ever compiled—was to apply the principle of the division of labor systematically to mental work, anticipating by over a century the creation of the modern office (see Text Box 3.1).

If de Prony, like Leibniz before him, was a pioneer in developing the software of digital computing that has enabled the rapid advance of code in our lifetime, then credit for pioneering the hardware of digital computing goes to another French revolutionary: a famed weaver and sometime soldier, Joseph Marie Charles, known as Joseph Marie Jacquard.[6]

IN 1801, FRENCH silk weavers in Lyon, concerned about the potential mechanization of their craft, gathered to destroy the model for a newly patented treadle loom that had been awarded the bronze medal for technical achievement at the Second Paris Industrial Exposition.[7] The loom's inventor, Joseph Marie Jacquard, later recalled, "The iron was sold for old iron, the wood for kindling, while I was delivered over to universal ignominy."[8] Fortunately, not only for Jacquard but for the rest of the world, his ignominy was short lived. Three years later he unveiled another loom that featured a novel control mechanism for a drawloom that would, over the coming century, not only dominate weaving but seed a far-reaching revolution in the organization of work and society.

The drawloom was invented in China during the second century BCE, and for nearly two millennia thereafter, silk weaving was a tedious and exacting process. To create a woven pattern, a silk weaver had to lift individual threads of the warp (the parallel threads that hold the pattern in place) to let each row of the weft (the threads that create the design) pass through perpendicularly. By the start of the nineteenth century, machine manufacturers had figured out how to build

Text Box 3.1 **The Birth of "the Office"**

By the twentieth century, the systematic approach to analyzing the division of labor that de Prony developed would have a name: management science. The first and foremost proponent of management science was Frederick Winslow Taylor, a child of privilege who found his calling in factories.

Born to a wealthy Philadelphia family and educated in his youth in Europe, Taylor's parents later sent him to boarding school at the exclusive Phillips Exeter Academy in Exeter, New Hampshire. However, following graduation, Taylor broke from the usual path taken by an Exeter graduate; he neither enrolled in an Ivy League university nor sought a position as a clerk in a Boston firm. Instead, much to his parents' astonishment and dismay, he accepted a position as an apprentice machinist in a hydraulic works.

This first experience of factory work gave Taylor an understanding of the habits of workers that was as intimate as it was, ultimately, unfavorable. Being highly organized and precise by nature, Taylor was appalled at the lax habits and absence of structure that characterized the early twentieth-century factory floor. Taylor would later assert that there is not a single worker "who does not devote a considerable part of his time to studying just how slowly he can work and still convince his employer that he is going at a good pace."[9] However, Taylor ultimately concluded that the blame did not lie in the workers but in the lack of rigorously considered management techniques. At the center of management, Taylor determined, was the capacity to precisely define the tasks of which a "job" was comprised.

What distinguished Taylor was his absolute conviction that workers could not be left on their own to define, much less refine, the tasks that comprised their work. He argued that authority must be fully vested in scientifically determined routine—which is to say, code. Defining such routines was the paramount task of management. Taylor wrote:

It is only through enforced standardization of methods, enforced adoption of the best implements and working conditions, and enforced cooperation that this faster work can be assured. And the duty of enforcing the adoption of standards and enforcing this cooperation rests with the management alone.[10]

To Taylor, workers' loss of autonomy was an essential element in achieving efficiency in the modern organization. He believed it was tied directly to the "how" of production—the specific work to be performed.

A disciple of Taylor's, W. H. Leffingwell, took on the task of extending Taylor's methodology from the factory to a domain of work growing in importance: the office. In two mammoth books, Leffingwell observed with horror the gross inefficiencies of the early twentieth-century office, describing in minute detail how imposition of the principles of scientific management could improve office productivity.

As Nikil Saval describes in his revelatory chronicle, *Cubed: A Secret History of the Workplace*, "besides demonstrating the mania of Taylorists for infinite subdivision of tasks and time study, Leffingwell's treatise unconsciously reveals the sheer novelty of office life itself—the fact that managers were mostly unsure of how to organize and run offices."[11] The nineteenth-century "counting house," familiar to readers of Melville in "Bartleby the Scrivener" or of Dickens in *A Christmas Carol*, had been replaced by a new and significant domain of productive work as significant as the factories. According to Saval, "the notion of 'the office' itself, as a separate world, with its own rules and atmosphere and culture, was being justified under the rubric of management. The office was no longer an administrative holding tank, parasitic on the 'real work' done in factories and fields, but the place where the real work was in fact getting done."[12]

automatic looms dedicated to specific designs. The innovation was to use rods with hooks on the end to lift particular threads in the waft in a precise sequence, taking the place of human arms and fingers. The shortcoming of such looms was that they were "hardwired" to produce single designs and could not be reconfigured to produce other ones.

As demand for Lyonnaise silk grew rapidly with the emergence of a middle class in France and elsewhere in Europe, the inefficient manual drawloom constrained the silk industry's ability to increase production and maintain its market dominance. Consequently, the industry was in crisis.

Joseph Marie Jacquard was an unlikely person to take on the challenge of saving his hometown through technological innovation. He had inherited his father's silk-weaving business at the age of 20 but managed it poorly and went through his entire inheritance. For a time he worked as a laborer, but he was rescued from his life of poverty by the coming of the French Revolution. He served as a soldier, fighting first, and briefly, against the revolutionaries and then deftly changing sides to fight with them. Jacquard did not even begin to work on an improved drawloom until he was 47 years old—already beyond the expected lifespan for a Frenchman of his era. However, once Jacquard put his mind to invention he quickly found his calling.

Jacquard's innovation was to combine the automatic function of hardwired drawlooms with a mechanism for controlling the loom that could be reprogrammed with relative ease using wooden cards perforated with precisely punched holes—a technology that came to be known as punched cards. The principle was simple. At every stage in the weaving process, an array of rods with hooks on their tips would descend to the punch card specified for that step. Where a hole was present, the rod passed through the card and lifted the specified thread, which allowed the weft to slide through perpendicularly. Where no hole was present, the rod encountered resistance and did not descend further (see figure 3.1).

The most important characteristic of the Jacquard loom was, of course, that it worked. It could produce designs of any complexity at more than 20 times the speed of a manual drawloom. In 1804, Jacquard patented his "loom for weaving brocade using punched cards to control the action of the warp threads and therefore to control every row of weaving." The following year, newly crowned Emperor Napoleon Bonaparte visited Jacquard's workshop in Lyon, just days after issuing a decree declaring the Jacquard mechanism to be public property. The inventor received an annual pension of roughly $100,000 per year in today's terms and a royalty for every loom sold.

(a)

(b)
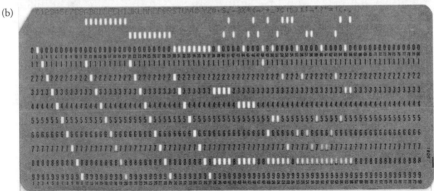

FIGURE 3.1 Punched Cards for a Jacquard Loom and IBM Computer. 3.1a. Punched cards in use in a Jacquard loom. German Museum of Technology, Berlin. 3.1b. This is the front of a blue IBM-style punch card. It shows the Latin alphabet character code.

The impact Jacquard's invention had on the silk-weaving industry in Lyon was sudden and strongly positive; production levels and wages both rose dramatically. By 1840, six years after Jacquard's death, the Count of Fortis would write in a book celebrating Jacquard's legacy that "the invention of Jacquard has produced a general and total revolution in the procedures for manufacturing; it has traced a great line between the past and the future; it has initiated a new era in general progress."[13] That same year, the city of Lyon erected a statue of Jacquard on the site where his first loom had been destroyed.[14]

Changes in the nature of production during the late eighteenth and early nineteenth centuries mirrored changes in the political system in Europe. Kings and craftsmen alike relinquished autonomy (and, as in the case of King Louis XVI, their heads) as codes of political order and production advanced in parallel, taking precedence over human judgment and whim to an unprecedented extent. While practices of modern democracy and automated production would take more than a century to mature, it is arguably no coincidence that they originated in the same places at the same time.

France led the advance of code during this era of revolutionary changes, but England was not far behind. At about the same time the citizens of Lyon were erecting their monument to Jacquard, his pragmatic invention was inspiring a new set of breakthroughs across the English Channel.[15] The protagonists in this round were an unlikely duo of mathematicians: the iconoclastic inventor Charles Babbage, and Augusta Ada King, Countess of Lovelace.

AS LONDON BEGAN to grow again following the great fire of 1666, it gradually absorbed surrounding towns and villages. Among these was the town of St. Mary at the Bourne on the banks of the Tybourne (later Tyburn), which, following a sequence of transfers in and out of royal hands and in the written form of its name, ended up as the London neighborhood of Marylebone. By the early 1800s, Marylebone was a hub of Bohemianism and creativity. Among its residents was an iconoclastic inventor named Charles Babbage.

Babbage was a force of nature. His list of accomplishments as compiled by the Computer History Museum in Mountain View, California, reads like random entries from an encyclopedia of technology. Babbage pioneered lighthouse signaling, invented the ophthalmoscope, proposed using "black-box" recorders to monitor railway conditions and help determine the cause of catastrophes, advocated for decimal currency, and proposed the use of tidal power to replace exhausted coal reserves. He also designed a cow-catcher for the front end of locomotives, a failsafe quick-release coupling mechanism for railway carriages, multicolored theater lighting, an altimeter, a seismic detector, a tugboat for winching vessels upstream, a hydrofoil, and an arcade game that enabled members of the public to challenge him at tic-tac-toe.[16]

Babbage was as comfortable, and apparently took as much joy in, advancing pure mathematics as he did in observing the activities on a factory floor in the most minute detail. Herbert Simon, a pioneer in the field of artificial intelligence and recipient of the 1978 Nobel Prize in Economics (see Text Box 3.2), once observed that Babbage, "perhaps more than any man since Leonardo de Vinci[,] exemplified in his life and work the powerful ways in which fundamental science could contribute to practical affairs, and practical affairs to science . . . He was one of the strongest mathematicians of his generation, but he devoted his career to the improvement of manufacturing arts, and—most remarkable of all—to the invention of the digital computer in something very close to its modern form."[17]

Inspired by Gaspard de Prony's success in calculating trigonometric tables through the division of labor, Babbage sought to embody the code de Prony had developed into a mechanical device. Babbage called his device the Difference Engine. An algorithm that had started as an idea in de Prony's head had, due to his exceptionally systematic approach to the division of labor, been converted into written rules—a form of "software"—to be followed by the human computers he recruited from among some unemployed hairdressers; Babbage, the genius tinkerer, in turn converted that software into hardware, the Difference Engine.[18]

Remarkable as it was on its own terms, the Difference Engine is remembered today not only as an ingenious machine for calculating trigonometric tables but as the predecessor to Babbage's subsequent invention, the Analytical Engine.

In his Marylebone home, Babbage had for years displayed the fraction of the Difference Engine he had managed to complete, which was a conversation piece at the many soirées Babbage hosted.[19] The Difference Engine was designed to tabulate polynomial functions, which was useful in generating the trigonometric tables used in navigation and engineering—domains of first-order economic significance in Georgian and Victorian England. Before he completed the Difference Engine, however, Babbage shifted his attention to a more ambitious project, the Analytical Engine, a general-purpose problem-solver that was the predecessor of modern programmable computers.

Text Box 3.2 "Over the Christmas holiday, Al and I invented a thinking machine."

One evening in January 1956, Herbert Simon took his wife and three children to his office at Carnegie Mellon University's Graduate School of Industrial Administration, where he was a professor, to get their help with a very particular project: running the first program ever developed to simulate human intelligence. The program was called the Logic Theorist, or LT. Earlier that month, Simon had walked into the first session of the semester for one of his courses and announced, "Over the Christmas holiday, Al and I invented a thinking machine." It was true: Simon and his colleague Al Newell were the first to realize the vision Gottfried Leibniz had expressed almost three centuries earlier for "a general method in which all the truths of reason would be reduced to a kind of calculation."[20]

Simon was slightly ahead of himself in making his pronouncement, as the LT wasn't actually running on a computer yet. However, as he later recalled, "we knew precisely how to write the program." That is where Simon's family came into the picture:

> While awaiting completion of the computer implementation of LT, Al and I wrote out the rules for the components of the program (subroutines) in English on index cards, and also made up cards for the contents of memories (the axioms of logic). To each member of [my family] we gave one of the cards, so that each person became, in effect, a component of the LT computer program—a subroutine that performed some special function, or a component of its memory. It was the task of each participant to execute his or her subroutine, or to provide the contents of his or her memory, whenever called by the routine at the next level above that was then in control.
>
> So we were able to simulate the LT with a computer constructed of human components. Here was nature imitating art imitating nature.[21]

In this manner, Simon's wife (not a trained mathematician) and his three children, then ages nine, eleven, and thirteen, were able to prove the first 25 or so theorems in Alfred North Whitehead and Bertrand Russell's *Principia Mathematica*. Proving theorems was to the early history of digital computation what calculating trigonometric tables was to the early history of mechanical computation: a proof of concept, using human computers, that had profound future significance.

That evening of family fun in 1956 launched the field of artificial intelligence.

Babbage's vision of the Analytical Engine was inspired by none other than French digital computing pioneer Joseph Marie Jacquard. Babbage eventually removed the Difference Engine from his hallway and replaced it with a portrait of Jacquard, then challenged his guests to guess the medium used to create the portrait. Most guests—including the Duke of Wellington—guessed that it was an engraving. Babbage was delighted by such incorrect guesses, for the portrait was in fact a finely woven tapestry produced using an automated Jacquard loom (see figure 3.2). For Babbage, the ability for a computer to produce a product indistinguishable from that of a human clearly suggested the potential power of the Analytical Engine he envisioned.[22]

Babbage did not labor on the Analytical Engine in isolation. He was aided by—indeed, worked collaboratively with—a woman 24 years his junior, who was an able mathematician in her own right. Her name was Augusta Ada King, Countess of Lovelace, or Ada Lovelace as she is now remembered. In a set of technical notes she authored in 1843 with some input from Babbage, Lovelace set forth a description that is more complete than any found in Babbage's writings of how the Analytical Engine might function as a general-purpose computer. Whereas the Difference Engine had been designed to calculate a specific set of nautical tables, Lovelace wrote, the Analytical Engine "is not merely adapted for tabulating the results of one particular function and of no other, but for developing and tabulating any function whatever . . . In enabling a mechanism to combine together general symbols, in successions of unlimited variety and extent, a uniting link is established between the operations of matter and the abstract mental processes." The "general

A LA MÉMOIRE DE J. M. JACQUARD.

Né à Lyon le 7 Juillet 1752 Mort le 7 Aout 1834

FIGURE 3.2 Joseph Marie Jacquard. This portrait of Jacquard was woven in silk on a Jacquard loom and required 24,000 punched cards to create (1839). It was only produced to order. Charles Babbage owned one of these portraits; it inspired him in using perforated cards in his analytical engine. It is in the collection of the Science Museum in London, England.

Source: Science Museum, London, England.

symbols" to which Lovelace referred were similar to the Universal Character Leibniz had envisioned, which were now tied more closely to practical application via the Analytical Engine. Lovelace was thus the first to envision the idea of code as executed by a computer—which is to say, software.

In their work on the Analytical Engine, Babbage and Lovelace were on the brink of a breakthrough, but neither would live to see it occur. Lovelace died of uterine cancer in 1851, at the age of 36. Babbage lived to be nearly 80, but he was never able to construct a working version of the Analytical Engine. Generations would pass before work on digital computing was to advance again in earnest.

When digital computing did advance, it did so far from the fashionable salons of Marylebone. Much like Gaspard de Prony, those who created the first digital computer worked within government bureaucracies and were motivated by the need to perform calculations in large quantities in the service of urgent national imperatives. Also like de Prony, those who developed the first digital computer first sought to solve the problem by delegating work among a large number of human computers.

This first installment in the history of digital computing illustrates the deep relationships that have existed from the beginning between the evolution of algorithms and the evolution of work. The next chapter will demonstrate that the fact that digital computers are able to outperform humans in performing mental tasks should come as no surprise.

They were designed to do just that.

4

Computers

Predicting the Weather

> Gains from algorithmic progress have been roughly fifty to one hundred percent as large as those from hardware progress. Improvements tend to be incremental, forming a relatively smooth curve on the scale of years.
> —Katja Grace, "Algorithmic Progress in Six Domains," 2013

THROUGHOUT HUMAN HISTORY—until 12pm on Sunday, March 5, 1950—predicting the weather was a practical impossibility.

In nearly all early civilizations, the terrible capriciousness of the wind and sky prompted people to concoct meteorological deities, which led to the powerful social roles shamans and early priests played in ancient times. In Egypt, Amun was the god of wind and creation; Anshar and An were the Mesopotamian god and goddess of the sky. Among the Māori, Tāwhirimātea was the god of weather, and in ancient Greece, Zeus was the ruler of Mount Olympus, king of the gods, and the god of sky, thunder, law, order, and fate.

However, awe and fear of the heavens did not prevent ancient people from seeking to mitigate the adverse consequences of meteorological variability.[1] The Sumerians were the first to manage the rains by implementing large-scale irrigation. This enabled them to create Uruk, among the world's first cities. The capital city of King Gilgamesh, hero of *The Epic of Gilgamesh*, Uruk was built on the Euphrates River. The Sumerians also invented the alphabet and were the first to encode computational procedures.[2] Interestingly, of the 1,255 logogram words and 2,511 compound words compiled in the most authoritative Sumerian lexicon, more than 140 pertain to water.[3] The Sumerian preoccupation with floods was sufficiently great that the Euphrates River is encoded in Sumerian as *buranun*, which is a concatenation of *bu* (to rush around), *ra* (to flood, overflow), and *nun* (great, noble). Moreover, a considerable fraction of existing Sumerian tablets pertain to hydrology. *The Epic of Gilgamesh* famously features a description of a Great Flood—similar, in at least one surviving version of *The Epic*, to that in the Old Testament—that further underscores the Sumerians' preoccupation with water and the weather.

Roughly three millennia after the ascendency of Uruk, Aristotle wrote *Meteorology*, the first systematic attempt to explain climatic phenomena. Theophrastus, Aristotle's contemporary and his successor as director of the Lyceum in Athens, wrote two short treatises on the topic of weather prediction that were titled "On Winds" and "On Weather Signs." Although fragmentary and inaccurate, these works by Theophrastus provided the framework for Western attempts to forecast the weather for the next two thousand years, until Enlightenment-era advances by Edmund Halley (for whom the comet is named) and George Hadley set the stage for scientific understanding of the weather.[4]

By 1922, meteorological theory had advanced to the point that British mathematician and physicist Lewis Fry Richardson could engage in wild speculation: "Perhaps some day in the dim future it will be possible to advance the computations faster than the weather advances . . . But that is a dream."[5] Richardson had fairly specific ideas about what it might take to realize this dream:

> In the tropics the weather is often foreknown, so that we may say [that the computation of global weather patterns will involve] 2000 active columns. So that 32 × 2000 = 64,000 computers would be needed to race the weather for the whole globe. That is a staggering figure. Perhaps in some years' time it may be possible to report a simplification of the process. But in any case, the organization indicated is a central forecast-factory for the whole globe, or for portions extending to boundaries where the weather is steady, with individual computers specializing on the separate equations.[6]

As Richardson continued to speculate about what he termed a "forecast factory," the "computers" he had in mind were neither mechanical nor electrical, analog nor digital. They were, in fact, just people performing mathematical computations by hand or with mechanical calculators, using sheets of paper to record their work—in other words, just the sort of "computers" Gaspard de Prony had used two centuries earlier. Recognizing the likely tedium of working in the sort of computational sweatshop he envisioned, Richardson offered an empathic qualification: "Let us hope for [the human computers'] sakes that they are moved on from time to time to new operations," by which he literally meant the calculation of different mathematical functions.[7]

At the time Richardson was writing, his concept was indeed closer to a dream than reality. But only 15 years later, a 24-year-old prodigy named Alan Turing published a paper in *The Proceedings of the London Mathematical Society* describing the fundamentals of a digital computing machine that had the potential to realize Richardson's far-fetched vision. "The idea behind digital computers may be explained by saying that these machines are intended to carry out any operations which could be done by a human computer," he wrote in a later paper.[8] He elaborated by describing the work of a human computer that was fully consistent with those used by Richardson and others in the 1920s and 1930s: "The human computer is supposed to be following fixed rules; he has no authority to deviate from them in any detail. We may suppose that these rules are supplied in a book, which is altered whenever he is put on to a new job. He has also an unlimited supply of paper on which he does his calculations."[9]

The outbreak of World War II in 1939 created a sudden and urgent need for just such human computers to perform computational work, but of a military rather than a meteorological variety. At the Ballistic Research Laboratory—the U.S. Army's primary weapons-testing facility—the demand for this specialized labor was so great that the military established a secret unit called the Philadelphia Computing Section (PCS) at the University of Pennsylvania's Moore School of Electrical Engineering. The army recruited one hundred human computers, mostly women, from the University of Pennsylvania and neighboring schools.[10]

Creating the PCS was an institutional innovation of precisely the same type, and within an order of magnitude of the scale, as that Richardson had imagined. Nonetheless, it turned out to be far from adequate to the task.[11] By August 1944, Herman Goldstine, a mathematician and Army lieutenant who was the liaison between the Ballistic Research Laboratory and the PCS, would lament, "The number of tables for which work has not yet started because of lack of computational facilities far exceeds the number in progress. Requests for the preparation of new tables are being currently received at the rate of six per day."[12]

Goldstine had not, however, placed all his bets on the PCS. A year earlier he had been prompted by a colleague to seek out John Mauchly, a physics instructor at the Moore School who had written a memorandum proposing that the calculations being performed by PCS workers could be completed thousands of times more rapidly using a digital computer built with vacuum tubes. Goldstine obtained funding for Mauchly's proposal and shortly thereafter engaged renowned mathematician John von Neumann to be its leader.[13] The effort to construct the world's first general-purpose digital computer was under way. On February 14, 1946, less than six months after the end of World War II, the Army announced the completion of the Electronic Numerical Integrator and Computer, or ENIAC.

With the war over, the Army dedicated its powerful new computing resource to a priority that had emerged directly from the war effort: determining the feasibility of the hydrogen bomb. From the outset, however, von Neumann had his eye on solving a problem even more challenging than that of computing nuclear chain reactions: predicting the weather. In May 1946, just three months after the ENIAC had become operational, von Neumann submitted a proposal for the creation of a meteorology group at the Moore School:

> The objective of this project is an investigation of the theory of dynamic meteorology in order to make it accessible to high-speed, electronic, digital, automatic computing, of a type which is beginning to be available, and which is likely to be increasingly available in the future. It is also expected that these investigations will give indications as to what further observations are necessary—both of the

laboratory type and of the field type—in order to make theoretical work, that is supported by such high speed computing, fully more effective.

The Navy funded the proposal immediately, and work began on July 1, 1946.[14]

Synthesizing all known meteorological science into a set of programs that conformed to the ENIAC's operational constraints was a far from trivial task (see Text Box 4.1). Nonetheless, little more than three years after they had gotten started, von Neumann and his team had come up with an approach they could test.

Text Box 4.1 The Determinants of Computational Speed

Scientists, including Lewis Fry Richardson and Carl-Gustaf Rossby, had long ago worked out the equations governing smooth atmospheric changes. The challenge lay in the scale of the earth and the sheer number of computations required to arrive at a numerical prediction. The specific problem the ENIAC solved in order to compute the first weather forecast was the "Numerical Integration of the Baratropic Vorticity Equation."

While the ENIAC was a powerful new tool for performing computations, it was not without its limitations. As von Neumann himself described at the time, the ENIAC was a quick thinker, but it had a terrible memory: "Imagine that you take 20 people, lock them up in a room for three years, provide them with 20 desk multipliers, and institute the rule: During the entire proceedings all of them together may never have more than one page written full. They can erase any amount, put it back again, but they are entitled at any given time only to one page. It's clear where the bottleneck . . . lies."[15]

Whether referring to human or machine computers, we can generally define three possible levels of memory. First, there is memory located adjacent to the processing unit that can be accessed very quickly. For humans, the processing unit is the brain, and this type of storage is called short-term memory; for computers it is called cache memory. We'll refer to both as Level 1 Memory. There is a limit to the amount of data the computer (human or machine) can retain in Level 1 memory, so the computer supplements it with the ability to read and write data on, say, a sheet of paper for a human or a Random Access Memory (RAM) device for a computer. To describe fully the bottleneck to which von Neumann refers, add one more constraint: each operator may have access to only a limited amount of such immediately available, but temporary, memory. We'll refer to this as Level 2 memory. To make life a bit easier for our processors, allow for the existence of a third level of memory. For the human, this could be a library in the basement where the human computers may go to look up information; for the computer, it's a hard drive or CD-ROM. Data stored in this format are more permanent, but also considerably more difficult to access. We'll refer to this third level of memory as storage.

For each processor, performing the work required to complete a single computational cycle requires the following:

- The function to be calculated
- Data on the weather in the neighboring zone during the previous 15-minute interval stored on some medium (for example, a set of numbers written on a sheet of paper from which to read)
- A processing unit with which to calculate the value of the function (for the human computer, a brain, potentially supplemented by a mechanical calculator)
- Some medium on which to store output data (a sheet of paper with blank space on which to write)

Given these elements of the computational cycle, it's clear that one dimension of computational speed has to do with computer hardware—the machine itself. The other has to do with the overall computational strategy employed, taking the hardware as given— the algorithm or computer program employed.

The speed of the processing unit determines how long it takes each individual unit to process the output once the relevant data are available, given the function to be computed. This will determine the minimum size of a computation cycle. If the problem is simple and the data inputs can be remembered easily, then the computation cycle can be the length of time required for the processor to perform a simple arithmetical computation in his or her "head" (literally or figuratively). But what if a processor is unable to recall the function from (short-term) memory and must refer back to the sheet of paper constantly while performing calculations? Or, even worse, what if the most condensed expression of the function to be computed is so lengthy that it doesn't fit on the allocated sheets of paper, so the processor must repeatedly run down to the data storage library to retrieve it in component parts? In that case, even if well organized and otherwise managed as efficiently as possible, the overall process could be very slow indeed.

The size of Level 1 and Level 2 memory and the time required to access storage, when required, will all have a direct bearing on the overall time required to perform our computation. Of even greater importance will be the ability of the overall organizational and technological design of the algorithm to work effectively within existing constraints.

At 12pm on Sunday, March 5, 1950, the ENIAC team set into motion the first weather forecast ever undertaken by a digital—rather than human—computer. The ENIAC's computation of the first digital weather forecast lasted 33 days and nights. Jule Charney, who led the meteorology group at Princeton's Institute for Advanced Study and oversaw the work with von Neumann, wrote of the outcome on April 10, 1950: "We returned from Aberdeen only Saturday, after having been given a week's extension on the ENIAC. The extra week made all the difference in the world. At the end of the four weeks we had made two 24-hour forecasts. The first, as you know, was not remarkable for accuracy . . . The second turned out to be surprisingly good."[16] The team was ecstatic. They had proved that weather prediction was possible, if within limits. As Charney, von Neumann, and their colleague Ragnar Fjortoft noted in their paper summarizing the experiment, "The computation time for a 24-hour forecast was about 24 hours, that is, we were just able to keep pace with the weather."[17]

Granted, being able to compute a weather prediction at about the same pace the weather is actually happening might not seem a great achievement, but even at that early stage the pioneers of computing knew something that the rest of us later learned: that computers have a tendency to get faster over time. Actually, a lot faster. As Charney later noted, "It mattered little that the twenty-four hour prediction was twenty-four hours in the making. That was a purely technological problem. Two years later we were able to make the same prediction on our own machine in five minutes."[18]

"BINARY" MEANS "SOMETHING made of, or based on, two things or parts." A binary computer is one that comprises information conveyed as lists of zeroes and ones. Consequently, the elementary unit of memory and storage in a binary computer is defined as the bit, which stores a value of either zero or one. The word "bit" is just a contraction of "binary digit,"[19] thus a "binary computer" is the same as a "digital computer."

Since it's not possible to do much that is useful with a single bit, computer scientists early on defined another fundamental unit, the byte, which is eight bits—the size of the eight-day binary weather record I described at the start of this passage. With a byte it is possible to specify a letter or a mark of punctuation (see Text Box 4.2).[20]

We can use binary numbers not only to encode data—such as, "it only rained on friday"—but also to encode instructions—such as, "do not run the sprinkler system after any rainy day" or "mix wet ingredients and dry ingredients separately, then combine."[21] Data, and instructions to take actions based on that data, are conveyed in the same binary language.

When it comes to the power of digital computers, industry analysts and journalists alike tend to focus on processor speed. That's partly because it's relatively easy to measure, but also because improvements in processor speed over the past half-century have been impressive (see figure 4.1). The famed Moore's Law, which originated in a paper published by Intel cofounder Gordon Moore in 1965, is all about processor speed.[22] Moore described a yearly doubling of the number of components per integrated circuit (later updated to a doubling every two years), which is directly related to increased processor speed. The specific quantitative relationship first described by Moore held for nearly a half-century. From the standpoint of fundamental technological possibilities, it explains the advent of

Text Box 4.2 **Binary Encoding**

Let us say I wanted to store information on whether any precipitation occurred at a particular location over the period of eight days. My rule for encoding the weather is: If any precipitation occurred at that location on that date, I write "1"; if not I write "0." At the end of eight days, beginning and ending, for example, on Sunday, I have recorded the following data: 00000100. This tells me that it rained only one day: Friday. Recording these data for eight days in this manner required 8 bits of information. This can be generalized: the number of distinct possibilities that can be expressed with a binary number n is 2 raised to the nth power, or 2^n. With one digit I can encode $2^1 = 2$ possibilities; with two digits, $2^2 = 4$ possibilities; with eight digits, $2^8 = 256$ possibilities.

The more bits I have, the greater amount of information I can convey. With one bit I can express only two possibilities: "Yes" or "No." With two bits I can express four possibilities: "Yes, Yes," "Yes, No," "No, Yes," and "No, No." With three bits I can express eight possibilities. "Yes, Yes, Yes," "Yes, Yes, No," "Yes, No, Yes," "Yes, No, No," "No, Yes, Yes," "No, Yes, No," "No, No, Yes," "No, No, No." And so forth.

Let's go back to my weather example. What would it mean to have "information" about the weather—even about as simple a question as whether or not any precipitation was experienced at a particular location on each day of a given eight-day interval. Without any information, anything is possible. Rain may have fallen every day. Rain may have fallen no days. Rain may have fallen some days, but not others. In all, there are $2^8 = 256$ possibilities. When I record the outcome "00000100" I have narrowed those 256 possibilities down to one. To convey that information requires eight binary digits. So, the message that it only rained on Friday contains eight bits of information.

Of course, I can also convey the same information by sending a message in type: "it only rained on friday." I can do this in binary code by expressing each digit as a binary number. How do we do this? Very simply: By assigning each binary number, from 1 to 26, to a specific letter of the alphabet. For example

- 00001 = a
- 00010 = b
- 00011 = c
- all the way to
- 11010 = z

In other words, 11010 is the binary representation of the decimal number 26, and "z" is the 26th letter in the alphabet. So with five digits it is possible to specify, among 26 possible letters, the one letter that we intend to communicate. In that sense, communication of a single letter requires 5 bits of information (the number of digits in 11010).

What this example illustrates is that there exist more and less efficient approaches to communicating the same message. To convey "00000100" requires eight bits. To convey the message "it only rained on friday" requires five bits for each character in the message. Since there are 24 characters in the message "it only rained on friday" (letters as well as spaces), communicating the message requires roughly 120 bits. (Note that I am deliberately keeping these messages in all lower-case letters, as additional bits are required to differentiate lowercase from uppercase letters.)

everything from laptop computers to mobile phones to the ubiquitous sensors connected throughout our environment that have come to be known as the Internet of Things. Put another way, Moore's Law has allowed the digital world as we know it to come into being.

However, just as cooking is more about what you do in the kitchen than what kind of oven you have, the real power of digital computers has more to do with your strategy for using the computer to accomplish a particular goal. Consider the fact that Charney and his team were able reduce the time required for a particular calculation from 24 hours to five minutes. That is a 30,000 percent (or 300x) improvement in speed in one year—much faster than Moore's Law—driven primarily by improvements in computational strategy (code) rather than hardware. A recent research paper by Katja Grace of the Machine Intelligence Research Institute finds that this result is quite general.

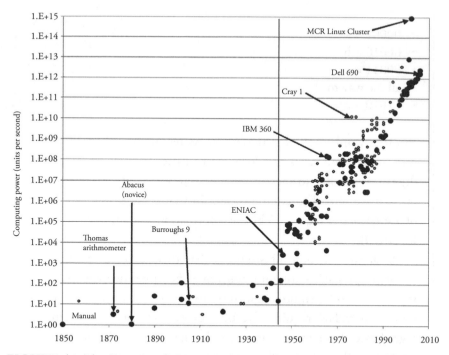

FIGURE 4.1 The Progress of Computing Power Measured in Computations per Second (CPS). Notes: The measure shown here is the index of computing power. For a discussion of the definition, see the text. The series is defined so that manual computing has a value of one. The large circles are estimates that have been judged relatively reliable, and the small circles are estimates in the literature that have not been independently verified. The vertical line is placed at 1944, which is the estimated breakpoint in productivity growth.

Source: William Nordhaus (2007), "Two Centuries of Productivity Growth in Computing," *The Journal of Economic History*, Vol. 67, No. 1 (March); pp. 143. Reprinted with permission of the publisher.

After assessing improvements in computation power in six specific areas, Grace found that "gains from algorithmic progress have been roughly fifty to one hundred percent as large as those from hardware progress." Furthermore, she continues, "improvements tend to be incremental, forming a relatively smooth curve on the scale of years."[23]

Grace's findings take away nothing from the power of Moore's Law: Moore's Law describes the increased power of the platform on which computation takes place, whereas "Grace's Law" describes increases in the power of the algorithms that run on that platform. The two are complementary.

Algorithmic progess of the type Katja Grace emphasizes is clearly an example of the advance of code. However, as I will describe more fully in chapter seven, the progress in hardware performance described by Moore's Law is equally an example of the advance of code. Progress in hardware performance is the result of improvements in "the recipe" for producing computer chips, and these recipes have advanced progressively in much the same way that recipes for producing Sumerian tablets improved more than five thousand years ago: through a relentless process of systematic tinkering with the "how" of production. That sort of systematic tinkering has been the primary driver in the advance of code and, as a consequence, in the advance of economies for as long as human societies have existed.

PART ONE HAS been about the advance of code—what code is and how it has been manifested at different stages in history. Chiseled axes, writing, culinary recipes, and the evolution of cities have all featured prominently. With the exception of Stone Age tools, they will, albeit in different forms, continue to do so as I proceed.

In this chapter I have described the evolution of a variant of code that is particularly relevant to our historical moment: code stored and executed by digital computers. The combinatoric "logic of invention" envisioned by Leibniz—a language for performing differentiation and recombination in the realm of ideas—has become a reality. Its power is as great as or greater than any of humanity's previous inventions, save perhaps writing and cities. The advance of code in the form of digital computation has enabled wonders like the accurate prediction of the weather, but it also has once again threatened to reduce individual authority and autonomy.

The power of digital computers is so great that a chess grandmaster was disqualified from a tournament in 2013 under suspicion of receiving computer-generated guidance via Morse code conveyed on his mobile phone.[24] How long will it be before a doctor is accused of malpractice for employing his or her medical best judgment instead of following the course of action recommended by an algorithm? To what limits will we allow code not only to displace human workers but also to usurp human authority?

It is with these questions that I begin Part Two.

PART TWO

CODE ECONOMICS

5

Substitution

The Great Man-vs-Machine Debate

I am convinced, that the substitution of machinery for human labour, is often very injurious to the interests of the class of labourers.
— David Ricardo, *On the Principles of Political Economy and Taxation*, 3rd edition, 1821

FANS OF THE Comedy Central series *South Park* will recall the 2004 "Goobacks" episode, in which Darryl Weathers calls a town meeting to protest the arrival of "The People from the Future"—immigrants fleeing overpopulation and poverty in the year 4035 who come to the town of South Park seeking work. (As they traveled back in time they accumulated goo on their backs—hence the name.) News reports describe the aliens as "a hairless, uniform mix of all races" who speak a sort of guttural Esperanto. They soon demonstrate a willingness to perform all manner of tedious jobs for low pay. "Now these people from the future are showing up and offering to do the same work for next to nothing," Weathers complains to his fellow citizens. "They took our jerbs [tr. jobs]!" A chorus of voices then takes up the chant, "They took our jerbs!"

After the broadcast of "Goobacks," the phrase "They took our jerbs!" took on a life of its own—which is to say, it became an Internet meme. A compilation of "They took our jerbs!" pronouncements from various *South Park* episodes that was posted on YouTube in 2008 has accumulated more than 1.4 million views and 4,700 comments over the past eight years.

This satiric *South Park* episode may have focused more on xenophobia than technophobia, but as a social commentary it is astute. It makes a fundamental and significant connection between immigration, artificial intelligence (AI), and economic vulnerability. As futurist Kevin Kelly has observed:

> AI could just as well stand for "Alien Intelligence" [as artificial intelligence]. We have no certainty we'll contact extra-terrestrial beings from one of the billion earth-like planets in the sky in the next 200 years, but we have almost 100% certainty that we'll manufacture an alien intelligence by then. When we face these synthetic aliens, we'll encounter the same benefits and challenges that we expect from contact with ET. They will force us to re-evaluate our roles, our beliefs, our goals, our identity. What are humans for? I believe our first answer will be: humans are for inventing new kinds of intelligences that biology could not evolve. Our job is to make machines that think differently—to create alien intelligences. Call them artificial aliens.[1]

Over the past few years, the onslaught of "artificial aliens" has become a national obsession. Picking up on themes first explored nearly two centuries ago by Mary Shelley in her 1818 novel *Frankenstein; or, The Modern Prometheus* and in Karel Čapek's 1920 science fiction play *R.U.R.*,[2] and further developed in Stanley Kubrick's *2001: A Space Odyssey* and Ridley Scott's dystopian masterpiece, *Blade Runner,* no fewer than a dozen major theatrical releases in the past two years have focused on the increasingly blurred boundary between man and machine—*Robot and Frank, Her, The Imitation Game, Big Hero 6, Chappie, Avengers: Age of Ultron,* and *Ex Machina* among them.[3]

Underlying the fascination with artificial aliens evidenced in popular culture is a widespread sense of apprehension about the viability of human work in a world increasingly dominated by digital computers. Entrepreneur and venture capitalist Marc Andreessen wrote in the *Wall Street Journal* in 2011, "Six decades into the computer revolution, four decades since the invention of the microprocessor, and two decades into the rise of the modern Internet, all of the technology required to transform industries through software finally works and can be widely delivered at global scale . . . More and more major businesses and industries are being run on software and delivered as online services—from movies to agriculture to national defense. Software is eating the world."[4]

As I noted in the Introduction to this book, recent observations regarding the impact of digital computing on the economy, and on human society more broadly, echo past debates on the impact of mechanization. Ada Lovelace and Herbert Simon, already mentioned, were early participants in the Great Man-vs-Machine Debate, which also has engaged important contributors to the history of ideas, including David Ricardo, the early nineteenth-century economist about whom we'll hear more shortly; John Maynard Keynes, who essentially invented the field of macroeconomics in the 1930s; Norbert Weiner, father of the field of robotics; and, most recently, Vint Cerf, co-inventor of the Transmission Control Protocol and the Internet Protocol (TCP/IP), which is the core architecture of the Internet. All of these people and many more, whose insights I will seek to convey in the coming pages, grappled with the difficult balance human societies must always find between the benefits of technologically enabled disruption and its cost in terms of a loss of human authority and autonomy.

Among the illustrious figures who have called attention to the potentially disruptive impact of mechanization and automation, the first was neither an economist nor a technologist nor a mathematician. He was a poet, George Gordon Byron, better known as Lord Byron.

ON FEBRUARY 27, 1812, Lord Byron delivered his first remarks before the House of Lords. The debate on that date concerned the Frame-Work Bill, which proposed that the destruction of mechanized looms known as stocking frames be deemed a capital felony, and hence punishable by death.

The Frame-Work Bill was prompted by a series of attacks on stocking frames that had begun in Nottinghamshire in November 1811. The attacks resembled similar acts of violence that had taken place in the French city of Lyon a decade earlier (see chapter three). The recent attacks were the work of a loose affiliation of textile artisans who called themselves the Luddites to suggest that they were followers of an imaginary Robin Hood-like character named General Ludd. Although the

Luddites' violence against property was met with predictable opprobrium among the Lords, their new member, Lord Byron, expressed sympathy for the Luddites and argued passionately against the imposition of capital penalties for the destruction of mechanized looms.

"By the adoption of one species of frame in particular, one man performed the work of many, and the superfluous laborers were thrown out of employment," Byron began. "Yet it is to be observed that the work thus executed was inferior in quality; not marketable at home, and merely hurried with a view to exportation." While the domestic market could not absorb the significant increase in output enabled by the mechanized loom, overseas markets could. Byron made the claim that the mechanization of production further intensified the waste and suffering caused by the disruption of trade brought on by the Napoleonic Wars: "Although the adoption of the enlarged machinery in that state of commerce which the country once boasted might have been beneficial to the master without being detrimental to the servant; yet, in the present situation of our manufactures, without a prospect of exportation, with the demand for work and workmen equally diminished, frames of this description tend materially to aggravate the distress and discontent of the disappointed sufferers."

Lord Byron's speech before the House of Lords on the Frame-Work Bill posed a fundamental question that has endured at the core of economic theory and in politics for two centuries: Is the adoption of "enlarged machinery" in fact "beneficial to the master without being detrimental to the servant" in some or even most cases? Or is it instead the case, as Byron asserted, that the advance of code—in this case mechanization—results only "in the enrichment of a few individuals" while throwing "the workman out of employment, and the laborer unworthy of his hire"?

In the field of economics, the Great Man-vs-Machine Debate began when one of the greatest figures in the history of economic thought changed his mind.

DAVID RICARDO WAS born in the City of London on April 18, 1772, the third of 17 children. His father, Abraham Ricardo, had emigrated to England from Holland in 1763 to expand the family's stockbrokerage business. David was sent back to live in Holland from age nine to eleven to learn Dutch and increase his connection to the Portuguese Jewish community there. When David was 14, his father brought him fully into the family business, where his responsibilities grew steadily. However, shortly after the family moved from London to the nearby town of Bow, David's connection to his family was severed suddenly when he announced his engagement to a neighbor, Priscilla Ann Wilkinson, one of three daughters of an eminent Quaker surgeon. Now on his own at the age of 21, Ricardo continued to work as a stockbroker and market speculator.

Ricardo was so successful in finance that he was semi-retired within a decade and free to dedicate much of his time to various intellectual pursuits, including the study of geology and mathematics. When Priscilla Ricardo fell ill in March 1799, the Ricardos traveled to Bath so Priscilla could recuperate in one of the town's famed spas. There he happened to spot a book by Adam Smith in a library and, after glancing through it briefly, requested that it be brought to his home. Priscilla Ricardo recovered, but the trajectory of her husband's life was altered: from the moment he encountered *The Wealth of Nations,* the study of what we now call economics became David Ricardo's primary preoccupation.

Ricardo's first analytical effort in the field of economics was an anonymous essay entitled "The Price of Gold," which was published in *The Morning Chronicle* in 1809. In the essay, Ricardo argued that directors of the Bank of England—of which he was one[5]—had been systematically devaluing the English pound for their own gain.[6] In 1813, when Parliament began to restrict trade in corn, Ricardo turned his attention from the debasement of the currency to the deleterious effects of trade restrictions. Here again he had the benefit of direct experience; he had, after all, been raised in two countries and spent a brief but lucrative career in the financial markets. The outcome of this effort was *On the Principles of Political Economy and Taxation,* published in 1817, a work of scope and significance comparable to Smith's *The Wealth of Nations*. In *Principles,* Ricardo introduced the concept of comparative advantage, which remains the primary framework through which economists understand gains from trade.

Principles was the summation of the first attempts to understand what Ricardo and his contemporaries referred to as political economy. For these early "classical" political economists, the primary domain of production in human society was what it had been for millennia: agriculture. While agricultural code did advance substantially during the era when Ricardo and his direct predecessors were writing, the fundamental technologies in use all involved one person using one piece of durable equipment—a plow, a hoe, or a scythe—in some cases powered by horses or oxen.

Ricardo's views on the primacy of land in the creation of wealth is evident from the first paragraph of the preface to *Principles*:

> The produce of the earth—all that is derived from its surface by the united application of labour, machinery, and capital, is divided among three classes of the community; namely, the proprietor of the land, the owner of the stock or capital necessary for its cultivation, and the labourers by whose industry it is cultivated.

The Ricardian view of the division of the returns from production among landlords, owners of capital, and workers is summarized in a cliché about real estate investing (attributed alternately to Mark Twain and Will Rogers): "Buy land, they're not making it any more." Ricardo saw laborers in all countries caught in a trap: the more productive their work, the greater the increase in their numbers and the less their ultimate happiness. In the long run, workers only got enough to reproduce themselves while landlords got . . . an awful lot.

As a result of this reasoning, Ricardo was not initially sympathetic to the views articulated by Byron and others who worried about the impact of new code, embodied as machinery, on the well-being of workers. Like the other leading economists of his generation—notably the Reverend Thomas Malthus—Ricardo believed that little could be done to improve the condition of the undifferentiated laboring masses fundamentally so long as their inclination was to expand their families whenever resources allowed them to do so. The nature of the evolution of work, and the possible substitution of machines for men in production, was not a question of great interest to Ricardo and other classical economists. If the introduction of new code were to increase national income by increasing productivity—that is, the output pie would grow—it would automatically increase the share of national income going to labor, as its slice of the pie would grow proportionately. Because proponents of this view held that the totality of wages were drawn from a national "fund" (a.k.a., slice of the pie) whose size would not change as the population changed, this line of argument became known as the wage fund theory (see Text Box 5.1).

Text Box 5.1 The Wage Fund Theory

When the English and Scottish political economists—Adam Smith, Jeremy Bentham, John Stuart Mill, the Reverend Thomas Malthus, and David Ricardo foremost among them—first considered what impact new machinery would have on the well-being of workers, their starting point was the work of the first political economists, the French Physiocrats. The Physiocrats' theories were in turn motivated by the dramatic, and generally positive, changes that occurred in France prior to the revolution in 1789—one or two generations before de Prony and Jacquard.

France at that time was a nation made prosperous from the bounty of the land. It was the first country to develop a large-scale middle class and the first to undergo the demographic phenomenon where rapid population growth is accompanied by an increase in income and a decrease in fertility rates. Agricultural production constituted 80 percent of France's income. Not surprisingly, the Physiocrats' view of the functioning of the economy took the total amount of land as a given, and assumed that it is from land that all wealth ultimately derives. Using the notation *"Output = F(Inputs)"* to denote "output is a function of 'inputs,'" we can write the following relationship:

$$Output = F\left(Land, Labor, Capital\right)$$

This equation says what happens in the process of agricultural production: land, labor, and capital combine in specific quantities to yield a specific quantity of output in the form of crops. It presumes that the farmer employs some method of combining labor with land and capital to yield the output. But the equation itself does not offer any particulars regarding that method—that is, how production takes place.

English and Scottish political economists largely accepted the Physiocrats' view of the economy as an essentially zero-sum game, one in which national capital is fixed and its bounty is necessarily shared within the population: land yields output, and that output is shared between landowners, laborers, and merchants in fixed proportions.

In sharp contrast to the Physiocrats, however, the British classical economists emphasized capital, rather than just land, as the productive wellspring from which national income derives.[7] Reflecting the different composition of the British and French economies at that time, the classical economists incorporated machinery into national capital.

The classical view of the allocation of wealth in the economy is summarized in the wage fund theory, which is expressed by the following relationship:

$$Wage = \frac{Capital}{Population}$$

Since the classical economists assumed that the stock of capital does not change in response to changes in the wage rate paid to labor,[8] a natural implication of this theory is that increases in population naturally drive down wages, and vice versa.[9]

The notion that both population growth and decreased wages are an inevitable consequence of increased "public prosperity" was developed two decades later by the Reverend Thomas Malthus in his 1798 book, *An Essay on the Principle of Population*. By adding the observation that increased income induces the poor to have more children, Malthus arrived at his well-known formulation: "No sooner is the laboring class comfortable again than the same retrograde and progressive movements with respect to happiness are repeated." Humanity is doomed to alternating boom and bust cycles, driven by the inverse relationship between population levels and per-capita income.[10]

While the wage fund theory may have been esoteric in its conception, it was nakedly brutal in its implementation. For one thing, it implied that any attempt to "assist" the poor was not only futile but counterproductive: any assistance provided to paupers in workhouses constituted a withdrawal from a fixed national wage "fund," and thus necessarily implied there was less in the fund to compensate employed laborers. The theory was made operational in the Poor Laws of 1834, which created the poorhouses whose existence would be decried decades later by Charles Dickens.[11] The miserable conditions in the poorhouses were a matter not of accident but of careful design: the intent was that life in the poorhouses should be so unpleasant as to make wage labor of any type seem more appealing than public assistance. It was directly in response to the Poor Laws that Dickens conceived the character of Ebenezer Scrooge in *A Christmas Carol*. At one point in the story, two gentlemen raising money for charity appear at the door of Scrooge's counting house, where he employs a single clerk, Bob Cratchit, as a human computer. After a brief exchange, one of the gentlemen challenges Scrooge's support of the poorhouses, stating that "many can't go there; and many would rather die." Scrooge replies, in a Malthusian manner, "If they would rather die, they had better do it, and decrease the surplus population."

As Ricardo wrote in the first edition of *Principles*, "Capital is that part of the wealth of a country which is employed in production, and consists of food, clothing, tools, raw materials, machinery, &c. necessary to give effect to labour . . . In proportion to the increase of capital will be the increase in the demand for labour; in proportion to the work to be done will be the demand for those who are to do it."[12] Think, for example, of one person operating a single plow: there is no way for the plow to function without a human operator. Under the assumption that capital and labor thus are perfect complements, there is no way for machines to displace workers because the two are always used in fixed proportions.

Having thus ruled out, a priori, substitution between capital and labor, classical economists held the view that the wages earned by workers were determined by immutable laws of demography. More people competing for their share of the "wage fund" would always mean that each person earned less. Since humankind had not (at least up to the end of the eighteenth century) devised a systematic method for keeping the human population from growing, other than the brute force of biological necessity, wages would always and everywhere be forced down to subsistence levels by demographic pressures. As a result, life was, as Hobbes famously noted, "nasty, brutish, and short." Code was not part of the story.

Within a few years, however, Ricardo's views had shifted. More than just a simple shift of opinion on an important public policy matter, his changing views on the Great Man-vs-Machine Debate anticipated a fundamental change in the way economists understood production, as agriculture gradually ceded to manufacturing the central role it had held in the economy for millennia.

AROUND THE TIME Ricardo wrote *On the Principles of Political Economy*, the end of the Napoleonic Wars caused a disruption of the economies of Europe, with severe consequences. The miserable conditions of urban laborers and workers' violent protests against the introduction of new machinery prompted a reconsideration of the wage fund theory. Could the introduction of automated production somehow constitute a threat to the well-being of workers?

The historical record confirms that the realities of the ongoing processes of mechanization and industrialization, as noted early on by Lord Byron, were very different from the picture adherents to the wage fund theory held in their heads. While the long-term impact the Industrial Revolution had on the health and well-being of the English population was strongly positive, the first half of the nineteenth century was indeed a time of exceptional hardship for English workers. In a study covering the years 1770–1815, Stephen Nicholas and Richard Steckel report "falling heights of urban- and rural-born males after 1780 and a delayed growth spurt for 13- to 23-year-old boys," as well as a fall in the English workers' height relative to that of Irish convicts.[13] By the 1830s, the life expectancy of anyone born in Liverpool and Manchester was less than 30 years—as low as had been experienced in England since the Black Death of 1348.

Responding to these contemporary realities, John Barton, a Quaker political economist, published a pamphlet in 1817 titled, *Observations on the Circumstances Which Influence the Condition of the Labouring Classes of Society*. Rather than challenge the classical economists' conclusions about the lived reality of industrialization, Barton challenged the assumptions on which the wage fund theory was based and indicated how this theory led to faulty conclusions. Barton began by targeting the Malthusian assumption that population grows in response to increasing wages. His argument is as straightforward as it was prescient. He began by noting that there was no a priori reason to believe that labor and capital were perfect complements, as classical economists implicitly assumed. The more sensible assumption was that, as wages increased, manufacturers and farmers alike would tend to substitute animals or machines for human labor.[14] Rather than increasing the birth rate, the higher wages brought on by the introduction of new machinery would increase intergenerational differences in income and thus delay childbearing.[15] Contrary to the Malthusian line of argument, this is exactly what happened.

Ricardo read and was persuaded by Barton's book. He considered the question of mechanization of such great importance that he added a new chapter, titled "On Machinery," to the third edition of *On the Principles of Political Economy*. In an astonishing reversal, he wrote in 1821, "I now, however, see reason to be satisfied that the one fund, from which landlords and capitalists derive their revenue, may increase, while the other, that upon which the labouring class mainly depend, may diminish, and therefore it follows, if I am right, that the same cause which may increase the net revenue of the country, may at the same time render the population redundant, and deteriorate the condition of the labourer."[16]

However, this conclusion did not alter Ricardo's view that society was improved by the adoption of improved machinery—and by the evolution of code with which it was inextricably linked. Linking his theories of trade with his observations about machinery, Ricardo noted that the most economically efficient machinery would certainly be adopted somewhere in the world and the wage would be affected accordingly: "Machinery cannot be worked without the assistance of men, it cannot be made but with the contribution of their labour."[17]

By incorporating the potential for substitution between capital and labor, Ricardo led the field of economics in rejecting the wage fund theory, along with its Dickensian implications for policy. He accepted the notion the introduction of new machinery would result in the displacement of workers. The upshot was that the workers were still assumed to be doomed, but the reason was now substitution of machines for labor, not scarcity of a Malthusian variety.

With that, the Great Man-vs-Machine Debate intensified, ushering in a wholesale change in the way economists thought of code, workers, and the returns from productive activity in the economy.

Nearly four decades later and six thousand miles away, the Great Man-vs-Machine Debate took another sharp turn, setting it on a direct course to the present day.

IN THE FALL of 1868, the city of San Francisco was flush with anticipation, as the First Transcontinental Railroad (also known as the Pacific Railroad) was within months of completion. However, not all believed that the coming of the railroad would bring greater prosperity. Among the skeptics was a 29-year-old typesetter named Henry George. George's work further challenged the classical economists' wage fund theory and introduced a new dimension to the Great Man-vs-Machine Debate that today resonates powerfully amid current controversies over the relationship between prosperity and inequality.

George worked for the *San Francisco Times,* in which he published an editorial in late 1868 titled, "What the Railroads Will Bring Us." Much like those today who are concerned about the social inequities brought on by the advance of digital technologies, George was concerned about the social inequity the advance of the railroad would bring. George began his piece by noting that "the California of the new era will be greater, richer, more powerful than the California of the past ... She will have more wealth; but will it be so evenly distributed? She will have more luxury and refinement and culture; but will she have such general comfort, so little squalor and misery?" His answer to these two questions was a resounding "no." With the coming of the railway, George predicted, California's fate would be the "crowding of people into immense cities" and "marshaling of men into big gangs under the control of 'captains of industry,' " neither of which "tend to foster personal independence—the basis of all virtue." He concluded: "A great change is coming over our State. We should not prevent it if we could, and could not if we would, but we can view it in all its bearings—look at the dark as well as the bright side, and endeavor to hasten that which is good and retard or prevent that which is bad."[18] George's editorial hit a nerve. It was widely read and reprinted at the time, and was required reading in California schools for decades to come.

In 1871, three years after publication of "What the Railroads Will Bring Us," George stopped to rest while on a horseback ride and sat overlooking San Francisco Bay. He later recalled the revelation he experienced: "I asked a passing teamster, for want of something better to say, what land was worth there. He pointed to some cows grazing so far off that they looked like mice and said, 'I don't know exactly, but there is a man over there who will sell some land for a thousand dollars an acre.' Like a flash it came over me that there was the reason of advancing poverty with advancing wealth. With the growth of population, land grows in value, and the men who work it must pay more for the privilege."[19]

George set about putting his insight into words. The task would take him the remainder of that decade and would bring his family to the brink of bankruptcy more than once. The book he ultimately completed and self-published in 1879 was titled *Progress and Poverty*. It would become the most commercially successful book ever published by an American up to that time, selling more than two million copies worldwide.

Progress and Poverty generalized the observations George had made earlier about the coming of the railroad. Anticipating by 150 years the theories of Jane Jacobs and the findings of the Santa Fe team that I described in chapter two, George asserted that increasing population density (not, as Malthus claimed, population decline) was the source of increased prosperity in human societies: "Wealth is greatest where population is densest ... the production of wealth to a given amount of labor increases as population increases."[20] The frequent interactions among people in densely populated cities accelerates the emergence and evolution of code. However, while population growth and increased density naturally bring increased prosperity, they also, just as naturally, bring increasing inequality and poverty. Why? Because the fruits of labor are inevitably gathered by the owners of land. "That [the] increasing productive power [of industry] does not add to the reward of labor is not because of competition, but because competition is one-sided," he writes. "Land, without which there can be no production, is monopolized, and the competition of producers for its use forces wages to a minimum and gives all the advantage of increasing productive power to land owners, in higher rents and increased land values."[21]

In sharp contrast with Karl Marx, whose *Das Kapital* appeared more than a decade before *Progress and Poverty,* George stated that "the antagonism of interests is not between labor and capital . . . but is in reality between labor and capital on the one side and land ownership on the other."[22] The implication of his analysis was as simple as it was powerful: to avoid concentrating wealth in the hands of the few, it was the government's responsibility to eliminate all taxes on capital and labor, the productive elements of the economy, and to replace those taxes with a single tax on land. Thus the Single Tax movement was born.

The Single Tax movement was far larger and more influential in its day than the recent Tea Party and Occupy movements combined. With adherents across the United States and around the world, the movement even spawned its own journal, *The Single Tax Review,* which was founded in 1901 (four years after George's death) and remained in print continually until 1921.

THE FIRST ROUND of the Great Man-vs-Machine Debate focused on mechanization. In that domain, the verdict of history was clear: machines turned out to be complements to human labor, not pure substitutes. This verdict is sufficiently conclusive that the argument to the contrary, exemplified by Lord Byron's remarks to the House of Lords, has come to be known as the Luddite Fallacy.

Generally we know that, from the mid-nineteenth century onward, the Industrial Revolution in England dramatically increased both wages and the standard of living for workers. In the aggregate, when workers left their villages to work in urban factories, inevitably submitting to the authority of managerially enforced code in their jobs and to the various constraints of urban life, the increased productive efficiency achieved by the advance of code did lead to genuine improvements in the median level of well-being, even if those improvements were inequitably distributed, as Henry George predicted. As George Mason University economist Alex Tabarrok has put it, "[If] the Luddite fallacy were true we would all be out of work because productivity has been increasing for two centuries."[23]

The generally beneficial impact on human communities of human labor being displaced by machines and factory workers by automated assembly is a matter of historical record. But what of cubicle dwellers displaced by digital computers? Is there any reason to believe that history will repeat itself? Will further concessions of individual autonomy in the service of increased efficiency continue to yield gains sufficiently large to improve median levels of well-being? If so, are we willing to accept the increasing inequality the continued advance of code will likely create? History's adverse judgment against the Luddites notwithstanding, these are serious questions. As former treasury secretary Larry Summers wrote in the *Wall Street Journal* regarding the displacement of workers due to digital disruption, "There are more sectors losing jobs than creating jobs. And the general-purpose aspect of software technology means that even the industries and jobs that it creates are not forever."[24] How can this be a positive development?

While these questions do not have easy answers, history does provide some guidance. Ours is not the first era in which people performing mental labor have faced threats to their livelihood due to automation. Eighteenth- and nineteenth-century countinghouse clerks—embodied in Charles Dickens' creation Bob Cratchit—toiled endlessly at standing desks performing arithmetical calculations. With the advent of the first adding machines, notably the Burroughs (see figure 5.1), the work of these clerks could be performed by people with far less training and natural computational acuity. By the 1920s it was no longer just artisans and laborers whose livelihoods were considered in jeopardy due to mechanization; clerical workers were at risk as well.

In 1926, University of Chicago economist Paul Douglas published an article in *System: The Magazine of Business*—the *Forbes* of the era—titled "What Is Happening to the 'White-Collar-Job' Market?" Douglas described a peculiar and potentially alarming trend: the wages of factory workers were catching up to the wages earned by salaried white-collar workers. This fact was peculiar because the growth rate of white-collar work during the interval Douglas studied, 1889 to 1922, was twice the rate for factory work. Given this strong growth in relative demand for white-collar workers, one might have expected correspondingly strong wage growth; the data instead revealed a moderate wage decline. The convergence of white-collar salaries and factory wages was potentially alarming, as white-collar work required a higher level of education than factory work and was viewed as a path toward a new, relatively more comfortable version of the middle-class life. With

157.38	157.38
762.91	762.91
435.75	435.75
800.76	800.76
43.02	43.02
987.25	987.25
500.00	500.00
1,003.50	1,003.50
245.65	245.65
82.47	82.47
4,250.86	4,250.86
1,014.75	1,014.75
243.92	243.92
914.75	914.75
5,475.80	5,475.80
14,850.07	14,850.07
410.25	410.25
.74	.74
9.10	9.10
27.72	27.72
896.35	896.35
1,238.63	1,238.63
7,800.00	7,800.00
10,000.00	10,000.00
127.34	127.34
77.01	77.01
303.24	303.24
3,808.89	3,808.89
458.92	458.92
1,456,789.34	1,456,789.34
11,025.22	11,025.22
600.10	600.10
2,250.85	2,250.85
14,823.45	14,823.45
8,207.12	8,207.12
2,100.00	2,100.00
1,552,723.11	1,552,723.11 *

| Facsimile of Figures Added and Listed by hand by the average Clerk in 9 minutes. | Facsimile of Figures Added and Listed by a Burroughs in 1½ minutes by an average operator. |

FIGURE 1

Why the Burroughs is a Necessity

Expert operators on a Burroughs can add and list 500 checks, different amounts, in 6 min. 18 sec.

48

FIGURE 5.1 "Why the Burroughs is a Necessity." This image is reproduced from a book published by the Burroughs Corporation in 1910, describing the history and societal impacts of the Burroughs Adding Machine. The left-hand side image is a facsimile of a set of figures added by hand, stated to require an average clerk 9 minutes to complete; the right-hand side is a facsimile of a set of figures added with a Burroughs Adding Machine, stated to require 1.5 minutes for an average operator to complete. Regardless of the accuracy of the time estimates, the key point is that the use of the Burroughs Adding Machine required considerably less training and mental acuity than adding the figures by hand.

Source: Burroughs Corporation (1910), "A Better Day's Work at a Less Cost of Time, Work, and Worry to the Man at the Desk," Detroit, MI: Burroughs Adding Machine Company. Digitized by Google.

the erosion of white-collar advantages then in process, Douglas warned that "not too many years in the future we may find the situation permanently like that of 1918–20, when the wage-earner [that is, factory worker] was frequently making more money than the office employee. Then the only advantage to the office job will be that of working in a white, clean collar instead of a pair of greasy overalls."[25] Analyzing the data, Douglas found three reasons for this convergence of white-collar salaries and factory wages. The first was simply that, while demand for white-collar workers had grown rapidly, the supply of white-collar workers had grown even more rapidly. This was due to a combination of workers' preference for clerical over factory jobs and an increase in workers' educational attainment, which created a larger pool of candidates for white-collar work. (Recent labor market dynamics in China have shown a similar trend.)[26]

The second reason had to do with machinery, as Douglas noted: "The increased use of mechanical appliances in offices has tended to lower the skill required. An old-fashioned bookkeeper, for instance, had to write a good hand, he had to be able to multiply and divide with absolute accuracy. Today his place is taken by a girl who operates a bookkeeping machine, and it has taken her a few weeks at most to become a skilled bookkeeper." In other words, the introduction of machinery displaced skilled workers for the very same reason it enhanced human capabilities: it allowed a worker with relatively rudimentary training to perform tasks that previously required a skilled worker.

There is more to the story, however. Douglas continues: "Another way of looking at it, is this: Where formerly the skill used in bookkeeping was exercised by the bookkeeper, today that skill is exercised by the factory employees who utilize it to manufacture a machine which can do the job of keeping books, when operated by someone of skill far below that of the former bookkeeper. And because of this transfer of skill from the office to the factory, the rewards of skill are likewise transferred to the wage-earner at the plant."

This is a vitally important point, to which I will return later in the book. The essence of this insight is that introducing more powerful machines into the workplace does more than simply encode into the machine the skills or capabilities that previously resided only in humans; it also shifts the burden of skill from one domain of work to another. As

Douglas reported, one such shift in the early twentieth century was from the skill of bookkeeping to the skill of manufacturing a calculating machine; the result was a relative growth in manufacturing wages. A comparable shift in recent decades has been from the skill of manufacturing computing machines (think IBM or Dell in their heydays) to that of creating improved instructions for computing machines; the result has been a relative growth in programmers' wages. The underlying process is the same. Improvements in technology will predictably reduce demand for the skills held by some workers, but they also will enhance the capabilities of other workers and shift the requirement of skill from one domain of work to another. (Later work by Douglas, in collaboration with the mathematician John Cobb, set the stage for the modern study of productivity and capital-labor substitution in the economy; see Text Box 5.2.)

In the manner described by Paul Douglas, work divides or "bifurcates" as code advances in a predictable and repeatable way. The bifurcation of work is a critical mechanism by which the advance of code yields improvements in human well-being at the same time it increases human reliance on code.

IN THIS CHAPTER I have described economists' first efforts to represent production processes and quantify the importance of code. In the next chapter I will describe how economists' efforts to understand the origins of organized commerce and novelty in economic systems finds a direct parallel in biologists' efforts to understand the origins of life and novelty in biological systems.[27]

Before we move on, a brief postscript to the story of Lord Byron, Charles Babbage, and Ada Lovelace, which anticipates themes in the next chapter concerning the challenge posed to the most highly educated workers by the "immigrants from the future" to whom I alluded at the start of this chapter—or, more precisely, the machine learning algorithms and digitally enabled systems for artificial intelligence that are today at the frontier of the advance of code.

In 1957, Herbert Simon delivered a talk to the Operations Research Society. He observed with delight "that physicists and electrical engineers had very little to do with the invention of the digital computer—the real inventor was the economist Adam Smith, whose idea was translated into hardware through successive stages of development by two

Text Box 5.2 The Cobb-Douglas Production Function

While lecturing at Amherst College in the spring of 1927, Paul Douglas began work on a paper titled simply, "A Theory of Production." At that time, Douglas had laboriously compiled data on American manufacturing during the interval from 1889 to 1922, including the total capital in use, the number of wage earners employed in manufacturing, and manufacturing output. When Douglas plotted the data, he noticed an unexpected regularity: the relative shares of capital and labor in output were consistent across the entire interval. Working with mathematician Charles Cobb, he determined that the data throughout the period covered by his study could be well represented by a variant of a generalized production function linking capital (K) and labor (L) inputs to produced output (Y). The specific variant that fit the data was the following:

$$Y = K^{0.25} \bullet L^{0.75}$$

Cobb and Douglas arrived at this particular functional form because it was known to have properties consistent with some commonsense reasoning about the economy. Specifically, this function exhibits "constant returns to scale," which means it describes a situation in which doubling all of the inputs into the production process (in this case, capital and labor) results in exactly double the output. In 1928 they published their joint work in the *American Economic Review*, the journal of the American Economic Association.[28]

That the Cobb-Douglas production function fit the data for manufacturing inputs and outputs was not what made it interesting. What was interesting was that the Cobb-Douglas estimates validated a particular theoretically derived prediction about the way output was shared by capitalists and laborers. The validated theory is today known as the "Just Deserts" theory of distribution in economics—which, although the spelling here is correct, might intuitively and by way of analogy make more sense if spelled "just desserts."

First advanced by John Bates Clark (namesake of the American Economic Association's annual award to an outstanding economist under the age of 40, the second most prestigious award in economics, after the Nobel Prize) in an address to the American Economic Association in 1888, the Just Deserts theory states that the distribution of output going to labor as opposed to capital is—in an economy free of "distortions" such as the bargaining power of labor unions or collusion among capitalists—determined by the fundamentals of technology. In his classic 1899 book, *The Distribution of Wealth,* Clark sums up the theory:

> It is the purpose of this work to show that the distribution of the income of society is controlled by a natural law, and that this law, if it worked without friction, would give to every agent of production the amount of wealth which that agent creates. However wages may be adjusted by bargains freely made between individual men, the rates of pay that result from such transactions tend, it is here claimed, to equal that part of the product of industry which is traceable to the labor itself; and however interest may be adjusted by similarly free bargaining, it naturally tends to equal the fractional product that is separately traceable to capital.

An additional hour added to the pool of labor is rewarded in accordance with the contribution that additional hour makes to output; the same is true with capital. As this additional, or "marginal," product of labor goes up, wages go up; as the additional, or "marginal," product of capital goes up, rates of return to capital go up. To both labor and capital the implication is clear: you get what you get and you don't get upset.

If Cobb and Douglas' estimates were correct, then the Just Deserts theory predicted that 75 percent of output of production during the interval from 1899 to 1922 should have gone to workers—where the 75 percent corresponds directly to the 0.75 exponent in the above function. The actual value? 74.1 percent. The absolute magnitudes of capital and labor thus determined the size of the total output pie, while the coefficients of the Cobb-Douglas production function determined the size of the slices going to capital and labor—25.9 percent of output went to capital owners and 74.1 percent was paid to workers as wages.

The fact that Cobb and Douglas' estimates matched the wealth data so closely was a major validation of neoclassical production theory. Nonetheless, as Douglas himself would later report, his paper with Charles Cobb "was very adversely received . . . Virtually no one had a good word for our efforts."

Over time, however, the approach Cobb and Douglas pioneered gained favor. By the 1950s, the general form of the function they had estimated in their 1928 paper became a mainstay of both empirical and theoretical economics. While it since has been superseded in economic theory by more complex and flexible functional forms, variants of the Cobb-Douglas production function remain the default framework for most empirical production analyses.

mathematicians, Prony and Babbage." Simon then recounted the tale of de Prony and the hairdressers that I related in chapter three, concluding that "it was Prony's mass production of the mathematical tables . . . that suggested to Babbage that machinery could replace human labor in the clerical phases of the task, and that started him on the undertaking of designing and constructing an automatic calculating engine."[29]

Seven years earlier, in 1950, Simon had given a talk to a group of business executives in which he focused on the advent of digital computers—then only five years old—that recalled the insights of Paul Douglas. Referring to advances in digital computing, Simon stated that, "in describing these developments, which are now engrossing the efforts of . . . scientists in a dozen locations, I do not wish to create undue anxiety about [the] prospective obsolescence [of business executives]. Before today's business executives take their place with the mastodons, quite a span of years, if not generations, is likely to elapse. Nevertheless, I think it is fair to regard these researches . . . as portents that we are in time going to have a theory in management—theory of the kind that predicts reality, and not of the kind that is contrasted with practice."[30]

If the business executives in attendance were discomfited by Simon's suggestion that digital machinery could progressively replace their labor, they might have taken comfort in the observations of Babbage's collaborator, Ada Lovelace. As you will recall, while Lovelace specifically

envisioned that computers could be used to write poetry or music—
in fact could compose "elaborate and scientific pieces of music of any
degree of complexity"—she did not believe that computers would be
capable of human thought or of undertaking higher-order tasks. "The
Analytical Engine has no pretension whatever to originate anything,"
she wrote. "It can do whatever we know how to in order to perform. It
can only follow analysis; but it has not power of anticipating any analytical relations or truths." Alan Turing would later term this assertion
"Lady Lovelace's Objection."

Where modern-day inheritors of the argument advanced by Lord
Byron before the House of Lords have kept alive his concern that automation of work results only "in the enrichment of a few individuals"
while it throws "the workman out of employment, and the laborer unworthy of his hire," Ada Lovelace posthumously counters these concerns by insisting on the existence of a boundary to the advance of artificial intelligence—a line beyond which human cognition, experience,
and creativity cannot be simulated by any computer.

In the Great Man-vs-Machine Debate, Byron and Lovelace thus,
ironically, end up occupying opposite ends of the spectrum—followers
of Byron arguing that the ability to substitute machines for human work
is all but unbounded, and those of Lovelace arguing to the contrary.
Why the irony? Because Ada Lovelace was Lord Byron's daughter.[31]

6

Information

"Reliable Circuits Using Crummy Relays"

Philosophy is written in that great book which ever is before our eyes—I mean the universe—but we cannot understand it if we do not first learn the language and grasp the symbols in which it is written.

—Galileo Galilei, *The Systems of the World*, 1661

ON JANUARY 5, 2015, on the second day of the annual meeting of the American Economic Association, extreme overcrowding at one session prompted the appearance of a Boston police officer. The officer promptly directed a number of participants to vacate the room to ensure compliance with the fire code.

What exceptional offering prompted this frenzy among economists? The session in question was titled, "Machine Learning Methods in Economics and Econometrics." The session did have some star power from the standpoint of the economics profession, as panelists included Stanford's Susan Athey, the 2007 recipient of the John Bates Clark Medal and the former chief consulting economist for Microsoft, as well as Harvard's Sendhil Mullainathan, a groundbreaking behavioral economist. However, the real draw of the session was that it was one of the few in which the application to economics of the emerging field of data analytics—or Big Data—took center stage.

To put this session in context, let's start with the term featured in its title, "machine learning." Machine learning finds answers based on computationally intensive but efficient pattern matching.[1] An example is Google Translate. Rather than mimic the process of human language acquisition, Google Translate employs a technique known as statistical machine translation. This technique involves first gathering a "training dataset" comprised of as much text as possible previously translated from one language to another, and then undertaking a thorough computational analysis of that translated text to arrive at a raw probability that a specific phrase or sentence in Language A—really, just a string of characters—corresponds to another specific phrase or sentence in Language B. That information is stored until someone types a phrase or sentence into Google Translate, at which point the program offers up the most likely corresponding phrase or sentence.

Google Translate doesn't "know" anything about grammar, syntax, or even vocabulary, and it doesn't attempt understanding at that level. It simply offers responses based on probable matches, based on large datasets, all previously created by human intelligence. The hour-by-hour weather predictions we can now access on our cell phones are generated the same way. Machine learning works well for translation and weather prediction—for now, better than any automated translator or weatherman that is based on the sort of brain-mimicking architecture envisioned by early artificial intelligence programmers like Herbert Simon and Al Newell.

Machine learning pioneer Leslie Valiant described the approach in his 1984 paper, "A Theory of the Learnable." "Humans appear to be able to learn new concepts without needing to be programmed explicitly in any conventional sense," Valiant observed. "In this paper we regard learning as the phenomenon of knowledge acquisition in the absence of explicit programming."[2] This process begins when "the learner has access to a supply of typical data that positively exemplify the concept," which is the training dataset. Using the training dataset, the machine learning algorithm matches patterns and estimates relevant probabilities. Additional test datasets can be used to evaluate and improve the performance of the algorithm.

Let us consider what it might mean for the field of economics that the "Machine Learning" session was so overcrowded—mostly with graduate students seeking insights into the new techniques shaping the future of economics. While the patterns sought by machine-learning algorithms may well begin as questions derived from theory, once the algorithms take over, theory and even detailed simulation take a back seat, as the algorithm and the data tell their own stories.

Of course, as noted data journalist Nate Silver is quick to point out, "no amount of data is a substitute for scientific inference and hypothesis testing, any kind of structured analysis of a system." Nonetheless, the introduction and rapid uptake of machine learning in economics places code at the center of economic inquiry as never before, and it challenges long-held notions of expertise and methodological validity. David Rothkopf, CEO and editor of *Foreign Policy*, recently wrote a piece for that publication titled "Requiem for the Macrosaurus," in which he stated:

> Whereas today's economic models rely on a relative handful of variables, future models will be able to utilize a limitless number, creating opportunities for policymakers to develop new tools. Many of these new models and tools will require not the insights of micro-economists, but those of nano-economists, superspecialists in the relationship between much smaller economic units and the larger economy as a whole. New economic theories will also emerge based on growing sources of real-time data about every aspect of markets and the factors affecting them—and new, ever more powerful tools will be created for analyzing that data.[3]

But if macroeconomists—the "Macrosauruses" in Rothkopf's piece—sense that their authority is being challenged by the power of these new analytic techniques in this manner, they can take comfort in the fact that they are not alone. Speaking at the National Academy of Sciences in 2015, University of Chicago economist and *Freakonomics* coauthor Steven Levitt noted, echoing Herbert Simon's remarks to a group of executives in 1950: "It's a very hard world for business—and I think also policy makers—to transform into, where the role of the executive goes from being, 'I am the expert, who knows everything,' to my job being 'Can I ask the right questions and can I marshal the right data and tell me what the answers are to those questions?'"[4]

The application of code to business decision-making represents the latest chapter in the evolution of code and learning—one that is changing not only the field of economics but the economy itself.

"THE DENSITY OF settlement of economists over the whole empire of economic science is very uneven, with a few areas of modest size holding the bulk of the population," Herbert Simon observed in his 1978 Nobel lecture. "The economic Heartland is the normative study of the international and national economies and their markets, with its triple main concerns of full employment of resources, the efficient allocation of resources, and equity in distribution of the economic product."[5] In contrast to this crowded "Heartland" in which questions about the allocation and distribution of resources dominated, the domain of study relating to the actual behavior of business firms—the creative actors whose existence largely defines "the economy," in contrast to human society more broadly—until World War II represented a remote and sparsely settled colony. "Such inhabitants as it had were mainly industrial engineers, students of public administration, and specialists in business functions, none of whom especially identified themselves with the economic sciences. Prominent pioneers included the mathematician, Charles Babbage, inventor of the digital computer, the engineer, Frederick Taylor, and the administrator, Henri Fayol."[6]

However, Simon continued, "during World War II, this territory, almost abandoned, was rediscovered by scientists, mathematicians, and statisticians concerned with military management and logistics, and was renamed 'operations research' or 'operations analysis.' So remote were the operations researchers from the social science community that economists wishing to enter the territory had to establish their own colony, which they called 'management science.'"[7] Management science is distinguished from economics in the Heartland by its focus on code: "These are theories of *how* to decide rather than theories of *what* to decide."[8]

Simon's Nobel Prize citation noted his work on "bounded rationality," a phrase Simon himself coined and around which he organized his contributions to economics. However, this phrase, much like Simon's metaphor of the Heartland versus the colonies, suggests a marginalization of systematic inquiry into the how of production rather than the what, and of the fundamental information processing that underlies all decision-making.

That Simon felt himself to be marginalized among economists—despite the fact that he had just been awarded a Nobel Prize in economics—is actually understandable. For one thing, he considered himself not an economist but a behavioral scientist. For another, he had little patience for those who failed to grasp truths that he himself saw as obvious. Furthermore, the trend of the discipline in the 1970s was strongly toward neoclassical choice models that emphasized the allocation of resources under assumptions of perfect information—and that mostly disregarded the algorithms of production that were his preoccupation.

That said, if we consider the discipline of economics in the context of broader trends in scientific inquiry in the twentieth century, we see the "sparsely populated" intellectual territory inhabited by Herbert Simon, Charles Babbage, and Frederick Taylor for what it really was at the time Simon delivered his Nobel address: the frontier.

THE ECONOMICS TAUGHT in undergraduate courses is a great example of history being written by the victors. Because the methodologies of neoclassical economics experienced numerous triumphs in the middle of the twentieth century, the study of the distribution of resources within the economy—choice rather than code and, to a lesser extent, consumption rather than production—came to be taught as the totality of economics. However, the reality is that choice and code have always coexisted, not only in the economy itself but in the history of economic thought.

The tendency toward selective memory among economists is nowhere better illustrated than in the story of William Jevons, widely recognized as one of three original architects of neoclassical choice theory—a father of modern economics.

Like David Ricardo, Jevons was first motivated to take up the study of economics by reading Adam Smith's *Wealth of Nations.* Also like Ricardo, Jevons devoted his twenties to business pursuits. Those experiences left him with a first-hand appreciation of the complex working of markets and, in turn, of the singular power of mathematics to simplify and organize a complex world.[9] "Such is the infinite complexity of causes and of effect that we cannot treat them in detail ... Economy, indeed, being concerned with quantities, has always of necessity been mathematical in its subject, but the strict and general statement, and the easy comprehension of its quantitative laws has been prevented by neglect of those powerful methods of expression which have been applied to most other sciences with so much success."[10]

The preferred tool of the time was optimization, using calculus. The use of calculus, along with the fundamental framing of economic experience as dominated by the need to make choices about the allocation of resources, led Jevons to devise the tools of marginal analysis that became the core of the new classical or neoclassical economic theory that is taught today in college courses.

And here the story usually ends. However, there was much more to Jevons.

Like his contemporary, Henry George, Jevons sought throughout his life to make sense of the fundamental contradiction in the history of his native city: evident progress on a societal level juxtaposed against wide variation in the fortunes of individuals and groups within that society.

Jevons was born in Liverpool on September 1, 1835, the son of an iron merchant and an artistically inclined mother. The city's rapid growth during the seventeenth century had been fueled by its central role in the slave trade. When slavery was abolished in the British Empire in 1807, anxiety among citizens over the city's future ran deep.[11] Forecasts of impending doom for Liverpool turned out to be ill-founded, however, as trade with the American colonies grew rapidly and filled the economic void left by the abolition of slavery. Indeed, from 1807 to the time Jevons was born, the volume of shipping flowing through the port of Liverpool more than doubled.

And yet, while both the city's population and workers' wages increased steadily, a severe economic rift occurred that separated the haves from the have-nots. As wealthy Liverpudlians moved away from the docks to newly fashionable districts on the edges of the city, those left behind in the center of town faced miserable conditions. From 1830 to 1850, life expectancy actually decreased in Liverpool proper from an already miserable 32 years to a shocking 25 years.

Faced with these realities, Jevons was highly sensitive to the inequities of the nineteenth-century system of industrial organization, rhetorically asking in his 1870 essay, "Does not every one feel that there is an evil at work which needs remedy? Does not the constant occurrence of strikes, and the rise of vast and powerful organisations of workmen, show that there is some profound unfitness in the present customs of the country to the progress of affairs?" Arguing for the imperative of institutional innovation as eloquently as any modern advocate of equity, Jevons stated, "If the masters insist on retaining their ancient customs; if they will shroud their profits in mystery, and treat their men as if they were another class of beings, whose interests are wholly separate and opposite; I see trouble in the future as in the past."[12]

While Jevons shared modern neoclassical economists' views that labor unions tended to restrict employment, he nonetheless saw unions as positive social institutions, stating that "association of some kind or other is alike the sign and means of civilisation."[13] Rather than ban or crush unions, as was widely advocated by his contemporaries, he proposed instead to create "a more useful and beneficial form of organization" based on profit-sharing, which he alternately termed a "partnership" or a "co-operative":

> I hope to see the time when workmen will be to a great extent their own capitalists ... I believe that a movement of workmen towards co-operation in the raising of capital would be anticipated by employers admitting their men to a considerable share of their profits.[14]

Compared with the default system in which industrial inequities were addressed by the actions of labor unions and arbitration boards, a system based on profit-sharing cooperatives would have the advantage of aligning the interests of factory owners and workers. Anticipating modern contract theory by a full century, Jevons observes that "in every work there are a thousand opportunities where the workman can either benefit or injure the establishment." He continues: "Could [the worker] really be made to feel his interests identical with those of his employers, there can be no doubt that the profits of the trade could be greatly increased in many cases." He concludes: "Partnerships of industry are, no doubt, an innovation, having hitherto existed only in exceptional trades and rare experiments; but I assert confidently that *they are an innovation of which the utility is evident and the necessity urgent.*"[15]

Whom does Jevons credit with having originated the idea of the profit-sharing cooperative? None other than the inventor of the Difference Engine and early code economist, Charles Babbage. "It does not seem to be so generally known as it ought to be that, as far as can be ascertained, the real author of the system I am advocating is Mr. Charles Babbage," he writes. "Nearly forty years ago his admirable work 'The Economy of Manufactures' was published, and it is truly difficult to overrate the genius which it displays."[16]

Regarding matters of economic theory rather than public policy, Jevons was as strongly influenced by the pioneering evolutionary theorist Herbert Spencer (see Text Box 1.1) as he was by the great classical economist Adam Smith. Matching Spencer in audacity but differing from him in methods, Jevons sought to discover and articulate natural laws through the application of mathematics and logic. This impulse led Jevons to invent the world's first machine capable of proving theorems—a successor to Babbage's Difference Engine, and a direct antecedent to Simon and Newell's pioneering Logic Theorist, or LT program (see Text Box 3.2).

In sum, while the contributions William Jevons made to neoclassical choice theory are a matter of historical record, even this architect of textbook economics was also, and importantly, a code economist.

TEXTBOOK ECONOMICS BECAME what it is today during the tumultuous 1930s, more than 80 years ago, as the battle between Fascism and Communism raged in Spain and threatened to erupt elsewhere in Europe. Surrounded by severe and seemingly worsening political polarization, a group of young academics (mostly at the London School of Economics, where Jevons taught, and at Cambridge University) sought admirably to steer economics away from subjectivity and ideology and toward objectivity and science. Their vision was to invoke the power of logical positivism, an approach toward the advance of understanding based on the power of deductive logic.

The project of the logical positivists working in mathematics— notably Bertrand Russell and Alfred North Whitehead—was similar to that which had led Jevons to invent a theorem-proving machine: to organize all mathematical understanding as the derived implications of a few core axioms. Taking inspiration from Russell and Whitehead, these vanguard economists sought to undertake, in the words of Nobel Laureate John Hicks, "a purge of economic theory" that eliminated all assertions that could not be justified as derived implications from axiomatic foundations.

In the intervening 80 years, the project of re-creating all of economics by deriving theories from core axioms and, where possible, testing them empirically—a project that came to be known as the neoclassical revolution in economics—has been successful along multiple dimensions. However, the same was not true of the logical positivist project in mathematics spearheaded by Russell and Whitehead. Indeed, even as the neoclassical revolution in economics was just getting started, German mathematician Kurt Gödel was publishing a paper proving that the logical positivist project in mathematics contained an irreconcilable self-contradiction and thus was doomed to fail. The publication of Gödel's theorem immediately disrupted the field of mathematics. New theories—from the Heisenberg Uncertainty Principle to fundamental discoveries made by Andrey Kolmogorov, Claude Shannon, Norbert Wiener, and Alan Turing—followed in its wake and came to define the core of scientific inquiry. Together they formed the foundation of a domain of inquiry that has come to be known as information theory.

Information theory places the problem of communication at the center of technological, biological, and social processes. A classic paper of Claude Shannon's, titled "Reliable Circuits Using Crummy Relays," serves to illustrate the practical application. At the time that Shannon wrote, large-scale communications networks (like the telephone system run by the Bell Telephone Company, Shannon's employer) comprised hundreds of thousands of error-prone components. The challenge was: How to encode the human voice, transmit it across the country, and decode it intelligibly at the receiver's end, using such a network of imperfect components—the "crummy relays" in the title of Shannon's paper.[17]

To get into the details of the problem, consider the diagram sketched by Claude Shannon decades ago, reproduced in figure 6.1. In his outstanding book, *The Information: A History, a Theory, a Flood,* James Gleick summarizes Shannon's model as follows:

A communication system must contain the following elements: (1) **The information source** is the person or machine generating the message, which may be simply a sequence of characters, as in a telegraph or teletype, or may be expressed mathematically as

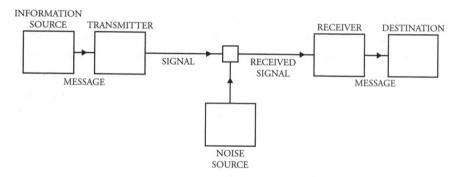

FIGURE 6.1 Claude Shannon's Diagram of the Fundamentals of a Communications System. *Source:* Taken from *Claude Elwood Shannon Collected Papers*, ed. NJA Sloane and Aaron Wyner. © 1993 IEEE, reproduced in James, Gleick (2011), *The Information: A History, a Theory, a Flood*, New York, NY: Random House, Inc.; p. 527.
Reprinted with permission of IEEE and Wiley.

functions—f(x, y, t)—of time and other variables. In a complex example like color television, the components are three functions in a three-dimensional continuum, Shannon noted. (2) **The transmitter** "operates on the message in some way"—that is, encodes the message—to produce a suitable signal. A telephone converts sound pressure into analog electric current. A telegraph encodes characters in dots, dashes, and spaces. More complex messages may be sampled, compressed, quantized, and interleaved. (3) **The channel**: "merely the medium used to transmit the signal." (4) **The receiver** inverts the operation of the transmitter. It decodes the message, or reconstructs it from the signal. (5) **The destination** "is the person (or thing)" at the other end. In the case of ordinary speech, these elements are the speaker's brain, the speaker's vocal cords, the air, the listener's ear, and the listener's brain.[18]

We see here immediately that the subject matter of information theory disappears if communication is costless and signal transmission is perfect. No noise, no problem. The nature of the world is just the opposite: noise is abundant, communication is costly, and signal transmission is imperfect. The challenge is to build a reliable economy with less reliable people. In this way, the economy is an information processing organism.

Information theory earned a central place among biologists decades ago, beginning in 1956 with the discovery of the structure of DNA. As Sydney Brenner, the 2002 Nobel Laureate in medicine, said in 1971, "I feel that this new molecular biology has to go in this direction—to explore the high-level logical computers, the programs, the algorithms of development. Where a science like physics works in terms of laws, or a science like molecular biology is stated in terms of mechanisms, maybe now what one has to begin to think of is algorithms. Recipes. Procedures."[19] The result of the transformation Brenner described was a revolution in the life sciences that continues to unfold today, with dramatic effects, including the advent of gene therapies and biomolecular computing.

When I assert that economics must properly be understood as a branch of information theory, I am referring to the centrality of the communications problem that exists whenever one person attempts to share know-how with another. I am referring, in other words, to the centrality of code.

OVER THE PAST two centuries, there has been much more to inquiry about the economics of production than is present in the ideas of the classical and neoclassical schools of economics, as dominant as both have been in their influence on research, instruction, and policy. Indeed, for at least 150 years, some of the most noted and respected contributors to the field of economics have advanced ideas that suggest a very different way of thinking about economic fundamentals than those represented by the standard textbook economics of neoclassical choice theory.

Renowned mathematical economist Alfred Marshall famously stated in his *Principles of Economics,* published in 1910, that "the Mecca of the economist lies in economic biology rather than in economic dynamics. But biological conceptions are more complex than those of mechanics; a volume on Foundations must therefore give a relatively large place to mechanical analogies; and frequent use is made of the term 'equilibrium,' which suggests something of statical analogy."[20] At about the same time, in *The Theory of Economic Development,* Austrian economist Joseph Schumpeter described the role of entrepreneurs as the economic agents responsible for "creating new combinations," where the "new combinations" were essentially recombinations of economically relevant code.[21] Thereafter, a series of economists, Herbert Simon foremost among them, put the challenges of gathering, sharing, and processing economically relevant information at the center of their work.[22]

Taken together and combined with foundational insights from other fields—notably evolutionary biology and molecular biology—the contributions of these economists constitute a distinct domain of inquiry within economics. These contributions have focused on people as producers and on the algorithms that drive the development of the economy.

This domain of inquiry is Code Economics.

7

Learning

The Dividend of Doing

If a machine is expected to be infallible, it cannot also be intelligent.
—Alan Turing, Lecture to the London Mathematical Society, 1947

THE FIRST MEAL Julia Child served to her husband, Paul, after they were married on September 1, 1946, was a dinner of brains stewed in a red wine sauce. It was inedible. This was not surprising, since Child, newly wed at the age of 34, had never learned to cook. Born to moderately wealthy parents in Pasadena, California, Julia had never stood on a stool to watch her mother prepare the family's meals. The cooking in the household was left to hired help, the output nourishing but artless. The family ate their meals regularly and dutifully, but the food was not discussed.

The turning point for Julia occurred two years into her marriage, when Paul was posted to the U.S. embassy in Paris. On November 3, 1948, having just arrived in France on the transatlantic ocean liner *America,* Paul, who had lived in France in the 1920s, introduced Julia to French cuisine at a restaurant in Rouen called La Couronne, which was housed in a medieval quarter-timber house built in 1345. "In Pasadena we used to have boiled mackerel for Friday dinners," Julia later recalled. "Codfish balls with egg sauce, 'boiled' (poached) salmon on the Fourth of July, and the occasional pan-fried trout when camping in the Sierras. But at La Couronne I experienced fish, and a dining experience, of a higher order than I ever had before. It was the most exciting meal of my life."[1]

Over the next four years, Child immersed herself ever more deeply in French cuisine—first as an enthusiastic restaurant patron, then as a home cook, and finally as an aspiring chef.

Despite her lack of experience in the kitchen, she persuaded the director of the renowned Cordon Bleu cooking school to permit her to enroll in a year-long course for professional restaurateurs. The class included 11 World War II veterans studying in Paris under the GI Bill ... and Julia. She distinguished herself from the outset with a methodical and determined approach:

> When I wasn't in school, I was experimenting at home, and became a bit of a Mad Scientist. I did hours of research on mayonnaise for instance, and although no one else seemed to care, I thought it was fascinating. When the weather turned cold, the mayonnaise suddenly became a terrible struggle, because the emulsion kept separating, and it wouldn't behave when there was a change in the olive oil or the room temperature. I finally got the upper hand by going back to the beginning of the process, studying each step scientifically, and writing it all down. By the end of my research I believe I had written more on the subject of mayonnaise than anyone in history ... In this way I had finally discovered a foolproof recipe, which was a glory![2]

Thirteen years and more than 10,000 hours of such experimentation later, Julia Child completed her first cookbook, *Mastering the Art of French Cooking*. Over the coming decades she inspired millions of people in the United States to undertake their own culinary experimentation at home and to learn at least one phrase in French: *"Bon appétit!"*

"TWO ROADS DIVERGED in a wood," wrote Robert Frost, "and I—I took the one less traveled by, and that has made all the difference."[3]

The history of science is full of such roads that diverge in the wilderness of inquiry. In the history of economic thought, an example of a road not taken "that has made all the difference" is a paper published in the inaugural volume of the *Quarterly Journal of Economics* (now the highest ranked economics journal) by Francis Walker, the first president of the American Economic Association.

Walker was a Civil War veteran who had risen to prominence among economists due to his groundbreaking statistical analysis—one might say he was an early data scientist in the field of economics. As superintendent of the 1870 U.S. Census, Walker oversaw production of the *Statistical Atlas of the United States,* a pioneering work in data visualization.[4]

Like his contemporary William Jevons, Walker was known as an incisive critic of the classical economists' wage fund theory (see Text Box 5.1). Where Jevons and Walker diverged was in the alternatives they proposed. Jevons' road led in the direction of viewing economics as "a science of motives." His assumption was that a firm's intention is to maximize profits, thus it follows that it will hire workers until it reaches the point where the bang-for-the-buck from employing the next unit of capital is equal to that from employing the next unit of labor. While this formulation makes it possible for firms to employ fundamentally different techniques, any such differences and the inherent complexity of production fade into the background as the problem of choosing the optimal allocation of capital and labor—a choice that economists refer to as allocative efficiency—is pushed to the fore. The possibility that some firms might consistently perform better than others by employing better code is ruled out.

Walker takes an altogether different approach.[5] "We have the phenomenon in every community and in every trade, in whatever state of the market," Walker observes, "of some employers realizing no profits at all, while others are making fair profits; others, again, large profits; others, still, colossal profits. Side by side, in the same business, with equal command of capital, with equal opportunities, one man is gradually sinking a fortune, while another is doubling or trebling his accumulations."[6] It would be nearly a century before data on firm profits were available on a sufficiently large scale to test Walker's intuition. When such data did become available, they clearly substantiated his claim. The distribution of profits among firms in the economy is indeed highly skewed in just the manner he suggested, with a large number of small firms earning little in the way of profits while a few very large firms earn enormous profits that persist over time—the exceptional profitability of Apple and Alphabet (the parent company of Google) providing obvious current examples.

So how do these profitable firms succeed? They do so by arriving at a combination of managerial actions that solves a difficult problem in a relatively effective manner:

> The excess of produce which we are contemplating comes from directing force to its proper object by the simplest and shortest ways; from saving all unnecessary waste of materials and machinery; from boldly incurring the expense—the often large expense of improved processes and appliances, while closely scrutinizing outgo and practicing a thousand petty economies in unessential matters; from meeting the demands of the market most aptly and instantly; and, lastly, from exercising a sound judgment as to the time of sale and the terms of payment.[7]

Walker argued that more profitable entrepreneurs are that way because they are able to solve a difficult problem more effectively than other entrepreneurs—and not simply because they are manipulators or cheats. In the intervening century, a growing body of work supporting this conjecture of Walker's has emerged. That work describes the three core mechanisms for the advance of code: learning, evolution, and the layering of complexity through the development of platforms. It spans economics, management science, aeronautical engineering, evolutionary biology, and, of course, the art of French cooking.

PRACTICE, IT TURNS out, does not make perfect. Practice brings improvement. On an individual level, this is not a great discovery, as learning is among the central functions our neural circuitry is designed for. Whatever we humans do most, we end up doing best. The capacity for individual learning is in fact fundamental to the success of the human species. However, humans also have evolved a capacity to learn together in our tribes, villages, cities—and our businesses.[8]

But if the human learning apparatus is formidable, so are the problems humans aim to solve. Julia Child's story illustrates that even seemingly routine productive activities—in her case, making mayonnaise—become hugely challenging tasks when the objective is not mere competence but mastery. This is where Julia's story connects to the hypothesis advanced by Francis Walker. Julia Child was not successful due to advantages conferred on her by birth or youthful experience; she was 34 years old before she even began to learn to cook! The capacity she brought to her work was a tenacious will to experiment, to learn, and (importantly) to document carefully the results of her learning.

Elsewhere in her autobiography, Julia relates her experience developing a workable recipe for baking a baguette in a U.S. home, which I use as the epigraph to this book's Introduction. Learning, as Child describes it so clearly, is a process of imagining and testing new "ways of combining." We typically stop learning not when we find the best possible approach—how would we even know what that was?—but when we find an approach that works well and cannot be improved by any minor modification.

However, learning as a group is more than—or at least fundamentally different from—the sum of learning as individuals. To link the lived experience of learning conveyed by Julia Child to the hypothesis advanced by Francis Walker regarding better and worse managers, we need to take a further step: we need to understand how a tenacious will to experiment, to learn, and to carefully document the results of learning might also be a successful strategy for a village or a business.

As we explore this question we will find that, in the empirical economics of production, few discoveries have been more universal or significant than that of the firm-level learning curve. As economist James Bessen notes, "Developing the knowledge and skills needed to implement new technologies on a large scale is a difficult social problem that takes a long time to resolve . . . A new technology typically requires more than an invention in order to be designed, built, installed, operated, and maintained. Initially much of this new technical knowledge develops slowly because it is learned through experience, not in the classroom. Throughout our history, workers have acquired their technical knowledge through a combination of formal training and experience, not in the classroom. They gained much of their important technical knowledge on the job, through 'learning by doing.'"[9]

In economics, as it turns out, the classic example of learning by doing in the process of production is not making mayonnaise but producing airframes. That story begins with Gene Vidal (father of author Gore Vidal), a larger-than-life figure who helped propel America into the Golden Age of Flight.

BORN IN SOUTH DAKOTA in 1895, Gene Vidal moved east to attend West Point, where he served as one of the first U.S. Army Air Corps pilots and became captain of the football team. He represented the U.S. as a decathlete at the 1920 Olympics and subsequently played football for the Washington Senators of the American Professional Football Association, a forerunner of the National Football League. In the early 1920s, working in partnership with Amelia Earhart and others, Vidal contributed to the launch of three companies that over the next half-century developed into leading U.S. airlines: Transworld Airlines (TWA), Eastern Airlines, and Northeast Airlines.

In 1933, Vidal was appointed director of the Bureau of Air Commerce within the U.S. Department of Commerce. In this new role he immediately set to work on his top goal: democratizing the world of flight with the production of a "poor man's airplane," much as development of the Model T had democratized access to automobiles. He pledged to put a half-million dollars behind the project of producing an all-metal two-seat aircraft that could be sold at a per-unit cost of $700, assuming a production run of at least 10,000 units. He proposed that the project be sponsored by the federal Depression-era Works Progress Administration as a way to put unemployed engineers and machinists to work. Their task would be to create a plane that would make aviation accessible to all.

Announcement of a design competition in November 1933 did not meet with a friendly reception. At the time, aircraft manufacturers were having considerable difficulty producing a fabric-covered two-seat aircraft for less than $1,000; they considered Vidal's vision of an all-metal plane produced at a unit cost of $700 to be so improbable that they derided it as the "all-mental" plane. Vidal's new colleagues in government—including the influential Harold Ickes—were not amenable to issuing a contract for the planes via the Works Progress Administration on the simple grounds that private planes were not public works.[10]

But Vidal was undeterred. The Bureau of Air Commerce did not have an R&D budget, but it did have a budget to procure aircraft for its inspectors. Using that budget as a lever, the bureau announced a competition for a "safety aircraft" that matched the specifications for the poor-man's airplane.

The controversy around Vidal's plan prompted Theodore P. Wright, an aeronautical engineer born the same year as Vidal, to compile and publish the 15-years of research he had undertaken on the variation of cost with quantity in the aircraft industry. True, the per-unit cost of $700 targeted by Vidal was unrealistic for a low-volume order, but Wright was interested in knowing if Vidal's cost target might not be so implausible if the assumption of a 10,000-unit production run was taken fully into account. Using data on the variation of cost with quantity that he had painstakingly gathered, Wright sought an answer.

The data published in hand-drawn charts on the first page of Wright's paper, "Factors Affecting the Cost of Airplanes," showed a striking empirical finding: as cumulative output increased, labor costs dropped with dramatic regularity. Indeed, for every doubling of output, the labor cost per unit tended to drop by 20 percent "on the assumption that no major changes [to the design of the output] will be introduced during construction." Put differently, if the average labor cost to produce the first one hundred planes was $1,000, then the average labor cost to produce the second hundred planes would be 80 percent of that, or $800. The reasons Wright offered for this cost reduction included refinement and standardization of processes, reduced waste, reduced per-unit overhead, and, of course, individual learning by the workers who produced the planes (see figure 7.1).

A plethora of studies documenting the decline of per-unit labor costs as a function of increasing cumulative output followed Wright's paper. The plot of this relationship entered the general lexicon as the "learning curve"; "a steep learning curve" came to suggest a process of intensive engagement in a new activity with the potential to yield significant gains in productivity. Remarkably, these studies affirmed not only the principle of organizational learning but also the specific quantitative result reported by Wright—that the doubling of output characteristically yields a 20 percent reduction in per-unit labor costs. The ubiquity of firm learning and the regularity of its observed quantitative features made it a centerpiece of corporate planning, particularly in manufacturing (see Text Box 7.1). Companies could price products based on a reliable estimate of actual costs subsequent to production at scale.

The impact of the learning curve was not limited to the commercial world. As Bessen relates in his 2015 book *Learning by Doing*, firm

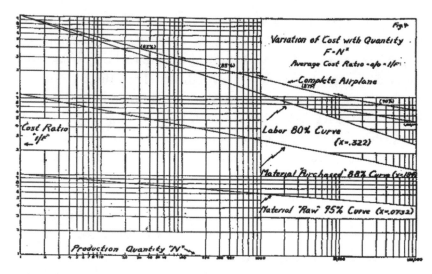

FIGURE 7.1 T. P. Wright's Estimate of Cost Reduction in the Production of Airframes. *Source:* Wright, T. P. (1936). "Factors Affecting the Cost of Airplanes." *Journal of the Aeronautical Sciences* 2, 122–128.

learning also played a central role in U.S. military history. The setting was the dire situation at the time the United States entered World War II. German U-boats—protected by Germany's Enigma code, which will be familiar to anyone who has seen the film *The Imitation Game*— were operating essentially unimpeded in the North Atlantic. As long as the Germans maintained this significant tactical advantage, the only way the United States could supply its allies was, literally, to build ships more rapidly than the U-boats could sink them. Accordingly, within months of the bombing of Pearl Harbor, Franklin Roosevelt issued a presidential directive calling for the construction of 24 million tons of merchant shipping capacity. Much like Vidal's $700 airplane, this mandate assumed that some sort of miracle would happen to sharply reduce per-unit shipbuilding costs as cumulative output increased. This particular miracle had a name: the learning curve. Fortunately for the war effort, the miracle was delivered. During the course of the war, shipyards increased their output per worker by a factor of four.[11]

T. P. Wright went on manage aircraft production during World War II. In 1941 he moved to Washington, D.C., where he assumed the role of assistant chief in the Aircraft Section of the Office of Production Management; he was subsequently appointed chair of the Joint Aircraft

Text Box 7.1 *The* **Learning Curve as a Strategic Tool**

Perhaps no company has employed the learning curve as a strategic tool over the past half-century more effectively than Intel, the world's dominant producer of computer chips. Generation after generation of Intel chips have been designed, priced, produced, and sold with careful estimates of future learning as a guide, and with deliberate factory-floor R&D strategies in place to ensure that learning progresses at the anticipated rate.

Some years ago, Gordon Moore, who cofounded Intel in 1968 and is universally known as the originator of Moore's Law, authored some reflections on his early years at Intel predecessor Fairchild Semiconductor to illustrate the direct relationship between code and firm-level learning curves:

> Eight of us left [Shockley Semiconductor] and ended up starting Fairchild Semiconductor ... We advertised for a general manager, and buried among the many salesmen who believed they could manage was an application from Ed Baldwin, the engineering manager for the Hughes Semiconductor operation, then one of the largest semiconductor companies in the world ... Baldwin taught us most of the simple things every M.B.A. knows. He taught us that different parts of the organization should be established with different responsibilities ... And everything was working fine: the development and the pre-production engineering for our process and first products was complete; we had a thick process-spec book that recorded all the detailed recipes; and we had interested customers.[12]

The relative quietude did not last long:

> One day we came to work and discovered that Baldwin, along with a group of people he had suggested we hire, were leaving to set up a competing semiconductor company (Rheem) just down the road. He and his group took with them the "recipes" for manufacturing that we had developed. But they left behind something more valuable. He had graduated a class of

engineer-managers who now had the ability to figure out how to do it alone. And we did. Our response to their departure was to compete technologically by improving upon (and manufacturing) the products that Baldwin had guided us to develop. Although a court eventually ruled that they had to return the copy of the spec book to us, it no longer mattered.[13]

With his reference to Fairchild's "thick process-spec book that recorded all the detailed recipes" for production of semiconductors, Moore offers a tangible example of the concept of the production recipe, which I have been using interchangeably with production algorithm. The existence of such a recipe book points to a missing element in the textbook representation of technological change as the simple outward movement of a "production possibilities frontier"—a term that refers to the maximum output attainable using a fixed amount of capital and labor, given existing technology. Moore's comments suggest that improvements in the recipes used to combine inputs into a reliable product that meets market-determined specifications underlie increases in productivity that show up as the downward slope of a learning curve. Production recipes can be thought of literally as the sort of "process spec-book" alluded to by Moore; alternatively, since Moore states that the principle that "different parts of the organization should be established with different responsibilities" is among the "simple things every M.B.A. knows," we can also think of production recipes as all of the decisions made in any time period by those different and distinct parts of the organization.[14]

Moore emphasizes the overriding importance to a firm's survival of its ability to improve on existing products and processes. He states that the response of Fairchild "loyalists" to Baldwin's departure was to "compete technologically by improving upon (and manufacturing) the products that Baldwin had guided us to develop." From the standpoint of growth and competitiveness in a dynamic environment, the mix of inputs that enter the production plan is less significant than the development of firm-specific technology—that is, the firm's complete production recipe.[15]

Committee. In that role, Wright was instrumental in measuring and increasing aircraft production during the war using the same learning curve-based methods that were successful in shipbuilding.

Over time, the firm learning curve influenced the work of economists and became for the production side of economics what downward-sloping demand curves were to the consumer side: a widely observed empirical regularity with potential to provide a reliable anchor for theory. In 1962, future Nobel Laureate Kenneth Arrow wrote a broadly influential paper titled "The Economic Implications of Learning By Doing," in which he specifically referred to T. P. Wright's airframe results. He incorporated into his model the same equation Wright employed in his 1936 paper. Just over three decades later, another future Nobel Laureate, Robert Lucas, wrote a comparably influential paper titled "Making a Miracle," which focused on understanding the rapid economic advance of countries in East Asia and used the Liberty Ships story to frame his description of the drivers of long-term growth. Many others contributed to the literature, documenting learning curves and examining the impact the phenomenon of learning by doing had on the evolution of the economy over time.[16]

Meanwhile, Vidal's competition to yield the Model T of the airplane world was successful up to a point: it did yield a winner. Moreover, access to commercial aircraft services was ultimately democratized, as Vidal had hoped it would be. However, despite the subsequent popularity of the Cessna and other low-cost, all-metal two-seater airplanes, the path to democratizing aviation services was not through do-it-yourself flying but through the development of the enormous array of products, services, and associated skills that would ultimately give the commercial aviation industry—including TWA, Eastern Airlines, and Northeast Airlines—a truly global reach.

IN 2010, A group of economists led by Nicholas Bloom of Stanford University made an offer to a randomly selected group of large textile firms in India: "Over the coming month, we will assess your current management practices, and make suggestions for improvement." To a randomly selected subset of these firms, the researchers made a further offer: "We will provide you with four months of intensive, onsite consulting on the implementation of the recommendations."

The results of the experiment, ultimately published in the *Quarterly Journal of Economics,* were dramatic. As the authors reported, the firms that received the additional four months of intensive onsite consulting showed significant improvement (and also fundamentally improved their management practices) over the "control group" through three mechanisms: "First, [they] raised average productivity by 11% through improved quality and efficiency and reduced inventory. Second, [they] increased decentralization of decision making, as better information flow enabled owners to delegate more decisions to middle managers. Third, [they] increased the use of computers, necessitated by the data collection and analysis involved in modern management."[17] Furthermore, the firms that received the additional support were able to increase their profits to an extent that would have made it worthwhile for them to pay for the consulting, had it not been provided free of charge. The results of the experiment thus raised a question: why had the firms not sought assistance in improving their management practices earlier?

Based on more than a decade of prior work studying management practices around the world, Bloom and coauthors offer a simple explanation that confirms that Francis Walker was right: managing a firm is not easy (see figure 7.2). A good manager must be able to solve challenging problems. This is a practice that can be learned, but only with considerable effort and (in many cases) expert guidance. As Alfred Marshall wrote in his 1910 masterwork, *Principles of Economics,* "Capital consists in a great part of knowledge and organization: and of this some part is private property and [an]other part is not. Knowledge is our most powerful engine of production."[18]

Whereas dominant variants of the neoclassical production model emphasize categories such as public knowledge and organization, which can be copied and implemented at zero cost, code economics suggests that such categories are unlikely to be significantly relevant in the practical work of creating the business entities that drive the progress of human society. This is because code at the level of a single company—what I term a "production algorithm"—includes firm-specific components. Producers far from dominant production clusters must learn to produce through a costly process of trial and error. Market-driven advances in production recipes, from which ventures with proprietary

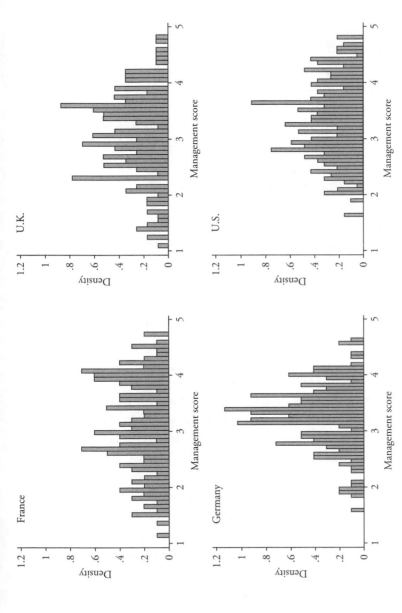

FIGURE 7.2 Distribution of Management Scores by Country Evidencing Dispersion of Practices. From Bloom and Van Reenen (2007): "These are the distributions of the raw management scores (simple averages across all 18 practices for each firm). 1 indicates worst practice, 5 indicates best practice. There are 135 French observations, 156 German observations, 151 UK observations, and 290 U.S. observations."

Source: (2007). Nicholas Bloom and John Van Reenen (2007), "Measuring and Explaining Management Practices Across Firms and Countries." *The Quarterly Journal of Economics* 122 (4): pp. 1351–1408.

Reprinted with permission of Oxford University Press.

value can be created, require a tenacious will to experiment, to learn, and to document carefully the results of that learning. Heterogeneity among managers—as postulated by Francis Walker and quantified by Nicholas Bloom, John Van Reenen, and colleagues—is thus central to understanding observed differences between regions and nations.[19]

While significant differences remain among firms in terms of the effectiveness of their respective productive algorithms, the professionalization of management that has occurred since World War II has had an equalizing effect. Developing complex supply chains required management approaches far more complex than the strategies employed by Gaspard de Prony. (Think, for example, of the development of total quality management.) In the first sentence of his widely influential 1974 work, *Management: Tools, Responsibilities, Practices*, business thinker Peter Drucker went so far as to state: "The emergence of management in this century may have been a pivotal event in history."[20] Even in light of the transformative impact of penicillin, the transistor, and the Internet, Drucker makes a valid point. Management and the development of technical standards combined to enable not just machines but organizations to be interoperable and collaborative. Companies thus could become far bigger and supply chains far more complex than ever before.

BY THIS ROUTE, we come at last to a resolution of the (admittedly minor) mystery of the overcrowded conference session on machine learning referred to in chapter six. The actual tools of machine learning have been in active use for three decades, thus the graduates who packed into that conference room to hear Susan Athey and others were not seeking an understanding of those tools. Their desire to be in that room reflects the fact that the advantage in using machine-learning tools in a competitive environment lies in the dimensions of interpretation, asking questions, and intuition that cannot be directly embedded into a machine-learning algorithm. Downloading a program is not enough to gain access to those dimensions of Big Data analytics; to access the insights of the people skilled in these dimensions of data science, one has to be in the room with them—in this case, literally.

In this sense, data science is like cooking. What brought Julia Child fame wasn't publication of *Mastering the Art of French Cooking*, which represented a decade-long attempt to codify every aspect of her culinary practice, but the success of her pioneering cooking program, which gave her non-expert audience at home the opportunity to be in the kitchen with her as she cooked. This format has proven enormously popular for the simple reason that there is much about cooking that can be conveyed in writing only with great difficulty. Showing is better. Doing is better still.

Julia Child's struggles to master the art of producing mayonnaise, Nicholas Bloom and John Van Reenen's compelling evidence on the persistent differences between firms' management practices, and T. P. Wright's documentation of the firm learning curve all serve to validate what might be referred to as the Cool Hand Luke Theorem of economic information: "What we have here is a failure to communicate."

Here is what I mean: If communicating economically relevant know-how were a perfect and costless activity as assumed in default textbook models of production, we would not see a skilled cook taking weeks to test and document the recipe for a simple condiment. We would not observe wide disparity in management capabilities among firms either within particular industries and geographies or across different industries and geographical contexts. And we would not see firms lowering their costs over time when producing a given good.

All of these examples underscore the following point, core to code economics: The imperfection of communication is not a theory. It is a ubiquitous and inescapable physical reality.

In the next two chapters we'll switch the focus from learning at the firm level—specifically, the systematic search for improved production recipes—to learning-driven evolution at the level of a city, a region, or an entire economy. Consider, in this broader context, the particular problem that must be solved by natural selection, as articulated in a 1977 *Science* essay titled "Evolution and Tinkering," by French biologist Francois Jacob (the recipient, with Jacques Monod and André Lwoff, of the 1965 Nobel Prize in Medicine):

> Natural selection is the result of two constraints imposed by every living organism: (i) the requirement for reproduction, which is fulfilled thorough genetic mechanisms carefully adjusted by special devices such as mutation, recombination, and sex to produce organisms

similar, but not equal to, their parents, and (ii) the requirement of a permanent interaction with the environment because living beings are what thermodynamicists call open systems and persist only by a constant flux of matter, energy, and information.[21]

Where genetic processes must favor convergence and conservation, the processes of learning and adaptation necessitated by constant interaction with the environment favor divergence and exploration. The expression of the genetic code as a fertilized egg that develops into a fully realized organism (what biologists refer to as epigenesis) depends upon predictable, error-free repetition. However, the survival of the realized organism requires learning and adaptation, which depend on exploration and change.[22]

A similar idea is expressed by noted ecologist Gregory Bateson in his 1978 book, *Mind and Nature: A Necessary Unity*; "We face, then, two systems [involving randomness and discovery] that are partly isolated from each other. One system is within the individual and is called *learning*; the other is immanent in heredity and in populations and is called *evolution*. One is a matter of a single lifetime; the other is a matter of multiple generations of many individuals."[23]

Literally and figuratively, the second of the processes—evolution—all starts with DNA.

8

Evolution

The Code of Life

If we wish to be guided by a natural science metaphor, I suggest one drawn from biology rather than physics. Obvious lessons are to be learned from evolutionary biology, and rather less obvious ones from molecular biology. From molecular biology, in particular, we can glimpse a picture of how a few basic mechanisms—the DNA of the Double Helix, for example, or the energy transfer mechanisms elucidated so elegantly by Professor Mitchell—can account for a wide range of complex phenomena. We can see the role in science of laws of qualitative structure, and the power of qualitative, as well as quantitative explanation.

—Herbert Simon, Nobel Lecture, 1978

LEGEND HAS IT that Ruth Wakefield, proprietress of the Toll House Inn in Whitman, Massachusetts, ran out of nuts while mixing a batch of cookies sometime in 1937. In their place she is said to have used broken pieces of Nestlé's semi-sweet chocolate, expecting the chocolate to melt and absorb into the dough to create chocolate cookies. Instead, when she removed the pan from the oven, the bits of chocolate remained embedded in the cookie and thus the chocolate chip cookie was born—or so the story goes.

The reality is that Wakefield was an experienced baker who published her first cookbook six years before the invention of the chocolate chip cookie. (That cookbook was a bestseller that grew into an 888-recipe volume and was reprinted 28 times.) Those who worked with Wakefield say that she understood full well that the semi-sweet chocolate would not melt into the dough. Wakefield's only account of the invention came in an interview she gave decades later: "We had been serving a thin butterscotch-nut cookie with ice cream. Everybody seemed to love it, but I was trying to give them something different. So I came up with the Toll House cookie." Another reporter's account from the same era stated that Wakefield "worked out the recipe on the way back from a trip to Egypt."[1]

Whatever the details of her moment of inspiration, it is clear that Wakefield and her husband Kenneth knew how to run a restaurant. They started the Toll House Inn in 1930, just months after the Black Tuesday stock market crash of October 29, 1929. By their third day of operation, their original $50 in operating capital was down to $10. In spite of their inadequate startup capital and inauspicious timing, their business grew throughout the Great Depression. Located on the road from Boston to Cape Cod, the Toll House Inn benefited from two significant trends: the ascent of automotive transport and the democratization of the concept of vacation. By the time Wakefield experienced her famed moment of inspiration, the restaurant employed over one hundred people, served one thousand customers a day, had earned the Wakefields more than a half-million dollars, and was known throughout the region. In the 1940s and 1950s, patrons included composer Cole Porter, actresses Ethel Merman and Bette Davis, baseball player Joe DiMaggio, and first lady Eleanor Roosevelt.

Service was, of course, as much a part of the recipe for success at the Toll House Inn as the food. A post-World War II pamphlet captures both the owners' aspirations and the spirit of a country fresh from military victory and consumed by industrial growth: "No military machine or factory production line was ever geared toward more smooth-running cohesion," the pamphlet stated. "Long-range planning and constantly studied personnel are reflected in an operating framework flawless in its unruffled perfection." The martial and industrial similitudes are given credence by the fact that every Toll House employee had to master a seven-page manual of standard service procedures at the restaurant.

The recipe that made the greatest difference in the success of the Toll House Inn arguably was not the one for chocolate chip cookies—which is still printed on every bag of Nestlé's semi-sweet chocolate chips and is the one I refer to in the Introduction to this book—but the administrative "recipe" the Wakefields employed in operating their restaurant. Their recipes for preparing meals can be thought of as "sub-recipes" of this encompassing organizational code—the practices that governed the dining experience at the Toll House Inn.

Production recipes—code executed on an organizational scale—are much like culinary recipes on an entirely different scale of activity. Production recipes are comprised of discrete tasks that, when performed in combination, yield clearly specified outputs. Each task can be refined and be the subject of experimentation; different arrangements of tasks (which is to say, different recipes) will result in different outputs. As pioneering evolutionary economist Sidney Winter wrote in 1968, " 'Knowing how to bake a cake' is clearly not the same thing as 'knowing how to bring together all of the ingredients for a cake.' Knowing how to bake a cake is knowing how to execute the sequence of operations that are specified, more or less closely, in a cake recipe."[2] In code economics, this distinction takes on first-order importance.

Sidney Winter's comments echo the nearly contemporaneous comments of Sydney Brenner, whom I quoted earlier: "Where a science like physics works in terms of laws, or a science like molecular biology, to now, is stated in terms of mechanisms, maybe now what one has to begin to think of is algorithms. Recipes. Procedures."[3] Knowing how to create life is not the same as knowing how to bring together the ingredients for life.

Much as DNA encodes the recipe of life, production recipes are the DNA of the economy.

AT THE SAME time T. P. Wright was engaged in research on learning curves, which I described in the last chapter, his brother Sewall Wright published a paper titled "The Roles of Mutation, Inbreeding, Crossbreeding and Selection in Evolution." The article would ultimately have at least as great an impact in the field of evolutionary biology as T. P.'s "Factors Affecting the Cost of Airplanes" did among management scientists and economists.[4]

Sewall Wright was a major contributor to the modern synthesis in evolutionary biology—that is, the systematic integration of the microgenetics of combination and recombination (first described by Gregor

Mendel) with the macro theory of evolution (first and most famously expounded by Charles Darwin, with significant contributions from Herbert Spencer) that described the changing character of populations over time. Sewall Wright's work constituted a significant advance over Darwinian theory and offered a bridge from evolutionary biology to other domains of inquiry.

He began "The Roles of Mutation" by distinguishing between two mechanisms by which genetic novelty might be introduced into particular populations. The first was single-point mutation, emphasized by Darwin, which would constitute incremental change for an offspring relative to a parent. The second was sexual or biparental reproduction, emphasized by Mendel, which would constitute large-scale, combinatorial change for an offspring relative to the parents. Wright noted the fundamentally unsatisfactory nature of mutation as the sole factor in the evolutionary process: "The observed properties of gene mutation—fortuitous in origin, infrequent in occurrence and deleterious when not negligible in effect—seem about as unfavorable as possible for an evolutionary process. [With] united bi-parental reproduction, however, a limited number of mutations which are not too injurious to be carried by the species may furnish an almost indefinite field of possible variations through which the species may work its way under natural selection." Wright supported his claim by describing the literally astronomical number of combinations of genes that are possible in higher organisms.[5] Due to the enormous combinatorial possibilities afforded by sexual reproduction, populations of higher organisms (including humans) demonstrate tremendous genetic diversity.[6]

To organize inquiry into how populations evolve over time, Wright introduced the idea of a "landscape" that assigns each genetic combination to a particular environmentally determined "fitness" level. "The problem of evolution," he states, "is that of a mechanism by which the species may continually find its way from lower to higher peaks in such a field. In order that this may occur, there must be some trial and error mechanism on a grand scale by which the species may explore the region surrounding a small portion of the field which it occupies. To evolve, the species must not be under the strict control of [mutation-driven] natural selection."[7]

Sexual reproduction provides such a mechanism, with which a population scans its fitness landscape for potentially improved variants. In a closed population, inbreeding combines with natural selection to shift the distribution of genetic combinations "uphill" in the landscape toward a fixed number of "peaks," a peak being defined as the local maximum for favorable adaptation to the environment. After sufficient time has elapsed to allow the population to converge on such peaks, a certain stasis sets in. While mutation may continue to introduce some variation after the population has reached the high points on the fitness landscape, "the species will occupy a certain field of variation about a peak ... The field occupied [on the landscape] remains constant although no two individuals are ever identical." Under such conditions, "further evolution can only occur by the appearance of wholly new (instead of recurrent) mutations, and ones which happen to be favorable from the first [instance it appears]."[8] Absent fortuitous encounters with entire new populations of the same species, the single most effective way out of this trap is for the species to subdivide into local subspecies that occasionally crossbreed. This allows the regular introduction of truly new combinations that fundamentally expand the field of variation occupied by the species.

Wright's primary conclusion is that evolution requires a balance among the various mechanisms for generating novelty on which it depends: mutation, selection, inbreeding, and crossbreeding. In the short run, narrow specialization leads to economies of scale and increased productivity; however, in the long run, narrow specialization leads to the exhaustion of possibilities for search and thus to evolutionary dead ends. Success for a species, as well as for a company and a region, depends on balancing these factors. The early history of one well-known global franchise corporation serves to illustrate.

IN 1956, A milkshake-mixer salesman by the name of Ray Kroc was running into difficulties. A company by the name of Hamilton Beach had come out with a new line of low-cost mixers that was threatening his business. Always on the lookout for a new opportunity, Kroc took note of an anomaly in his sales records: a single restaurant in San Bernardino, California, had ordered eight of his Multimixers, each with the capacity to produce five milkshakes. What restaurant needed to produce

40 milkshakes at a time? Intrigued, Kroc traveled to San Bernardino to visit a small hamburger and hot dog restaurant run by two brothers, Dick and Mac McDonald.

The restaurant was unlike any Kroc had every seen. In contrast to the drive-in restaurants popular at the time, the McDonald brothers' restaurant had no waitresses or seating, and it offered only cheeseburgers, hamburgers, french fries, sodas, and milkshakes. All meals were prepared in an assembly-line manner and delivered to customers within a minute of ordering.[9]

Like Ruth Wakefield, the McDonald brothers had gotten their start in the food service business during the Great Depression. With a $5,000 loan, they opened the Airdrome hot dog stand in 1937 in Arcadia, California. In 1940 they moved their operation to San Bernardino and changed the name to McDonald's Barbeque.[10] Eight years later, as the postwar economy took off, the brothers undertook a radical experiment: they shut down their restaurant entirely and reopened a month later with a new business model that was optimized to deliver meals with assembly-line efficiency. They called their design the "Speedee Service System."

Kroc, whose gift was knowing a good idea when he saw one, was hooked. He brokered a deal with the brothers to license the McDonald's name and method. Kroc opened his first McDonald's restaurant in 1955 in Des Plaines, California. Within five years he had opened two hundred new franchises across the country. He pushed his operators obsessively to adhere to a system that reinforced the company motto: "Quality, service, cleanliness, and value." In 1961 he bought the company from the founders and a franchising empire was born.

In his 1987 autobiography, Kroc described the essence of the franchise-based system behind the growth of McDonald's:

> It's all interrelated—our development of the restaurant, the training, the marketing advice, the product development, the research that has gone into each element of the equipment package. Together with our national advertising and continuing supervisory assistance, it forms an invaluable support system. Individual operators pay 11.5 percent of their gross to the corporation for all of this, and I think it's a hell of a bargain.[11]

The process of operating a McDonald's franchise was engineered to be as cognitively undemanding as possible. As Kroc stated, "a person doesn't need to be super smart or have more than a high school education, but he or she must be willing to work hard and concentrate exclusively on the challenge of operating that store."[12]

Kroc created a program that could be broken into subroutines. A single operator could run a subroutine by following the instruction manual provided to him or her as a franchisee. Acting like the DNA of the organization, the manual allowed the Speedee Service System to function in a variety of environments without losing essential structure or function.

Meanwhile, far from Arcadia, California, a pair of young scientists were seeking the structure of a code of a different type. Their discovery would change science and shape the way we humans see our place in the world.

ON THE EVENING of Sunday, March 1, 1953, James Watson and Francis Crick went out to a pub, The Eagle in Cambridge, England. That morning, Watson had experienced a moment of insight that promised to be a breakthrough in the duo's attempt to solve the puzzle of the structure of DNA. Working with cardboard cutouts of the base pairs that featured centrally in their still-incomplete model, Watson noticed an unexpected symmetry that suggested a solution, but on the cusp of great discovery he was suddenly and frustratingly stuck. Why? The cardboard cutouts did not provide sufficient precision for Watson and Crick to be confident of their structure. They had ordered metal models of the base pairs from a local machine shop, but delivery had been delayed. "That night . . . we could not firmly establish the double helix," Watson later recalled. "Until the metal bases were on hand, any model building would be too sloppy to be convincing." Without a physical scale model against which to test possible configurations and confirm the conjectured symmetry, Watson and Crick could not persuade themselves—much less anyone else—that they had hit upon the correct structure.

There really was no time to waste. Fully cognizant that a Nobel Prize was at stake, Watson and Crick—24 and 36 years old at the time, respectively, and relatively unknown in the scientific world—were engaged in a David and Goliath-like contest with Linus Pauling, the greatest chemist of the era. The goal toward which they were racing was a precious one: to be the first to discover, literally, the code of life.

Watson, a student of biochemistry, and Crick, a physicist turned biologist, had both been motivated to study the structure of the genetic code after reading a slim collection of lectures written by famed quantum physicist Erwin Schrödinger, titled *What Is Life?* Pauling, many years earlier, had been Schrödinger's student in Zurich. In *What Is Life?* Schrödinger articulated the fundamental challenge inherent in understanding life. In a world governed by the Second Law of Thermodynamics, which dictates that any closed system must tend from order toward disorder over time, how is it that we can observe self-perpetuating islands of order that not only persist but also grow in complexity—which is to say, life itself? Put differently (and borrowing imagery from Norbert Wiener), if the entropy of the universe is ever increasing, how does life manage its trick of swimming upstream against the cosmic tide of chaos and disorder?[13]

As Schrödinger saw it, roughly summarizing what was known of molecular biology at the time, the instructions for life must take the form of an "aperiodic solid." Unlike a periodic solid, such as a crystal, in which the same pattern is repeated again and again like "ordinary wallpaper," this aperiodic solid would be like "a masterpiece of embroidery, say a Raphael tapestry, which shows no dull repetition, but an elaborate, coherent, meaningful design traced by the great master."[14] Referring to this aperiodic solid as the "hereditary substance," Schrödinger explained the way out of the entropic conundrum he had posed: "To reconcile the high durability of the hereditary substance with its minute size, [nature] had to evade the tendency to disorder by 'inventing the molecule,' in fact, an unusually large molecule which has to be a masterpiece of highly differentiated order."[15] In this way, the code of life does not contravene "the natural tendency of things to go over into disorder" and instead reveals how nature allows the existing order to be maintained and replicated (see Text Box 8.1).

What Is Life? constituted an open challenge to the scientific community to search for the structure of the genetic code. Watson, Crick, and Pauling were among those who responded to that challenge. Both teams—Watson and Crick's and Pauling's—were working from roughly the same evidence: (1) X-ray diffraction photographs that offered

Text Box 8.1 **The Difference between Artificial and Natural Objects**

"The difference between artificial and natural objects seems immediately and unambiguously apparent to all of us." So begins Jacques Monod's 1972 book, *Chance and Necessity*. "We know the knife was man-made for a use its maker visualized beforehand. The object renders in material form the preexistent intention that gave birth to it, and its form is accounted for by the performance expected of it even before it takes shape" (p. 3). In contrast, we perceive natural objects to have been "molded by the free play of physical forces to which we cannot attribute any design, any 'project' or purpose." Our presumption that a hard and fast distinction exists between artificial and natural objects begins to weaken once we seek an objective and repeatable method for distinguishing between the two. Imagine that the Mars rover was equipped with an apparatus of this type. What could be more fascinating than to inspect extraterrestrial objects to see if they show indications of having been the products of nonhuman intelligent life? In order to detect evidence of the past presence of intelligent beings, Monod states, "we would have to search and be able to recognize its products, however radically unlike the fruit of human industry they might be" (p. 4).

We might note upon brief reflection that, outside of the microscopic realm, natural objects rarely incorporate simple geometries—shapes with right angles or regular triangles, for example—while artificial objects frequently do. The internal structure of leaves, the branching pattern that characterize a river delta or venous network, and the swirling patterns made by smoke all exhibit design complexity that far exceeds that of artificial objects. We might, therefore, start with a test that would look for macroscopic regularity and repetition as a feature of artificial construction. Trying out our program on territorial objects, however, we would soon run into trouble. Crystals, for example, incorporate basic geometries that repeat themselves. Likewise a honeycomb, which is constructed from repeated hexagonal cylinders.

At this point, Monod notes, we will determine that an approach to distinguishing between natural and artificial objects on the basis of observed structural characteristics is unlikely to be successful. At that point we might return to our original insight and seek to build a new machine, distinguishing between natural and artificial objects in terms of their exhibited purpose. "Programming the machine so that henceforth it studies not only the structure but the eventual performance of the examined objects, we end up with still more disappointing results." It would be both "arbitrary and pointless . . . to deny that the natural organ, the eye, represents the materialization of a 'purpose'—that of picking up images—while this is indisputably also the origin of the camera. It would only be more absurd to deny it since, in the last analysis, the purpose which 'explains' the camera can only be the same as the one to which the eye owes its structure" (p. 8).

All of this leads Monod to his core point, which has nothing to do with the Mars rover: "Every artifact is a product made by a living being which through it expresses, in a particularly conspicuous manner, one of the fundamental characteristics common to all living being without exception: that of being objects endowed with a purpose or project, which at the same time they exhibit in their structure and carry out through their performances (such as, for instance, the making of artifacts)" (p. 9).

Having been the corecipient of the Nobel Prize in Physiology or Medicine for "discoveries concerning genetic control of enzyme and virus synthesis," Monod knew something about the relationship between code and life. As discussed in chapter six, DNA codes for life through exactly the mechanism that was the subject of the discoveries by Monod and his colleagues: the synthesis of enzymes (proteins and RNA) and viruses.

DNA builds products with a purpose. So do people. This is Monod's insight.

low-resolution images of the shadows of DNA, and (2) the basic laws of chemistry that dictated which structures could have the "high durability" that Schrödinger had noted would be required of "the hereditary substance." Watson and Crick had a significant advantage over Pauling

FIGURE 8.1 James Watson (left) and Francis Crick (right) with their Original Model of the Double Helix. © Photo Researchers, used with permission.

in that their colleague Rosalind Franklin had recently generated newly revealing X-ray diffraction photographs that provided additional evidence to guide them in their model building. With that discovery, the pace of the race intensified.

Watson recounts that, on the day of their March 1 outing to The Eagle, he "wandered down to see if the [metal-working] shop could be speeded to produce the purines and pyrimidines later that afternoon. Only a little encouragement was needed to get the final soldering accomplished in the next couple of hours."

With the required model pieces in hand, Watson went straight to work: "The brightly shining metal plates were then immediately used to make a model in which for the first time all the DNA components were present. In about an hour I had arranged the atoms in positions which satisfied both the X-ray data and the laws of stereochemistry."[16]

Following two years of progressive search and discovery, that morning's work settled the puzzle of the structure of DNA (see figure 8.1). Within months the pair had published a paper in *Nature* that announced their discovery. On the role of DNA as the carrier of the code of life, they noted simply, "It has not escaped our notice that the specific pairing we have postulated immediately suggests a possible copying mechanism for the genetic material."[17]

Seven years later, James Watson and Francis Crick were in Stockholm to accept the Nobel Prize in Physiology or Medicine, awarded for the discovery of the structure of DNA.[18]

A CENTURY AFTER Herbert Spencer introduced the term "survival of the fittest," a half-century after Sewall Wright introduced the idea of adaptive fitness landscapes to evolutionary biology, and a quarter-century after Watson and Crick discovered the structure of DNA, two young scientists named Stuart Kauffman and Simon Levin further advanced evolution theory. Their model of evolutionary fitness landscapes incorporated two characteristics shared by both genes and the evolutionary process itself: complexity and interdependence. By abstracting the essential features of the evolutionary process in a general modeling framework, Kauffman and Levin's theoretical framework provided a bridge to the study of technology that ultimately would link the work of two Wright brothers: Sewall Wright's work on adaptive landscapes and T. P. Wright's work on the dynamics of learning that he documented in "Factors Affecting the Cost of Airplanes."

Kauffman and Levin began their 1987 paper, "Towards a General Theory of Adaptive Walks on Rugged Landscapes," with the following statement: "Adaptive evolution, to a large extent, is a complex combinatorial process." Complexity in this context means that the relationship between changes in genetic code and resultant fitness is complicated by the fact that genes express themselves in combinations, so that a mutation of one gene is likely to affect the function of many genes. This interdependence in evolutionary biology is known as epistatic interactions among genes. Epistatic interactions make the problem solved by evolution a sort of "Rubik's Cube from Hell," whereby a change that improves fitness locally may result in reduced fitness globally. Kauffman and Levin went on to note the similarity between the structure of the problem solved by evolution and that of complex combinatorial problems in computer science and physics.[19]

Kauffman and Levin introduced their model by making reference to the essay by Francois Jacob that I cited at the end of the last chapter, which advanced the idea that evolution as a process was much more like tinkering than optimization: "Natural selection does not work as an engineer works . . . It works like a tinkerer—a tinkerer who does not know exactly what he is going to produce but uses . . . everything at his disposal to produce some kind of workable object."[20] This process is progressive, moving from simpler to more complex forms: "Evolution does not produce novelties from scratch. It works on what already exists, either transforming a system to give it new functions or combining several systems to produce a more elaborate one [as] during the passage from unicellular to multicellular forms."[21] The very fact of progressive evolution means that the living systems that are the result of evolutionary processes face an increasing number of constraints as their complexity increases: "The constraints to which systems are subjected vary with the level of complexity. There are always some constraints imposed by stability and thermodynamics. But as complexity increases, additional constraints appear—such as reproduction for living systems, or economic requirements for social systems."[22] To be viable in the world, a new molecule originating in the primordial swamp need only conform with fundamental physical laws. To be similarly viable, a new genetic combination, however, must not only conform to physical laws but also increase the "fitness" of its carrier within its given environment. A new technological combination must improve upon existing technologies and provide sufficient value to people that it is recorded, shared, and copied.

The Kauffman and Levin model was as simple as it was powerful. Imagine a genetic code of length N, where each gene might occupy one of two possible "states"—for example, "0" and "1" in a binary computer.[23] The difficulty of the evolutionary problem was tunable with the parameter K, which represented the average number of interactions among genes. The NK model, as it came to be called, was able to reproduce a number of measurable features of evolution in biological systems. Evolution could be represented as a genetic walk on a fitness landscape, in which increasing complexity was now a central parameter.

Might the same model, derived from evolutionary biology, explain the evolution of technology?

LIFE IS NOTHING else but the capacity for invariant reproduction. An organism, a process, or an organization create the circumstances for their own self-replication, both through time and across space. The story of McDonald's illustrates. The success of Ray Kroc was essentially that of creating code—in this case, a franchise manual—that could propagate across space and time. The fact that "billions and billions" of McDonald's hamburgers have been sold defines a certain type of success in code economics. Yet, as evidenced by the challenges McDonald's has faced in recent years as consumer tastes have changed, an organism's success in self-replication does not obviate the need for learning and adaptation. Indeed, in order for more complex forms of life to be viable, they must possess a capacity for learning and adaptation—mostly of an involuntary, unconscious variety.

By this route we arrive not only back to the cases of Dick and Mac McDonald and the Speedee Service System, but also to the seven-page manual of standard operating procedures that Ruth Wakefield generated for her employees at the Toll House Restaurant and the recipes tested and documented with great effort by Julia Child in *Mastering the Art of French Cooking*—not to mention the beer recipes recorded in 5,500-year-old Sumerian tablets. In each of these instances, the objective of encoding production recipes was invariant reproduction; in the first case the objective was the reliable reproduction of a franchise business; in the second that of a service experience; in the third that of a authentically prepared dish; and in the fourth, beer.

To the extent that the analogy holds, technology may also be nothing else but the capacity for invariant reproduction. However, in order for more complex forms of technology to be viable over time, technology also must possess a capacity for learning and adaptation.

Evolutionary theory as applied to the advance of code is the focus of the next chapter. Kauffman and Levin's *NK* model ends up providing a framework for studying the creation and evolution of code. Learning curves act as the link between biology and economics.

9

Platforms

The Role of Standards in Enabling Increased Complexity

Everywhere, economic activity is turning outward by embracing shared business and technology standards that let businesses plug into truly global systems of production.
—Sam Palmisano, The Globally Integrated Enterprise, 2006

IF THE SUGGESTION I have made repeatedly that the economy is "alive" seems fanciful or far-fetched, it is much less so if we consider the alternative: that it is dead.

What would it mean if the economy were dead? It would mean that it was inert. It would mean that it lacked the capacity to reproduce itself. It would mean that it decays and loses structure over time.

But, as we can readily observe, the economy—which exists beyond the control or direction of any single person and develops order and structure on a timeline that far exceeds a human lifespan—*is not*, in fact, inert. The economy *does* have the capacity to reproduce itself. And the economy *gains* in structure and complexity over time.

Those familiar with the study of such physical phenomena as a rolling boil in a pot of water, or a hurricane twisting high in the atmosphere,[1] will counter that the presence of structure in the economy does not necessarily suggest that the economy is alive. All that is required for such persistent "dissipative" structures to exist is that they process large amounts of energy throughput. The only additional explanation required for the order observed in the economy is its own observably large energy throughput—analogous to the flame under the pot of water that keeps it in a rolling boil.

The scaling laws that relate a city's "metabolism" to its size, which I described in chapter one, lend some credence to this energy-centric line of argument. Regular, predictable relationships exist between the internal structure of both organisms and economies, and in the fact that both require energy and "nutrients." However, the existence of such regularities on a macro scale are little more than shadows on the wall when it comes to understanding the micro-scale structural changes that actually are responsible for the evolution of the economy. In this chapter I will explore in more detail what it means for the economy to be alive and why contrary conceptions—including those woven deeply into the fabric of the classical and neoclassical schools of economics—are inconsistent with both logic and experience.

As I stated in the Introduction, the primary reason that I chose "code" as the most appropriate term to describe the mechanism by which technological information is stored and transmitted is not because code is a synonym for computer software but because it is used to describe genetic material—material that both preserves structure and enables organic change. That is the operative analogy. Indeed, as I have insisted throughout, this is more than an analogy: the introduction of production recipes into economics is—by structural parallel if not by magnitude of historic insight—exactly what the introduction of DNA is to molecular biology. It is the essential first step toward a transformation of economics into a branch of information theory.

IN THE SPRING of 1993, a professional dream came true for me: I was accepted to attend the Complex Systems Summer School at the Santa Fe Institute (SFI), where a small group of scientists from an array of disciplines—theoretical biologist Stuart Kauffman, economist Brian Arthur, and Nobel Prize-winning physicist Murray Gell-Mann among them—were cloistered in a former monastery where they collaborated on an array of grand projects relating to complexity in physical, biological, and social systems.

I had come to Santa Fe specifically in the hope of working with two of the leaders of the emerging field of complexity theory: Kauffman and Arthur. By the time I arrived at the school I had read and re-read everything they had published on the economy as an evolving complex system.

While I dedicated considerable effort that summer to a joint project on the self-organization of cities,[2] my greatest preoccupation—shared with my fellow summer school student José Lobo—was finding a way to integrate the framework of the Kauffman-Levin *NK* model into neoclassical production theory. Economics had a lot to say about how to optimize the level of inputs to get output, but what about the actual process of turning inputs into outputs? What is the difference between a "high-tech" and a "low-tech" firm anyway? In the Wonderful World of Widgets that is standard economics, ingredients combine to make a final product, but the recipe by which the ingredients actually become the product is nowhere explicitly represented. It seemed that the Kauffman-Levin *NK* model could be a start toward such a representation.

Economist Michael Porter long ago quipped, "There's no such thing as a low-tech industry. There are only low-tech companies."[3] This comment has the ring of folksy truth to it. But, if accurately applied to the economy of the present, it also reflects a profound shift in the nature of the economy over the past five hundred years. Consider the economy of the Middle Ages. We would have a hard time arguing that most production at that time was "complex." Returning to the biological analogy, most production was carried out by the equivalent of single-celled organisms. Even as late as the end of the nineteenth century, technological artifacts (which is to say, physical products) and the social arrangements that created them were primitive compared with those of today.

All of that changed in the early twentieth century, with the advent of large-scale production by single firms. The emergence of the great corporations of that era—from Ford, to Thyssen, to the even more ambitious project of state socialism in the USSR—represented a new form of social and economic organization. The complexity of production itself suddenly became a significant barrier to entry for new firms. General Motors may have been an entrepreneurial startup in the early twentieth century, but by mid-century it was an organizational behemoth operating on an unprecedented scale.

What do we mean by complexity in this context? It may be measured most simply in terms of the number of parts in a technological artifact.[4] The John Deere tractor sold today is clearly more complex than McCormick's reaper, which in turn was more complex than a plow. The social arrangements required to produce each of these products have also correspondingly increased in complexity over time.[5]

Understood in this way, complexity emphasizes the difficulty of the problem that is solved by a particular production recipe. A more complex problem is simply one for which finding a good solution is more difficult. (Think again of Julia Child's search for the perfect mayonnaise recipe—more difficult than it might seem at first!) The concept of solving hard problems can be defined quite formally; as applied to production recipes, it represents a special case of algorithmic complexity that is at the heart of information theory.

The primary causal pathway by which complexity affects the evolution of industries and the economy is via the obstacles to imitation that complexity creates. The greater the complexity of technology, the lower the correlation between the effectiveness of a given production recipe (e.g., the leader's method) and that of the same recipe altered slightly (i.e., an imperfect imitation). Using this algorithmic definition, the complexity of a production recipe can be represented in terms of both the number of "operations" or distinct units involved in the production process and (critically) the extent of the interdependence between those units. Before imitating a simple technological/organizational routine, a firm can predict its future performance characteristics with some reliability. Based on those estimated characteristics, a simple technological/organizational routine will be adopted—or not.

Complex technologies cannot be imitated in this manner, for two reasons. The first is that different components of a complex technological problem are typically interdependent, so changing one part of the organizational routine when searching for a solution will affect other parts. Finding a solution to a complex technological problem is thus like solving Rubik's Cube: you can't address one part of the problem at a time (analogous to one color on the Cube) the way you can with a simple problem. The second reason is that complex technological problems are more likely to have elements that are not encoded in any manual, patent, or book of specifications. People "just know" how to perform certain parts of the organizational routine.

For these two reasons, complex technological/organizational routines cannot be "adopted" in the way economists customarily employ this term. Imitation of such routines is almost always imperfect—sometimes disastrously so—because modifications in the practices of one unit within the firm (alleles, in the DNA analogy) will affect the effectiveness of multiple other units. Because a simple technological/ organizational routine can be easily imitated, it is not likely to yield persistent profits to an early adopter. Enduring technological leadership is based on activities that require the greatest coordination and have the greatest inherent complexity. These activities are the most potentially disruptive to the internal operations of innovating firms, but also the most difficult to imitate when successfully implemented.

If this way of looking at the world is accurate, then the Porter quote above becomes immediately intelligible. We may look at both Walmart and a "mom-and-pop" corner store as existing in the retail sector of the economy, but they are in fact in different lines of business. Walmart is above all a logistics operation; it gets products where they need to be at a low cost. Corner store owners are effectively in the real estate and relationship business; those who succeed generally do so not because they charge exceptionally low prices or offer unusual products but because they save their customers time, and because they give their customers an experience of human connection—essentially the pleasure of being recognized. Retail is therefore not an inherently low-tech sector of the economy, although it may include low-tech firms—understood through the lens of code economics as "easy to imitate."

DURING THE SUMMER and fall of 1993, Kauffman, Lobo, and I made some initial progress toward the goal of using an evolutionary model of technology, based on the *NK* framework, to differentiate high-tech and low-tech firms and describe the evolution of industries. Our joint efforts received a significant boost when noted macroeconomic theorist Karl Shell volunteered to join our team in winter 1994. Shell immediately suggested that we focus our attention on what we all soon agreed was the single most significant unanswered question in the microeconomics of production: How do firms learn? In particular, what specific search process for better production processes within firms over time could explain the emergence of learning curves, as was observed so consistently across industries? While companies like Intel routinely used learning curves as a practical guide to strategy, economists had done little to explain their origins. This was the problem Kauffman, Lobo, Shell, and I set out to solve.

After two years of programming, testing, and iterating models, we ended up with a variant of the *NK* model that we could use to simulate learning curves. The results: using the simplest default implementation and search of a wide range of potential values for the critical parameters, we identified the subset of parameter values that yielded not only the qualitative characteristics of learning curves but also a number of their quantitative characteristics. We found that observed learning curves corresponded to production processes that exhibited some interconnection between component parts, but not maximal organizational complexity. Further simulations at the scale of industry suggested that the most appealing industries for entry by new firms were those in which production was characterized by intermediate levels of complexity. That is, they were neither so mature that the most effective production recipes had all been discovered by incumbent firms, but also not so young that systematic learning about production was not yet possible, which meant that experience could not yet provide a competitive advantage. This theory lined up with entrepreneurial intuition, as evidenced in Gordon Moore's story about the early history of Fairchild Semiconductor (see Text Box 7.1): the complexity of production is a factor that limits a new firm's ability to copy the practices of an incumbent firm.

Kauffman, Lobo, Shell, and I had employed code economics to advance understanding of an important economic phenomenon—as the structural origin of the learning curve surely is—for which classical economics had provided only a very general explanation (for example, Adam Smith's division of labor in a pin factory) and neoclassical economics provided no real explanation at all. Others, notably Brian Arthur, had taken the application of code further. Yet the efforts of Santa Fe Institute economists in the early 1990s collectively constituted no more than a rudimentary proof of concept for code economics.

Those who contributed to the intellectual ferment during the early days of the SFI planted seeds of inquiry that took more than a decade to germinate and grow. From the mid-1990s until the mid-2000s, progress in code economics was limited. Complexity theory had failed to yield the empirically robust "killer app" that the work of Paul Douglas had provided for neoclassical production theory (see Text Box 5.2).

But while code economics stagnated, the code economy itself took off. The fundamentally new essence of the code economy that Brian Arthur, Stuart Kauffman, and others all had glimpsed from a distance in the early 1990s had come roaring out of the mist, carried by the Internet. In some cases, algorithmic reality and theory were linked. Abstract work in the early 1990s at SFI and elsewhere on the discrete mathematics of social networks had, via a group of Stanford-based academics, turned into Google's Page Rank algorithm. Esoteric attempts to use "agent-based" models to simulate the dynamics of city formation had found their way into tens of millions of households via highly popular games such as *SimCity* and *Civilization*. Research on the potential for herding and speculative bubbles in financial markets vaulted from the back pages of scholarly journals to the front pages of major newspapers when the financial crisis hit in 2008. Stuart Kauffman's notion of technological search occurring in the space of the "adjacent possible"—a concept derived from the application of the *NK* model to innovation, and thus close to our joint work on learning curves—was popularized by author Steven Johnson in his book *Where Good Ideas Come From.* More generally, as discussed at the start of chapter six, Big Data and the Internet of Things had hit the worlds of business and government with force, washing away the foundations of default economic methodologies and challenging the field of economics to respond.

The time had come for a group of us who had been part of those early days at the SFI to try again to define and develop code economics.

In August 2013, nearly 20 years to the month since my first visit to the Santa Fe Institute, I returned there to join a group of economists, anthropologists, corporate technology managers, and others to discuss the very topic I'd worked on at the Complex Systems Summer School: the nature of technology and innovation in economic systems. The occasion was a three-week-long meeting organized by my former coauthor, José Lobo, and his colleague Deborah Strumsky on the representation of technology "inside the black box"[6] of the neoclassical production function.

Oxford University physicist Doyne Farmer presented work under-taken with collaborators on learning curves and economic food webs. Giovanni Dosi of the Scuola Superiore Sant'Anna in Pisa, Italy, pre-sented research on the knowledge and organizational practices behind input/output relations. Brian Arthur presented his powerful theory of the recombinant nature of technological change, elaborating on work presented in his 2011 book, *The Nature of Technology*. I presented a paper representing the early stages of this book.

At the same meeting, Harvard macroeconomist Ricardo Hausmann presented his work with MIT Media Lab-based physicist César Hidalgo on the evolution of complexity at the scale of a country. Developed in a sequence of coauthored publications, beginning with a paper published in *Science* in 2007,[7] that work bears directly on the distinction between low-tech and high-tech goods with which I opened this chapter, and helps develop the concept of technology platforms that is central to this book. Later in this chapter I'll refer back to the work by Doyne Farmer and his team on learning curves and economic food webs. In com-bination, these papers explain how the economy manages increasing complexity by "hard-wiring" solutions into standards, which in turn define platforms.

HAUSMANN AND HIDALGO'S work on economic complexity begins with data on the actual imports and exports of certain countries across time, which are available for most countries in the world. They use these data to map the progression from simplicity to complexity, across not time but geographical space. Affirming the principle that I stated at the outset, that there is literally no "what" of output without a "how" to produce that output, they observe that products of increasing complex-ity naturally reflect increasingly complex code.

Using the word "capability" to refer to the possession and execu-tion of the code required to produce a given good, Hausmann and Hidalgo describe their method using the analogy of building with Lego blocks: "We can create indirect measures of the capabilities available in a country by thinking of each capability as a building block or Lego piece. In this analogy, a product is equivalent to a Lego model, and a country is equivalent to a bucket of Legos. Countries will be able to make products for which they have all the necessary capabilities, just as a child is able to produce a Lego model if the child's bucket contains all of the necessary Lego pieces."[8] This is almost literally the way programs are written: blocks of simpler code are combined to yield more complex code. It is also almost literally the way complex products are assembled: simpler modules are combined to yield more complex final products. The country—in most cases including one key city or a small number of central cities—provides the platform on which individual exporting companies execute code, much as the operating system provides the platform for individual programs that execute code on a digital computer.

To elaborate further on the connection between Hidalgo and Hausmann's Lego analogy and the language of this book, the Lego pieces constitute snippets of code that have the potential to be combined and executed in the economy. If you have the snippet of code to create mayonnaise and you have the snippet of code to cook chicken, then you can combine those two snippets of code—production subrecipes, if you will—with the code that enables you to cut up a stalk of celery, which yields the code to produce chicken salad. However, if you only have the code to cook chicken but not the code to produce mayonnaise, then you will need to import mayonnaise to produce chicken salad. Furthermore—and crucial to Hausmann and Hidalgo's results— the fact that your country exports mayonnaise proves that your country has the code to produce mayonnaise.

Note that, in code economics, a given country's level of "development" is not sensibly measured by the total monetary value of all goods and services it produces—which is the definition of gross domestic product. It is also not sensibly measured by the total capital or educational level of the workforce. Rather, the development of a country consists of nothing more or less than its capacity to execute more complex code. Relatively more developed countries are those with the code to produce more complex products. Such countries will import raw materials (single Lego pieces) and intermediate products (relatively simpler assemblages of Legos). They will also export complex products in order to pay for the required imports.

Less-developed countries that lack the code to produce complex products will import them, and they will export simpler intermediate products and raw materials in order to pay for the required imports.[9]

In this manner, the table of imports and exports over time provides a direct and economically revealing map of the unfolding patterns of specialization, based on the underlying complexity of the code that countries have the capacity to execute. Hidalgo and Hausmann state that the challenge of mapping variations in underlying capabilities (code) across countries with trade data "is equivalent to asking whether we can infer properties such as the diversity and exclusivity of the Lego pieces inside a child's bucket by looking only at the models that a group of children, each with different Legos, can make." In this way, "connections between countries and products signal the availability of capabilities in a country, just like the creation of a model by a child signals the availability of a specific set of Lego pieces."[10]

Clearly, most of what is produced in any given country is not exported. What data on traded goods reveal far better than data on overall production are the relative advantages to a country of producing various goods. The existence of these relative advantages emphasizes the point documented by Bloom and Van Reenan: that countries, just like companies, have very different code, which leads to very different outcomes.[11] The historical record suggests that what matters for large-scale development progress is not only the quantity of trade but the type. Places that have companies that can contribute to and benefit from global supply chains seem to have the potential to prosper; those that are disconnected from global supply chains and can contribute only basic resources, but produce nothing complex, seem to lag. As Hausmann put it, "My theory is that inequality comes from differential connectedness."[12]

How have an increasing number of nations overcome the obstacle of "differential connectedness" to achieve genuine development and expand the opportunity for ever-greater numbers of their populations to contribute productively to the twenty-first-century economy? One answer is, through the development and widespread adoption of standards, which enables code created in different places to be executed on different platforms as never before.

OF THE DRIVERS of beneficial trade, international standards are at once among the most important and the least appreciated. Both writing and weights and measures were standardized by the first emperor of China, Qin Shi Huangdi (221 BCE to 206 BCE), whose aim was to increase trade within the newly unified country. From the invention of bills of exchange in the Middle Ages, to the development of universal time in the late nineteenth century, to the creation of twenty-first-century communications protocols, innovations in standards have lowered the cost and enhanced the value of exchanges across distance. In the process, they have created new capabilities and opportunities on a global scale.

Standards of a company-specific variety also underlie routines of production that are the essence of global supply chains. From the sourcing of raw materials to the marketing of final goods, contracts between buyers and suppliers depend on clearly communicated expectations and specifications, all facilitated by standards. For entrepreneurs in developing countries, demonstrated conformity with international standards—particularly those established and maintained by the International Organization for Standardization and the International Electrotechnical Commission—is a universally recognized mark of organizational capacity that substantially eases entry into global production and distribution networks.

Ask yourself what the greatest inventions were over the past 150 years: Penicillin? The transistor? Electric power? Each of these has been transformative, but equally compelling candidates include universal time, container shipping, the TCP/IP protocols underlying the Internet, and the GSM and CDMA standards that underlie mobile telephony. These are the technologies that make global trade possible by making code developed in one place interoperable with code developed in another. Standards reduce barriers among people and shrink the world. They are now so embedded in global exchange that their impact cannot be separated from economic dynamics in general.

Standards turn a firm-level recipe into a subroutine of a larger process comprising many different recipes, which enumerates the full instructions for the operation of a supply chain. As Paul Agnew, an early proponent of international standards, pointed out, compatibility standards resolve the difficulties that arise "at the transition points—points at which the product passes from department to department within a company, or is sold by one company to another or to an individual."[13] From the sourcing of raw materials to the marketing of final goods, procurement contracts between buyers and suppliers depend on expectations and specifications that are clearly communicated, all facilitated by standards.[14] Standards thus have become increasingly important as the economy has become increasingly complex, because they enable the interoperability of firm-level recipes.

Adam Smith long ago noted the correspondence between the increasing complexity and interdependence of a society and its shared well-being: "It is the great multiplication of the productions of all the different arts, in consequence of the division of labour, which occasions, in a well-governed society, that universal opulence which extends itself to the lowest ranks of the people."[15] He famously offered the example of the woolen coat as a seemingly simple item that in fact was "the produce of the joint labor of a great multitude of workmen" (see Text Box 9.1). Yet the complexity and interdependence of the economy today is orders of magnitude greater than two centuries ago. Apple, for example, has 786 suppliers located in 31 countries around the world for the production of the iPhone. A disassembled iPhone is its own miniature "United Nations General Assembly" with representatives from most of the countries that have the capacity to produce cellphone hardware and software for global supply chains.

As I described in greater detail in a recent work with Hezekiah Agwara and Brian Higginbotham, the phenomenon known as globalization really describes the increased interdependence among nations and in overall economic complexity.[16] Shared standards and business practices have been a precondition for this process of economic integration. It is not a great stretch to state that globalization is standardization.[17]

IF ECONOMIES ARE a form of food chain, then raw materials are the plankton that exist at the bottom of the chain. They are simple in structure. They don't change much. They don't learn much. They are essential to the overall functioning of the system, but the more we evolve the less we think about them. That, indeed, is precisely the point made by Alfred North Whitehead: "Civilization advances by extending the number of operations we can perform without thinking about them."[18]

In biological ecosystems, each level of the food chain depends for energy on the one below. Nanoplankton eat dissolved organic matter and particulate organic matter. Zooplankton eat nanoplankton. Small fish eat zooplankton. Large fish eat small fish. Humans eat large fish.

Text Box 9.1 Adam Smith's Description of an Eighteenth-Century
Supply Chain

"The woolen-coat, for example . . . is the produce of the joint labor of a great multitude of workmen. The shepherd, the sorter of the wool, the wool-comber or carder, the dyer, the scribbler, the spinner, the weaver, the fuller, the dresser, with many others, must all join their different arts in order to complete even this homely production. How many merchants and carriers, besides, must have been employed in transporting the materials from some of those workmen to others who often live in a very distant part of the country! How much commerce and navigation in particular, how many shipbuilders, sailors, sail-makers, rope-makers, must have been employed in order to bring together the different drugs made use of by the dyer, which often come from the remotest corners of the world! What a variety of labor too is necessary in order to produce the tools of the meanest of those workmen! To say nothing of such complicated machines as the ship of the sailor, the mill of the fuller, or even the loom of the weaver, let us consider only what a variety of labor is requisite in order to form that very simple machine, the shears with which the shepherd clips the wool. The miner, the builder of the furnace for smelting the ore, the feller of the timber, the burner of the charcoal to be made use of in the smelting-house, the brick-maker, the brick-layer, the workmen who attend the furnace, the mill-wright, the forger, the smith, must all of them join their different arts in order to produce them."[19]

Organisms at the top of the food chain are, generally, also the most recently evolved. Nanoplankton have been around longer than zooplankton. Zooplankton have been around longer than small fish. Small fish have been around longer than large fish. And large fish have been around longer than humans. In this manner, trophic levels represent not only a gradation of structure from the simplest to the most complex organisms, but also the gradation in evolutionary history from the earliest to the most recently evolved. To a point, the inverse correlation between the historical age of a species and its complexity is obvious: since life requires a constant throughput of energy, organisms at higher trophic levels could not have come into being if organisms at the lower trophic levels had not been there first.

In more or less the same way, it is obvious that we can't have a time-keeping or heart-monitoring app on a smartphone without an operating system for the phone. Thus the operating system is a platform that allows the apps to run. The operating system in turn is built on a platform of standards that convert the programs in which the operating systems are written (e.g., C, C++, or UNIX) into the binary "machines language," in which computer hardware understands instructions and stores information. The computer hardware in turn requires a constant flow of energy in order to maintain its structured state (in particular, it turns out, to reset so it can perform new functions). This requires electric power. Electric power provided through the grid is a platform technology that required decades to refine for even small geographic areas, and it continues to spread gradually across the globe. The electric power infrastructure in turn depends on a transportation infrastructure, and on technologies for extracting raw materials, that enable the generation of power.

The economy consists of the provision of ever more services, delivered over platforms on top of platforms. The platforms are the trophic levels of the economic ecosystem.

If goods and services are built on platforms, one atop the other, then it follows that learning at higher levels of the system should be faster than learning at lower levels, for the simple reason that learning at higher levels benefits from incremental learning all the way down. This is exactly what Doyne Farmer and his team found in their research on learning curves in an array of industries, which they presented at the 2013 Santa Fe Institute meeting I referred to above. When industries are ordered according to their place in an economic food chain, their characteristic rates of learning correlate with trophic levels: rates of learning in the production of "raw materials" are relatively slow, whereas they are relatively rapid for complex goods and services (see figures 9.1 and 9.2).

Awareness of this fact helps resolve some persistent disagreements among informed technology scholars. Those who focus on the extraction of raw materials will observe a high degree of volatility in prices around a gradually increasing trend, which suggests that learning is slow and

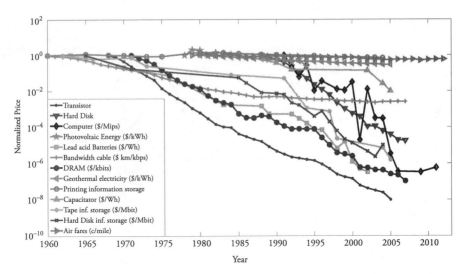

FIGURE 9.1 Price Reductions in a Set of Commodities and Complex Products, 1960–2013.

Source: Talk given by J. Doyne Farmer at Nanyang Technological University on March 3, 2014, "An Evolutionary View of Technological Progress."

scarcity dominates. Those who look at the delivery of services over layers of infrastructure—for example, the rates at which wireless networks share data—see exponential growth in every direction, which suggests that learning is fast and abundance dominates. The two layers coexist; indeed, the more complex layers depend on the less complex. Like the pace of biological evolution at different trophic levels, the pace of technological advance at different platform levels is slow and fast, depending on whether we focus our attention on simple or complex products.

BEFORE I BRING this discussion of standards and platforms to a close, I must elaborate on the development of a top-level platform with particular significance for code. The story begins with Vannevar Bush, a titanic figure of mid-twentieth-century science in the United States. Bush is best known for his work during World War II as director of the U.S. Office of Scientific Research and Development, where he led some of the most ambitious and large-scale R&D programs ever undertaken at that time (notably including the development of the atomic bomb); for his part in the development of analog computers; and as the author of *Science: The Endless Frontier,* which provided

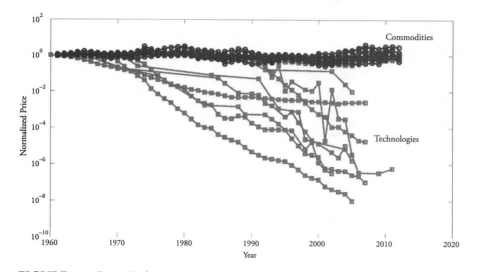

FIGURE 9.2 Price Reductions in a Set of Commodities and Complex Products, 1960–2013: Clustered by commodities and complex products ("technologies").

Source: Talk given by J. Doyne Farmer at Nanyang Technological University on March 3, 2014, "An Evolutionary View of Technological Progress."

the rationale for the creation of the National Science Foundation. However, one of Bush's most powerful and enduring contributions may be one that seemed relatively trivial at the time: an *Atlantic Monthly* article published in July 1945, just weeks before VJ Day—the end of World War II.

In that article, titled "As We May Think," Bush looked ahead to the frontier of societal advance in the postwar era. His emphasis was not on the products of publicly funded science but on the capacities of privately produced tools: "The world has arrived at an age of cheap complex devices of great reliability; and something is bound to come of it."[20] In that essay, he envisioned how existing low-cost technologies might be further advanced and networked into a system for the storage and retrieval of ideas, which he called the memex: "Wholly new forms of encyclopedias will appear, ready made with a mesh of associative trails running through them, ready to be dropped into the memex and there amplified." This tool would allow the forward progress of human inquiry: "[Man] has built a civilization so complex that he needs to mechanize his records more fully if he is to push his experiment to its logical conclusion and not merely become bogged down part way there by overtaxing his limited memory."[21]

Among those who read this essay in *Atlantic Monthly* was a 25-year-old aerospace engineer named Douglas Engelbart, who at the time the article reached him was sitting in a hut in the South Pacific. Engelbart was so taken by the vision set forth in "As We May Think" that he redirected his career toward making that vision a reality. While working as a staff researcher at Stanford Research Institute, Engelbart published a report, produced with funding from the U.S. Air Force Office of Scientific Research, titled "Augmenting Human Intellect: A Conceptual Framework," which summarized his 15 years of reflection prompted by Vannevar Bush's article. "Man's population and gross product are increasing at a considerable rate, but the complexity of his problems grows still faster, and the urgency with which solutions must be found becomes steadily greater in response to the increased rate of activity and the increasingly global nature of that activity," he wrote. "Augmenting man's intellect, in the sense defined above, would warrant full pursuit by an enlightened society if there could be shown a reasonable approach and some plausible benefits."[22]

Among the small group of people who shared Engelbart's vision of computers as enablers of human creativity was a psychologist and computer scientist named Joseph Carl Robnett Licklider, known to all as J. C. R. Licklider or, simply, "Lick." After receiving a triple bachelor of arts degree in 1937 from Washington University in St. Louis in physics, mathematics, and psychology, Licklider continued on to Harvard, where he received a PhD in psycho-acoustics and undertook a postdoctoral fellowship at the psycho-acoustics laboratory. Licklider moved to MIT in 1950, where he became interested in the new field of information technology, and from there, in 1957, to the legendary engineering firm of Bolt Beranek and Newman, Inc. (BBN), where he developed the first time-sharing computer.

In 1960, while at BBN, Licklider published a paper titled "Man-Computer Symbiosis," in which he, like Engelbart, described how computer networks might evolve to help humans solve complex problems. Emphasizing the complementarity of human and machine capabilities and citing the Newell-Simon-Shaw General Problem Solver as an example, Licklider wrote the following:

Man-computer symbiosis is an expected development in cooperative interaction between men and electronic computers. It will involve very close coupling between the human and the electronic members of the partnership. The main aims are 1) to let computers facilitate formulative thinking as they now facilitate the solution of formulated problems, and 2) to enable men and computers to cooperate in making decisions and controlling complex situations without inflexible dependence on predetermined programs. In the anticipated symbiotic partnership, men will set the goals, formulate the hypotheses, determine the criteria, and perform the evaluations. Computing machines will do the routinizable work that must be done to prepare the way for insights and decisions in technical and scientific thinking.[23]

In 1962, Licklider was appointed director of the Information Processing Techniques Office at the Advanced Research Projects Agency (ARPA). He immediately set about building a network of researchers who shared his vision at university laboratories and think tanks. Among them was Engelbart. On April 23, 1963, Licklider sent a memo to this group, lightheartedly addressed to "Members and Affiliates of the Intergalactic Computer Network." Licklider started by apologizing for the rushed nature of his communication, then stated his objective: "I shall try to set forth some background material and some thoughts about possible interactions among the various activities in the overall enterprise for which, as you may have detected in the above subject, I am at a loss for a name."[24] Among the most urgent needs as Licklider saw them was a reliable communication protocol to link different computers on a network. "Consider the situation in which several different centers are netted together, each center being highly individualistic and having its own special language and its own special way of doing things. Is it not desirable, or even necessary for all the centers to agree upon some language or, at least, upon some conventions for asking such questions as 'What language do you speak?'"[25] This question would seed an ARPA project to develop just such a network.

In 1968, ARPA announced that it had awarded the contract to build what was by then called the ARPAnet to BBN. (Licklider had left ARPA in 1964, so he did not oversee the creation of the ARPAnet.) Later the same year, at the fall Joint Computer Conference, a semi-annual meeting of the then-major computing societies held in San Francisco, Engelbart took those ideas further toward practical implementation.

He offered more than a thousand participants a demonstration of the core elements of the user architecture that would define the information revolution in the decades to come: the computer mouse, text editing, hypertext, windowing, and video conferencing. The talk became known as "The Mother of All Demos." Five years later, Vint Cerf and Bob Kahn codeveloped the TCP/IP (the standard that underlies the global platform we know today as the Internet), improving on the communications protocol the ARPAnet had been constructed on.

Even as he was leading some of the largest scale scientific endeavors in history, Vannevar Bush had the vision to look ahead to an era when the greatest progress in science-based discovery would be enabled by dramatically lowering the cost of storing and sharing ideas. Douglas Engelbart further democratized that vision, prototyping an architecture of collaboration through standardized interfaces that has become a global infrastructure of interaction. The Internet today is a platform that enables human creativity and collaboration on a global scale.

Whereas much of Great Man-vs-Machine Debate focused on the substitution of machine for man, Bush, Engelbart, and Licklider were among those who—like Ada Lovelace—envisioned a deep complementarity between computer and human work. This potential for complementary human and machine work, as well as for substitution, is the starting point for Part Three.

PART THREE
THE HUMAN ADVANTAGE

10

Complementarity

The Bifurcation Is Near

Mathematical reasoning may be regarded rather schematically as the exercise of a combination of two faculties, which we may call intuition and
ingenuity.

—Alan Turing, *Systems of Logic Based on Ordinals*, 1938

ON NOVEMBER 16, 2014, before a crowd of 60,000 people gathered at
Sardar Vallabhbhai Patel Stadium in Mumbai, India, the Jain monk
Munishri Ajitchandrasagarji accomplished a rare feat: he perfectly recalled five hundred unrelated facts in succession. From early morning
to midday, spectators approached the stadium stage, one at a time.
Each showed the young monk a random object, posed a math problem, or spoke a word or phrase in one of at least six languages. After
the last of these five hundred participants had conveyed their random
fact, the 24-year-old prodigy opened his eyes and began to recite them
back. Detouring only once to fill in a blank he had left aside, he recalled
every fact without error. According to his guru, the young monk had
matched a feat last accomplished six centuries earlier by a Jain monk in
the Mughal court of the Subahdar of Khambhat.[1]

"Munishri's mind is like a computer during the download process,"
said his mentor, P. P. Acharya Nayachandrasagarji. "Many processes can
happen in his mind at one time."

From a human standpoint, the young monk's achievement is indeed
astounding. An average person can reliably remember no more than

five to nine unrelated facts at a time.[2] Since Munishri can recall five hundred, his short-term memory capacity is 50 to 100 times that of the average human.

Now consider the first digital computer, the ENIAC, whose development I described in chapter four. Constructed of 17,468 vacuum tubes and occupying a 33-by-55-foot space, the ENIAC was a formidable apparatus. Yet for all its bulk it could only hold 20 numbers it its memory at a time, better than the average person but still only 1/25th the capacity of Munishri (see Text Box 4.1). Like a human forced to take repeated trips to the library to look up essential facts, the ENIAC operators supplemented the computer's memory using punch cards that took it one to five seconds to read.

Where the ENIAC excelled was not in memory but in the speed at which it was able to perform computations. While a human can generally average no more than three distinct computational cycles per minute, the ENIAC could maintain a pace of 300,000; in other words, even the first digital computer could perform raw computation at 100,000 times the speed of a human.

The attainments of Jain monks notwithstanding, it turns out that humans are not very good computers.

RICARDO HAUSMANN, WHOSE work I discussed in the previous chapter, once said to me during a conversation at the Santa Fe Institute, "What has happened over time is an increase in the amount of knowledge. What has not happened is an increase in the ability of humans to hold knowledge in their heads. Since we have limited brain space we embed tacit knowledge into code, and code into modularized hardware."

Technology—the how of production—begins as an idea. Some ideas are spread as unwritten recipes, procedures, and routines, whereas others are encoded as blueprints, manuals, patents, or standard operating procedures. Still others may be directly encoded as hardware. Hardware that can be programmed—a general purpose computer, for example—thus becomes a new platform for encoding ideas. The process then repeats, as I described in the last chapter, and platforms are built on other platforms.

Consider the story of Gaspard Clair François Marie Riche de Prony that I related in chapter three. De Prony began with a set of mathematical operations—procedures for converting one set of numbers into another set of numbers, which was useful in tax assessment. To perform such operations at the required scale, he converted them into routines that could be managed by human calculators, whose skill level was below that of the mathematicians who derived the original formulae. These routines were the "software" that allowed for the computational work to occur. Lewis Fry Richardson (see chapter four) imagined creating similar software for the computation of numbers that would be useful in predicting the weather. In both cases, these routines were useful enough that they ultimately were encoded into hardware. The ENIAC team converted a known routine for integrating the Baratropic Vorticity Equation into hardware that was capable of performing the calculation, which enabled Richardson's dream of predicting the weather to become a reality (see Text Box 4.1). Paul Douglas described how the widespread availability of mechanical calculators reduced the skill level required of clerks (see chapter five).

Julia Child experimented with the production of mayonnaise and encoded the results in a recipe she included in *Mastering the Art of French Cooking*. Publishing this recipe enabled home cooks of lesser ability than Child to prepare mayonnaise of a quality comparable to hers. Ruth Wakefield had an idea of how to make a chocolate chip cookie. After considerable experimentation, she encoded the results into a recipe that still appears on the Nestlé chocolate chip bag. She also had ideas about how to run a restaurant, which she encoded in a manual for her employees.

At each stage of production—from initial invention through repeated innovations to automation and digitization—people's capacity to create value progresses and the role of the human worker is redefined. As organizational theorist Geoff Moore puts it, "At the end of any arc of innovation, when we have gone all the way from entrepreneur to automation, goods and services that used to be scarce and very expensive to acquire have now been made plentiful and cheap. That makes them a perfect platform upon which to build the next wave of innovation. Entrepreneurs are the ones who catch on to the implications of this new state the fastest. They kick off the next round of innovation, they launch the next arc."[3] The journey from idea to algorithm thus arguably typifies the evolution of any technological innovation and the new work it creates as it evolves from the spark of an idea to an ubiquitous platform.

At every stage in this process, elements of the work formerly done by humans can be done by a machine or computer. At the same time, humans are empowered to do work of a type or at a rate that was previously not feasible. This is what I mean by the sequential "bifurcation" of work (See figure 10.1.).

WANT AN EXAMPLE? Look at the watch on your wrist. The first spring-driven clocks began to appear in Italy and Germany in the late 1400s. By 1524, master locksmith Peter Henlein was regularly manufacturing pocket watches in his Nuremberg shop. The technology to produce watches gradually spread to other parts of Europe, and by the seventeenth century watch production was centered in London, Paris, and the French cities of Blois and Lyon. As it turned out, many of the most accomplished watchmakers in sixteenth-century France were members of the beleaguered Protestant minority known as the Huguenots.[4] Beginning with a General Edict issued on January 29, 1536, that remained in effect for the next 60 years, France undertook an ill-considered and bloody campaign to expel or eliminate its Huguenot population.

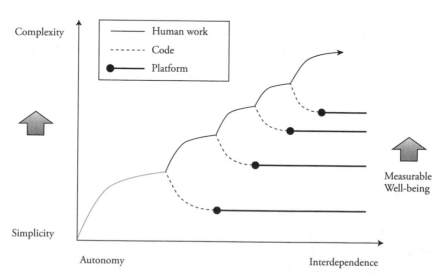

FIGURE 10.1 Sequential Bifurcations. *Source:* Author.

Many Huguenots fled to Switzerland—primarily to French-speaking Geneva—where their freedom of worship was protected. When they fled to Geneva, they took their watchmaking skills with them. As a result, Switzerland—a landlocked, mountainous, and fiercely independent nation—suddenly had a watch industry.

Buyers in Europe regarded the first watches produced by the nascent Swiss industry much as Americans viewed Japanese cars in the 1970s: crude compared to those manufactured at the established production centers in London and Paris but redemptively cheap and functional. Consequently, also like Japanese cars, the early Swiss watches found a market niche and sold well.

In Geneva, following a pattern prevalent in other industries, the most successful watchmakers soon organized themselves into a guild. Their aim was to govern market entry and restrict competition among existing firms. As the city prospered further from the watch trade, incumbent producers successfully enacted laws that excluded both immigrants and women from employment in watchmaking and reserved work in the trade exclusively for *citoyens* (citizens) and the *bourgeois* (burghers). An interval of remarkable if concentrated prosperity for Geneva ensued. Watchmaking created a Protestant middle class in democratic Switzerland that was in the vanguard of change during Europe's Age of Enlightenment, which is generally dated from the early seventeenth century to the late eighteenth century. Jean-Jacques Rousseau—author of *The Social Contract,* an early scientific theorist and an inspiration to both the French Revolution and Mary Shelley's *Frankenstein*—was the son of a third-generation Genevan watchmaker.[5]

As Geneva's watch industry developed through the late 1600s, the city faced a challenge: with the watchmaking talent among the citoyens and bourgeois already fully employed, how could the industry continue to grow without relaxing the restrictions on employment, which had helped watchmakers earn their high incomes and elevated social standing? The solution, of course, was to outsource. (If you're starting to read "Geneva ca. 1650" as "USA ca. 1995," you're getting the subtext.) Rather than permit immigrants or women to be employed in the workshops of Geneva, the Swiss standardized watchmaking tasks and sent piecework out to people living in the poor villages and towns in the Jura Mountains. These were inconsequential places, including one by the name of Neuchâtel.

The guilds held little sway in these mountain villages. Paying no mind to Genevan employment restrictions, producers in Neuchâtel and elsewhere in the Jura organized watch production around a model that suited their circumstances and predispositions. Rather than bringing workers together in a single workshop, they broke the piecework down into repetitive tasks that created production efficiencies best attained by a division of labor. Once the door of opportunity was opened to the shepherds of the Jura, they did not hesitate to rush through it. Entire families participated in making watches, including children, of course, who were adept at assembling small, delicate mechanisms.

Fast-forward to 1967. It was in Neuchâtel, at the Centre Electronique Horloger, that the first prototype quartz wristwatch was unveiled. The Japanese firm Seiko released a prototype quartz wristwatch the same year. Quartz watches were as accurate as mechanical timepieces but far easier to construct, and by the 1980s quartz wristwatches were dominating the market. They were produced by the millions on assembly lines, and reliable timekeeping became a commodity. As early as 1982, the journal *Assembly Automation* published a paper titled "Robots Start to Assemble Watches."[6] Further disruption of the watch industry occurred in the 1990s due to the availability of a low-cost alternative—mobile phones. As cell phones began to be sold widely in the 2000s, timekeeping became one app among many on the portable digital computers we have come to know as smartphones.

The average watch had completed a 500-year journey from a delicate timepiece assembled high in the Jura mountains to lines of code stored and processed on a smartphone. Did this end the Swiss watchmaking industry? Well, not exactly. Switzerland—once the dominant watchmaking nation—today produces fewer than 5 percent of the timepieces manufactured for export globally. In 2014, Switzerland exported 29 million watches, as compared to China's 669 million (the global leader in terms of volume). But what of value? That is a different story: Swiss watch exports were worth $24.3 billion in 2014, nearly five times as much as all Chinese watches combined. It turns out that the highest quality handmade watches are more valued than ever—as is the craftsmanship of the most capable watchmakers and designers who produce those watches.

As a sequence of new technologies delivered timekeeping services at rapidly diminishing costs—first through quartz watches then via smartphones—the Swiss watch industry managed not only to survive but to thrive. The creation of a low-price, high-volume timekeeping option strengthened the market for a differentiated higher price, low-volume option.

In short, the market bifurcated. Such bifurcations have occurred across time and across industries. Movies are one good example: as a sequence of new technologies have appeared to deliver home entertainment at a rapidly diminishing cost—first through videotapes, then DVDs, then online streaming—movie theaters have managed not only to survive but to thrive. They have done so by providing a lower volume, higher-priced option that incorporated a sequence of amenities not available at home, from Dolby Surround Sound to IMAX to 3D.

Visual art services are another example of a sequence of new technologies that deliver services at rapidly diminishing costs—first through photocopying and then digitization. Like movie theaters, the fine art market also has managed not only to survive but to thrive, as the very ubiquity of copies increased the value of authenticity.

The music industry, too, welcomed a sequence of new technologies, which delivered music with visuals at a rapidly diminishing cost—first through CDs and then through streaming services—while the live performance market has not only survived but thrived. Digital music creates a kind of personal connection between fan and musician—both global pop stars and YouTubers—and demand for in-person contact is intense.

In each instance, disruptive advances in code followed a consistent and predictable pattern: the creation of a new high-volume, low-price option creates a new market for the low-volume, high-price option. Every time this happens, the new value created through improved code forces a bifurcation of markets, and of work.

IF THERE IS one place in the United States that has come to define the implosion of the U.S. manufacturing-based economy, it is Detroit,

Michigan. Detroit's challenges are so well known that they do not require recounting here. But one Detroit story that is worth telling has to do with a recent manufacturing success—one that doesn't have to do with cars but with a much older consumer technology: watches.

In a building that once housed the General Motors design studio, craftspeople at a four-year-old company called Shinola hand-assemble high-end watches from Swiss parts. The company grew rapidly in the two years following its founding; in its third year it assembled 150,000 high-end watches and earned $60 million. Shinola's success is due in equal measure to the quality of its product and the power of its story. The company gives its employees and its customers an opportunity to be part of an undertaking that conveys a purpose beyond a minute-to-minute tracking of time.

If Shinola's success seems like an anecdotal aberration that does not reflect larger trends, then consider again what happened to the Swiss watch industry after the introduction of the low-cost, highly reliable quartz watch. Were it not for market bifurcation, the Swiss watch industry would have disappeared, crushed by the low-cost, high-volume capacity of Asian producers. Yet, as described above, the development of quartz watches did not eliminate the mechanical watch industry but instead forced a bifurcation of markets and of work. This process is the norm, not the exception, when technology disrupts work.

We can take this as far back as we like. Ten thousand years ago, agricultural technologies forced a bifurcation of work. Four hundred years ago, the bifurcation was caused by trade technologies. One hundred years ago, manufacturing technologies forced a bifurcation of work, and today's automation technologies and artificial intelligence are doing the same.

Because work is fundamentally algorithmic, it is capable of almost limitless diversification through both combinatorial and incremental change. The algorithms of work become, fairly literally, the DNA of the economy. Such bifurcations can, and do, occur without limit.

The question is, therefore, not whether opportunities for meaningful work will exist but how they will be compensated. As Geoff Moore puts it, "Digital innovation is reengineering our manufacturing-based product-centric economy to improve quality, reduce cost, expand markets, increase profits, and reward investment—all of which are very good things. It is doing so, however, largely at the expense of traditional middle class jobs. This class of work is bifurcating into elite professions that are highly compensated but outside the skillset of the target population and commoditizing workloads for which the wages fall well below the target level."[7]

The counterintuitive but pervasive reality is that technological advances have humanized work in the past and should do so in the future. Therefore, adapting to a world where computers can think is just the beginning.

The hard part for humans, of course, will be to redefine what it means to be human in the first place.

ONE CLICHÉ OF the technology world is that, if you're not paying for a service, you're the product. While the negative implications of this sentence may or may not hold for Internet services such as Gmail, Twitter, and Facebook, it does a pretty good job of explaining the relationship between insured patients and the U.S. healthcare system. This is because, while insured patients certainly pay for healthcare via their premiums, they do not bear the full cost of the procedures performed on them. (That, of course, is the point of having insurance.) As a result, healthcare providers have a strong incentive to maximize the revenue they can generate through any interaction with a patient. "Better" insurance only makes this dynamic worse.

The way out of this dilemma is simple: Turn the patient into the doctor. Allow individuals and communities to be the authors of their own healthcare. Far from utopian, this vision of a distributed health-service delivery system is in the process of becoming a reality, thanks to an array of loosely connected innovations in code, one of which takes the form of a 600-year-old technology: yes, the watch.

Prompted by the popularity of the first-generation wearable computers capable of gathering basic health data, first Apple and now Google have developed multifunction watches that integrate health analytics into users' daily lived experience. A parallel race is ongoing among major technology and healthcare companies, with the full support of the government, to develop increasingly powerful diagnostic aids that mine troves of anonymized data to identify patterns of health and illness. Such diagnostic aids are not yet, and will not be for the foreseeable future, a full substitute for the judgment and discretion of trained health professionals. However, they can provide guidance to a new generation of healthcare coaches whose role will not be to initiate medical interventions but to help people gain a greater awareness of their own health status and guide them toward behaviors that, in the current model, fall in the domain of prevention rather than treatment.

If this seems too good to be true, consider the story of Stephen Keating. In 2007, during a routine scan, Keating's doctors noticed a slight abnormality in his brain. He was advised that it was nothing to worry about but that he should monitor it. So he did, educating himself on the structure of the brain and obtaining a follow-up scan in 2010. Again, the scan showed no abnormalities.

However, in the summer of 2014, Keating began to smell vinegar when no vinegar was present. He was aware from his research that his particular abnormality was near the part of the brain responsible for smells, so he had another MRI. This time doctors found a cancerous tumor the size of a tennis ball, which they removed.

Throughout the process, Keating had aggressively sought data on his condition. By the time doctors removed the tumor from his brain, he had collected over 70 gigabytes of medical documentation on his case. The data were so detailed that he was able to model and print a 3D scale model of his tumor.

Granted, Keating had a considerable advantage in patient-led monitoring and diagnostics, as he is a doctoral student at the MIT Media Lab. But code-enabled diagnostic tools have the potential to reinforce and accelerate the rapid growth of peer-to-peer service provision, which is finally reaching healthcare. One example is the rapid growth of the Village Movement, a new approach to delivering healthcare services to people over 60 years of age that allows them to stay in their homes. The village model allows people to live at home past the point when they might otherwise have had to move to an institutional care facility, and does so without creating undue burdens for their families.[8]

While pharmacological and surgical approaches to treating illness will continue to advance as the global population ages, analogies to other mature industries strongly suggest that the greatest advances in the provision of healthcare services will come from a combination of wearable technologies, diagnostics supported by Big Data applications, peer-to-peer operations, and other innovations in code that distribute healthcare delivery away from the highly centralized models that came to dominate in the twentieth century.

In considering how code and work will coevolve in the next two to three decades, the case of healthcare provision is a particularly important one for the United States. As is well known, the growth of healthcare and education costs has outpaced inflation for decades; healthcare now comprises 17 percent of U.S. GDP, compared with 7 percent in 1970.[9] Healthcare and education are the only two sectors in the economy in which job growth has remained consistently strong following the Great Recession.[10] As a result, as is much discussed, technological trends affecting these sectors are those likely to have a significant macroeconomic impact.

However, the changes underway in the healthcare system also illustrate broader trends in the coevolution of code and work that are relevant across sectors. The entire network of services I have described as representing the future of healthcare delivery is built on platforms of earlier code-based innovations that have become sufficiently ubiquitous and reliable that they now constitute a shared infrastructure for future innovation. Foremost among these is the complex set of standards, contracts, hardware, and conventions that we refer to as the Internet, and the separate set of institutional and technological innovations that have enabled mobile telephony. Layered on these platforms are operating systems that allow specific devices to run programs, on which are layered the programs and data-access protocols that allow the device to serve alternately as a health monitor, a coach, an alarm . . . or, simply, a watch.

THE DIFFUSION OF simple machines invented in the nineteenth century gradually increased the efficiency of agricultural production and construction processes during the first half of the twentieth century, thus reducing the need for agricultural workers and non-farm laborers, respectively. Industrial production based on increasingly sophisticated management routines and machinery first drew workers into factories as it increased in scale, then beginning in the 1990s it sent them away as the efficiency of those processes increased further through automation and required fewer physical laborers (see figure 10.2). Knowledge work based on increasingly sophisticated management routines and technology has drawn workers into office cubicles as it has increased in scale; will it now send those workers away as algorithms become more powerful and data

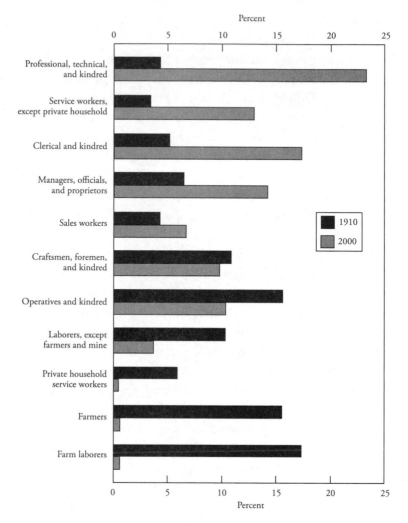

FIGURE 10.2 Proportional Employment in Occupational Categories, 1910 and 2000. *Source:* Ian D. Wyatt and Daniel E. Hecker (2006), "Occupational changes during the 20th century", *Monthly Labor Review* (Bureau of Labor Statistics), March; p. 36, chart 1.

more ubiquitous? Will machines driven by increasingly powerful computers end up being our liberators, or will they become our unbeatable competitors in the workplace of the future? More generally, does technology destroy or create jobs? The answer, of course, is that it does both.

The advance of code empowers us at the same time it permits algorithms and machines to replace us.

Following David Ricardo's argument that countries lacking an absolute productive advantage in the production of any good can nonetheless find mutual profit in trade on the basis of comparative advantage, Herbert Simon posited that we humans will always find domains of comparative advantage for our own labor relative to machines, regardless of how productive machines become. "Human employment will become smaller in those kinds of occupations and activities in which automatic devices have the greatest comparative advantage over humans," Simon predicted in 1960. "Human employment will become relatively greater in those occupations and activities in which automatic devices have the least comparative advantage."[11]

Exceptionally among his contemporaries, Simon understood that "automation" would extend well beyond the factory floor: "We should not make the simple assumption that the higher status occupations, and those requiring the most education, are going to be the least automated. There are perhaps as good prospects technically and economically for automating completely the job of a physician, a corporate vice-president, or a college teacher, as for automating the job of a man who operates a piece of earth-moving equipment."[12]

And yet, more than a half-century ago, Simon also understood intuitively what research has since established: as the power of computers increased, work would bifurcate, with computers performing the tasks most readily subject to algorithmic definition while humans perform those most resistant. He stated:

> It may seem paradoxical to think we can increase the productivity of mechanized techniques in all processes without displacing men somewhere. Won't a point be reached where men are less productive than machines in all processes, hence economically unemployable? The paradox is dissolved by supplying a missing term. Whether man or machines will be employed in a particular process depends not simply on their relative productivity in physical terms, but on their cost as well. And cost depends on price. Hence—so goes the traditional argument of economics—as technology changes and machines become more productive, the prices of labor and capital will adjust themselves as to clear the market of both. As much of each will be employed as offers itself at the market price, and the

market price will be proportional to the marginal productivity of that factor.[13]

While this description of comparative advantage derives directly from David Ricardo, Simon advances the conventional story of comparative advantage significantly with a subtle decision to use the word "process" rather than "occupation" in this critical passage: "By operation of the market place, manpower will flow to those processes in which productivity is high relative to the productivity of machines; it will leave those processes in which its productivity is relatively low."[14]

In other words, as technology evolves, the processes of work—code—undergo sequences of bifurcations, with humans focusing on the tasks in which their skills are *comparatively* strong, while machines (now computers) take on the tasks in which their skills are *comparatively* strong. Furthermore, such bifurcations occur not by chance but as the result of an inexorable evolutionary logic that constantly shifts the landscape of opportunity.

The best labor market analyses supporting Simon's line of argument come from a sequence of papers and one book published over the past dozen years by MIT economists David Autor, Daron Acemoglu, and Frank Levy, and Harvard economist Richard Murnane, in various combinations and with other coauthors. In a seminal 2003 paper published in the *Quarterly Journal of Economics,* Autor, Levy, and Murnane summarized their findings based on an analysis of three decades of census data:

> We contend that computer capital (1) substitutes for a limited and well-defined set of human activities, those involving routine (repetitive) cognitive and manual tasks; and (2) complements activities involving non-routine problem solving and interactive tasks. Provided these tasks are imperfect substitutes, our model implies measurable changes in the task content of employment, which we explore using representative data on job task requirements over 1960–1998. Computerization is associated with declining relative industry demand for routine manual and cognitive tasks and increased relative demand for non-routine cognitive tasks.[15]

From the Autor, Acemoglu, Levy, and Murnane (or "AALM") perspective, the impact of digital disruption on the future of work depends critically on the nature of the work itself—in other words, the how of production and not just the what (see figure 10.3). Routine tasks that can easily be encoded will be performed by computers, and those that cannot will continue to be performed by people. The jobs of the "human computers" at the Philadelphia Computing Section I described in chapter four are a case in point: because the human computers were performing exactly the same rule-based logical computations that are the essence of computer programs, they were also literally the first people to lose their jobs to digital computers. Summing up a decade of research, Autor writes, "The interplay between machine and human comparative allows computers to substitute for workers in performing routine, codifiable tasks while amplifying the comparative advantage for workers in supplying problem solving skills, adaptability, and creativity."[16]

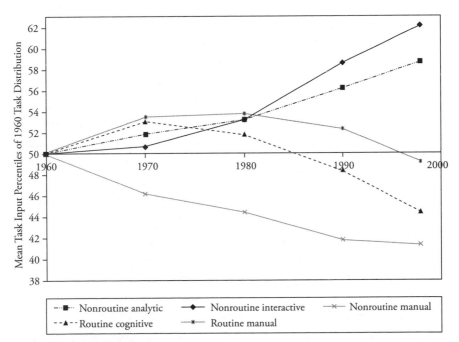

FIGURE 10.3 Trends in Routine and Nonroutine Task Input, 1960 to 1998. This figure "is constructed using *Dictionary of Occupational Titles* [1977] task measures by gender and occupation paired to employment data for 1960 and 1970 Census and 1980, 1990, and 1998 Current Population Survey (CPS) samples. Data are aggregated to 1120 industry-gender-education cells by year, and each cell is assigned a value corresponding to its rank in the 1960 distribution of task input (calculated across the 1120, 1960 task cells). Plotted values depict the employment-weighted mean of each assigned percentile in the indicated year."

Source: Autor, David H., Frank Levy and Richard J. Murnane (2003). "The Skill Content of Recent Technological Change: An Empirical Exploration." *The Quarterly Journal of Economics* 118 (4): 1279–1333.

Complementing the work by the AALM team, the most thoughtful historical and microeconomic analysis of the coevolution of code and work has been done by James Bessen, whom I quoted in chapter one. Bessen is something of a modern-day David Ricardo, having been successful as an entrepreneur before putting his energies into being at the forefront of economic theory. In 1983, Bessen wrote the first What-You-See-Is-What-You-Get (WYSIWYG) desktop publishing program (a category dominated for the past couple of decades by Microsoft Word), which ran on the first IBM PC with a luxurious 64K of RAM and a special graphics card.

In his insightful book, *Learning by Doing: The Real Connection between Innovation, Wages, and Wealth*, Bessen describes the impact the introduction of automated teller machines (ATMs) had on the banking industry. The name of the technology itself suggested that ATMs would be a major job destroyer: after all, their purpose was to automate the work of tellers. President Barack Obama articulated a widely held perspective when he stated in a 2011 interview that "there are some structural issues with our economy where a lot of businesses have learned to become much more efficient with a lot fewer workers. You see it when you go to a bank and you use an ATM, you don't go to a bank teller, or you go to the airport and you're using a kiosk instead of checking in at the gate."[17] Yet an analysis of the data tells a very different story: while the number of ATMs installed grew from barely 50,000 in 1985 to over 400,000 in 2010, the number of human bank tellers actually also increased, from 485,000 in 1985 to slightly over 600,000 in 2010. How did this happen? The fact that ATMs took over many routinized tasks allowed tellers to focus on more complex tasks: "ATM technology did not eliminate bank tellers, it did change the way tellers work and the skills they require," Bessen explains. "They now perform relatively fewer simple transactions in favor of complex ones, and they provide the personal service that is an important part of 'relationship banking.'" The creation of ATMs also—counter-intuitively perhaps—sparked a rapid growth in the number of bank branches. "Because ATMs perform many teller transactions, fewer tellers are needed to operate a bank branch. But because it costs less to operate a branch office, banks dramatically increased the number of branches in order to reach a bigger market. More bank branches means more tellers, despite fewer tellers per branch."[18]

Trends were similar for bookkeepers (presumably displaced by accounting software), sales clerks (presumably displaced by online shopping), and even independent booksellers (presumably displaced by Amazon). Bessen reports: "Amazon may have eliminated jobs at Borders and other national book chains that relied on bestsellers, but the number of independent booksellers has been growing and with it, more jobs for sales clerks who can provide selections and advice that Amazon cannot easily match."[19]

LET US SAY that the economy evolves through a sequence of bifurcations in the way I have described in this chapter, which at each stage of discontinuous advance in code creates both a new low-cost, high-volume option and a high-cost, low-volume option. What does that process tell us about the relative returns to workers and the owners of capital? Even if work is humanized by the advance of code, as I claim, that does not mean it will be remunerated equitably. Even if the median quality of life continues to improve, as I claim, that does not mean the gap between the wealthiest and the poorest will shrink or that everyone will have the opportunity to contribute productively to society.

A widely discussed study conducted in 2013 at Oxford University concluded that 47 percent of workers in the United States have jobs in categories that will be vulnerable to automation in the next decade.[20] While an apparently startling finding (if accurate even on its own terms), it actually tells us very little about how many jobs within those categories will be eliminated as a consequence of automation, and it tells us even less about the manner in which code within those occupations— the daily practice of work—will shift as a result of new technological capabilities or whether and how people will adapt to those shifts.

This imperative of adaptation at the personal level is the subject of the next chapter.

II

—————⊶◦◦◦⊷—————

Education
The Game of Life

Learn how to cook—try new recipes, learn from your mistakes, be fearless, and above all, have fun!

—Julia Child, *My Life in France*, 2006

IN 1960, U.S. game-manufacturer Milton Bradley introduced its classic version of *The Game of Life,* which has been played by millions of people in the decades since. You may recall how the game is played: At the start, in your "youth," you decide whether or not to go to college. This choice, combined with a part-of-the-game desire to maximize income and an element of randomness, determine which career you select. You acquire an automobile and, in time, a spouse and children. (The car has room for four children, but you can get a second car at no cost.) You proceed through various adventures, earning a regular salary and steadily accumulating wealth along the way. At the end of the game you retire—presumably precisely at the prescribed age of 65. Upon retirement you have the option of entering the exclusive "Millionaire Estates" community or settling for the relatively modest but perfectly adequate "Countryside Acres." There is little doubt as to which of these is preferable.

Aggregate data on occupational choice and the returns from education in the decades since 1960 seem to validate the assumptions underlying *The Game of Life:* since the late 1970s, the economically fortunate among us have been those who made the "go to college" choice. This group has seen its income grow rapidly and its share of

the aggregate wealth increase sharply. Those without a college education have watched their income stagnate and their share of the aggregate wealth decline. Among white males age 45 to 55 in the United
States today—the economically dominant segment of the population in previous generations—the economic contrast between college graduates and those without a degree has been particularly grim.
Middle-age white male college graduates (my cohort) have done
very well: their incomes have grown in real terms and they are living
longer than previous generations. Middle-age white men without a
college degree have been beset by sharply rising death rates—a phenomenon that contrasts starkly with middle-age Latino and African
American men, and with trends in nearly every other country in the
world.[1]

This divergence between the expected outcomes for college graduates and for those without a college education reinforces an economic
theory about the optimal life path known as the permanent income hypothesis, which was developed by Nobel Laureate in Economics Milton
Friedman three years before the introduction of *The Game of Life*. This
hypothesis mirrors the premise of the game: Early in life we optimize
our lifetime earnings by going into debt to invest in education, which
delivers the foundational skills on which we build a career. When we
begin our career we stop investing in education and start to save, and
we continue to save until we retire. When we retire we spend down our
savings while doing the only other thing left: we prepare to die. Ideally
we do this on schedule, as living longer than expected is a problem in
this model (not enough savings!).

The model Friedman developed is as technically sound today as
it was in 1957. Furthermore, the permanent income hypothesis—
somewhat like the efficient markets hypothesis, which was developed
at the University of Chicago at about the same time—has become
encoded not only in the widely played board game but in the operating system of the U.S. economy in such fundamental ways that we
barely notice its influence. From the Pell Grants that sustain college
students to the 401(k)s that enable employees to save for retirement,
the experience of workers from youth to death remains framed by the
notion that institutions are changing sufficiently slowly and we are
sufficiently short-lived that we can make a one-time investment in

education at the start of our lives to reap a reward that we enjoy at the end of our lives.

AN UPDATED AND empirically validated version of *The Game of Life* remains the way that the most prominent economists look at the world of work today. In 2008, Harvard's Claudia Goldin and Lawrence Katz published *The Race Between Education and Technology*, the most comprehensive treatment to that point of the relationship between education, the advance of technology, and the evolution of work. Picking up on the research by Paul Douglas on the decline in the wage premium for white-collar workers that I discussed in chapter 5, and employing a variant of the Cobb-Douglas production function (see Text Box 5.2) as the basis for their data analysis, Goldin and Katz find that, while machines did substitute for skilled labor in nineteenth-century manufacturing by replacing artisans with factory workers, by the early twentieth century, technology and worker skill had become complementary. Furthermore, while the wage premium for high school- and college-educated workers continued to fall for nearly two-and-a-half decades after Paul Douglas published his 1926 study, in 1950 the trend reversed sharply and the wage premium for educated workers expanded at a rapid pace for the rest of the twentieth century.

What drove Goldin and Katz's results and made possible what they refer to as the "Human Capital Century in America"? They focus on two historical discontinuities that occurred at the end of the nineteenth century and the beginning of the twentieth century in the United States. The first discontinuity was the shift from artisan production (craft, with little division of labor) to "batch and continuous-process production" (the modern factory floor, including the assembly line, as well as the factory-like clerical work that was the focus of W. H. Leffingwell's work).[2] The second discontinuity was in changes in the minimum educational attainment required of workers. Working on a farm, or as an apprentice to a craftsman, did not require the sort of education provided in high school, let alone at a college. But working in a factory, and certainly as a clerk, did increasingly require a high school education—and, later, a college degree. Considering the joint impact of these two discontinuities, Goldin and Katz find that the real returns from investment in formal education have been high for decades, and remain so. The takeaway for young people is clear: Go to college. For policymakers the takeaway is comparable and equally direct: Invest in formal education and thereby obtain greater levels of technological advance, increased productivity, a more rapid rate of economic growth, and a higher standard of living.

Delving more deeply into the specifics of factory-floor processes during the early industrial era in the United States, however, James Bessen arrives at a very different picture of the relationship between education, the advance of technology, and the evolution of work—both in the past and in the present.

Bessen takes issue with the finding by Goldin and Katz that the mechanization of production in the late nineteenth century was "deskilling" in the sense that skilled artisans were replaced in the labor force by unskilled factory workers. Instead, he finds the first factory workers were hackers and tinkerers who were very much involved in the actual work of developing the production algorithms that drove the first industrial revolution in the United States.[3] Using detailed micro data on textile production in the United States in the nineteenth and early twentieth century, Bessen is able to approximate closely the actual factory-level production recipe that mills employed at different points in time, evidencing "how the mills actually responded to changes in interest rates and prices, how different inventions affected the amount of labor time a weaver needed to spend on each loom, and how output grew with weaver skills." With the same datasets, Bessen is further able to construct a learning curve over the period of decades, finding that while a handloom weaver in 1800 required nearly forty minutes to weave a yard of coarse cloth using a single loom, a weaver in 1902 could do the same work operating eighteen Northrop looms in less than a minute, on average. This striking point relates to the relative importance of the accumulation of capital to the advance of code: "Of the roughly thirty-nine-minute reduction in labor time per yard, capital accumulation due to the changing cost of capital relative to wages accounted for just 2 percent of the reduction; inventions accounted for 73 percent of the reduction; and 25 percent of the time saving came from greater skill and effort of the weavers."[4] Bessen concludes: "Technology was, by far, the most important factor driving the growth in output per worker in cotton weaving. Skills were important, too, but the role of capital accumulation was minimal, counter to the conventional wisdom."[5]

What was the role of formal education in this process? Essentially nonexistent. The processes in question were new and still evolving, so learning and training by necessity happened on the job. This point generalizes, with important implications for our anticipation of the future as well as our understanding of the past: "Formal vocational education is difficult to conduct during the early stages of a technology, but easier later on, when knowledge becomes more standardized. Conversely, workers who are more adept at learning, perhaps because they have more general education, are more valuable early on. But as a technology matures, demand for workers with advanced general education often declines, while the supply of workers with vocational education rises."[6] A lag exists between the introduction of a new technology and the development of the standards and institutions that are a prerequisite for formal education. Until sufficient experience within an industry has accumulated to define the "best practices" that can form the basis of formal educational programs, there is a high reward for experience and general-purpose problem solvers. Only after tasks have been routinized does opportunity open up for workers with less experience or capacity to tinker and hack. For this reason, "it takes a long time for technical knowledge to be developed, longer for it to spread, and even longer for institutions to emerge, such as new labor markets, that allow ordinary workers to benefit from their new knowledge. Such learning on a mass scale was and is a difficult problem for society."[7]

New, transformative technologies tend not to be simple and easy to copy. Instead, such technologies tend to be complex and difficult to master. This perhaps obvious fact has far-reaching implications that run against the implications of a range of default models in both micro- and macroeconomics. "Complexity explains in the first instance why learning by doing takes time: complicated technologies involve many parameters that must be controlled," not to mentioned codified. "Finding efficient combinations of these parameters takes a lot of searching. As a consequence, knowledge of new technologies is often initially tentative and uncertain: Much of the knowledge is gained through experience and experiment and cannot be easily communicated; much of it may be tacit."[8]

Bessen provides original data and insightful analysis regarding the relationship between the advance of code and the evolution of work over the past century. For Bessen, formal education and basic research are not the keys to the development of economies that they are often represented as being. What drives the development of economies is learning by doing and the advance of code—processes that are driven at least as much by non-expert tinkering as by formal research and instruction. "Many people fail to appreciate the complexity and slow pace of the current transition [in the world of work, due to the advance of digital technology] because they confuse technology with inventions and they confuse skill with education," Bessen states.[9] "Technology is more than just inventions because implementation involves a lot of mundane technical knowledge and specialized skills, often among diverse people."[10]

VINT CERF IS worried about the Internet—specifically about how it is going to affect the well-being of workers in the future.

Cerf is particularly well placed to comment on the Internet, since he played a central role in creating it. His particular contribution was to solve the problem posed by J. C. R. Licklider in his 1963 memo (see chapter nine) by developing, with Bob Kahn, the TCP/IP, which constitutes the Internet's core architecture and is the standard that allows computers to communicate with each other.[11]

In 2012, Cerf and physicist-turned-journalist David Nordfors co-founded a network called Innovation for Jobs—I4J—that is focused on determining how innovation might be directed toward net job creation. Meetings of the group have included more than two hundred leaders in business, government, nonprofits, academia, and media, all of whom are seeking to understand how the continued advance of code will affect the future of work.

Cerf and other I4J members are motivated by a shared understanding that humans are not particularly good at being computers, and thus that a large number of current jobs that involve tasks that can be converted to code and automated will soon no longer provide viable salaried work. Indeed, many of the frontier business models shaping the economy today are based on enabling a sharp reduction in the number of people required to perform existing tasks. As venture capitalist and

I4J member Steve Jurvetson puts it, "We only invest in businesses that reduce labor. They're always massively more efficient than their predecessor, or we wouldn't invest in them."[12] For the total number of jobs involved in providing goods and services to increase rather than decline in the future, Jurvetson would have to be wrong. He isn't. This means that if people are to have opportunities for meaningful work in the future to an extent comparable to today, new forms of work must evolve.

"How do I educate people for jobs that don't exist yet? This is a real challenge for people who are in the business of education," Cerf observed recently to a group of I4J members. "There is a fairly long pipeline . . . How do the parties who are supposedly educating us, or how do we as the parties who are supposedly learning something, prepare for jobs that don't exist yet?"

Cerf relates this point to the default mode of the education system: "This whole model of 'I get educated, I work, I retire' may in fact be dead."

Cerf is not alone in questioning whether education in its current form is the answer to the workforce challenges posed by digital disruption. In a recent column in the *New York Times,* Robert Shiller wrote, "Most people complete the majority of their formal education by their early 20s and expect to draw on it for the better part of a century . . . But a computer can learn in seconds most of the factual information that people will get in high school and college, and there will be a great many generations of new computers and robots, improving at an exponential rate, before one long human lifetime has passed." Colleges and universities have yet to respond adequately to these changes, Shiller concluded. "We will have to adapt as information technology advances . . . We must continually re-evaluate what is inherently different between human and computer learning."[13]

OVER THE PAST decade, a plethora of economic analyses and books have made the case for a fundamental discontinuity between the coming economic future and the recent economic past. Depending on how this transition is framed, we are experiencing the onset of the Sharing Economy, the Gig Economy, the 1099 Economy, the Freelance Economy, the On-Demand Economy, or the Platform Economy. In a separate category but closely related are the relocalization of production and the return to craftsmanship—the Farm-to-Table Movement, the Slow Food Movement, and the Maker Movement. Each of these movements, and the analyses that accompany them, are describing different dimensions of very real shifts in the nature of code and the world of work.

Among those who have written recently about this transition, none has better understood and conveyed its core dynamics than Robin Chase, cofounder of the ride-sharing platform Zipcar. "Over the past two centuries, the industrial economy rewarded a specific type of capitalist," she observes in her book, *Peers Inc.* "To survive and thrive involved becoming just a smidge smaller than a monopoly, controlling the market while avoiding regulation . . . Products and services were standardized because high volumes led to economies of scale and the ability to offer lower-priced products. Higher volumes also meant increased market share. Then the Internet happened."[14]

What the Internet did was turn what had been a source of strength for market-dominant companies—their scale and proprietary knowledge—into a potential weakness. The result has been a shift from the corporate-centric economy of the twentieth century to the increasingly peer-to-peer economy of the twenty-first century.

To be sure, until the latter third of the nineteenth century, the peer-to-peer economy in the United States *was* the economy: Large corporations providing consumer services simply did not exist. Regulation governing consumer services was minimal. People provided services personally to other people who were very much like them. There were no call centers, no focus groups or strategic-planning retreats. The archetypal nineteenth-century entrepreneur hung up a shingle on Main Street and set to work.

Markets up through the nineteenth century were not the anonymous and abstract entities they sometimes appear to be today. They were physical spaces where people met to trade items they often had created or harvested themselves. This of course is what markets were originally about: realizing the productive possibilities of people.

At its human core, then, the peer-to-peer or sharing economy is not a new phenomenon. Were Alexis de Tocqueville to write about the United States of today, he likely would see a distinctly American character in peer-to-peer businesses. The question, therefore, is whether there is anything fundamentally new about the sorts of peer-to-peer businesses that have been proliferating over the past five years. The answer is yes. The difference between the past and the present is the platforms people use to find one another, conduct transactions, and establish reputations.

The triad of revolutions in computation, communications, and algorithmic power that have unfolded over the past half-century have dramatically lowered the cost of finding providers of a service, assessing their reliability, and concluding a contract to engage their services. A quarter of a century ago, the first Internet commerce companies brought consumer markets into new "virtual" spaces. Companies like eBay and Amazon (via Amazon Marketplace) made it newly possible for regular folks to find and exchange goods across large distances. Peer-to-peer businesses employ the same sort of powerful platforms to enable the exchange of services. Since services make up more than 84 percent of the U.S. economy and an increasingly comparable percentage in countries elsewhere, this is a big deal.

Lisa Gansky, author of *The Mesh* and cofounder of the photo-sharing site Ofoto, was among the first to illustrate the popularity of peer-to-peer business models by comparing the established hotel chains with the room-sharing site Airbnb. The Intercontinental Hotel chain, for example, has been around for 65 years and has an inventory of 650,000 hotel rooms, of which they own 100 percent. In contrast, Airbnb has been around for eight years and has an inventory of 1.5 million listings, of which it owns none. This means that Airbnb has unlocked latent assets comparable to 65 years of cumulative investment within the corporate world, and it has done so with essentially no capital outlay beyond the cost of the platform itself.

Participants in peer-to-peer marketplaces are clearly drawn by the ease of search and low transaction costs. Simply put, buyers pay less than they would without the service and sellers earn more—if only because they often would not be able to bring their service to market without the peer-to-peer platform.[15] Furthermore, buyers have access to options previously unavailable in the marketplace, while sellers have opportunities to diversify their sources of income and increase their financial resilience.

Of course, new business models that gain market acceptance almost invariably invite challenges from incumbents. New peer-to-peer businesses are no exception. Wherever peer-to-peer platforms have gained traction across the country, regulatory challenges have followed. Invoking regulatory equity, for example, licensed taxicab drivers have led challenges to the legality of Uber's business model in city after city. Invoking consumer and production safety, hotel and restaurant owners, respectively, have sought to slow the growth of room-sharing services like Airbnb and the proliferation of food trucks in urban areas (which has been accelerated by ratings platforms such as Yelp).

But there is more to the peer-to-peer economy than pushback from threatened incumbents. The deeper trend has to do with the return to an earlier model of personal productive activity—creating directly for other people. "This is not the familiar question of whether our machines will put us all out of work," writes technology investor Esther Dyson about the rise of the peer-to-peer economy. "The question is whether we will start doing more and more intellectual work for free or for barter, becoming more like our ancestors. Instead of producing food or housing for ourselves or for barter, we will be producing content and amusement for one another, without engaging in explicit (taxable) financial exchange."[16] Consider Wikipedia, an educational resource comprising over 40 million webpages, written in 292 languages, and used by more than 370 million people per month globally. The paid staff involved in the maintenance of this resource number two hundred, of whom only 40 are involved in the editorial aspects of the work. These 40 are not engaged directly in creating content but rather are focused on supporting a community of more than 70,000 "Wikipedians"—the volunteers who write and edit Wikipedia's articles.

Where both the classical and neoclassical schools in economics have, for over two centuries, focused on material scarcity and the desire for happiness through consumption, the actual economy is increasingly driven by algorithmic abundance and the desire for happiness through production.[17]

THE GAME OF LIFE and the permanent income hypothesis present some reflexive notions on how to respond to the differential outcomes between college graduates and those without a college degree, to which I just alluded, and to associated societal challenges such as the explosion of student debt, the aging population, and the crisis facing Social Security and other so-called entitlement programs:

- Bad outcomes for people without college degrees implies a need to increase the number of college graduates.
- An excess of student debt implies the need to increase the supply of subsidized student loans.
- Too little stability in the labor market implies the need to protect jobs and slow the automation of work.
- An aging population with inadequate aggregate saving implies the need to improve health insurance and expand economic supports to people over 65.

A significant share of government spending in the United States and in other advanced industrialized countries is allocated in a manner consistent with these premises. They are as widely believed as they are increasingly obsolete.

Changes in the world of work are undermining the premises on which these decades-old policy notions are based. Formal education does not ensure economic security in the way that it did in recent generations. Increasingly, life expectancy is challenging the norm of retirement at age sixty-five. And large asset-owning corporations that previously earned persistent profits and offered steady employment are increasingly being challenged by peer-to-peer platforms like Airbnb and market-enabling platforms like Uber, transforming labor markets in the process.

Of course, these companies represent just the beginning of the disruption in the world of work that will occur as a consequence of the latest phase in the advance of code. The peer-to-peer business models in local transportation, hospitality, food service, and the rental of consumer goods were the first to emerge, not because they are the most important for the economy but because these are industries with relatively low regulatory complexity. In contrast, there has been relatively little peer-to-peer business innovation in healthcare, energy, and education—three industries that together comprise more than a quarter of the U.S. GDP—where regulatory complexity is relatively high.

What will happen to the world of work when these industries become monopolized by a few dominant platforms the way Uber has come to dominate urban transportation?

That is the topic of the next chapter.

12

Equity

Progress and Poverty

The great fact that poverty and all its concomitants show themselves in communities just as they develop into the conditions toward which material progress tends—proves that the social difficulties existing wherever a certain stage of progress has been reached, do not arise from local circumstances, but are, in some way or another, engendered by progress itself.
—Henry George, *Progress and Poverty*, 1879

ON PAGE 56 of volume 2, number 2, of *The Single Tax Review*, published in autumn 1902, an item of some enduring interest appears. The item reads, "Miss Lizzie J. Magie, a single taxer of Washington, D.C., has invented an ingenious game, played with checkers and dice as in Parcheesi, and thus describes it for the *Review*: 'It is a practical demonstration of the present system of land-grabbing, with all its usual outcomes and consequences. It might as well have been called 'The Game of Life,' as it contains all the elements of success and failure in the real world, and the object is the same as the human race in general seems to have, i.e., the accumulation of wealth.'" Magie goes on to describe the rules of her game: "Representative money, deeds, mortgages, notes and charters are used in the game; lots are bought and sold; rents are collected . . . The railroad is also represented, and those who make use of it are obliged to pay their fare . . . There are two franchises: water and lighting . . . There are two tracts of land on the board that are held out of use—are neither for rent or for sale—and on each of these appear the forbidding sign: 'No trespassing. Go to Jail'" (see figure 12.1).

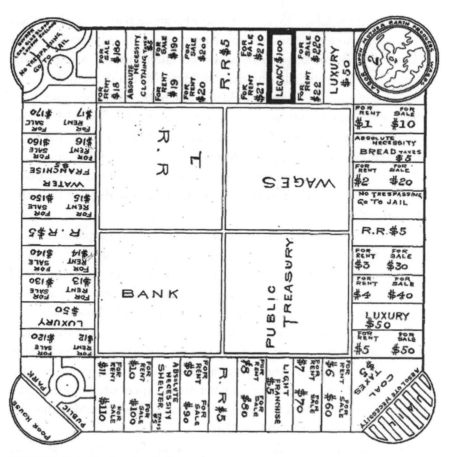

FIGURE 12.1 *The Landlord's Game.*

Magie called her game *The Landlord's Game*, since her original intention was "simply to work out a demonstration of how the landlord gets his money and keeps it." She published her description of *The Landlord's Game* in *The Single Tax Review* because the game was intended to advance the ideas of Henry George, the newspaper editor turned economist whose work I introduced in chapter five.

Magie was particularly enthused about the game's pedagogical value for children. "Children of nine or ten years and who possess average intelligence can easily understand the game and they get a good deal of hearty enjoyment out of it," she reported. "They learn that the quickest way to accumulate wealth and gain power is to get all the land they can get in the best localities and hold on to it." She notes that this lesson is not without its risks: "There are those who argue that it may be a dangerous thing to teach children how they may get the advantage of their fellows, but let me tell you there are no fairer-minded beings in the world than our own little American children. Watch them in their play and see how quick they are, should any one of their number attempt to cheat or take undue advantage of another, to cry, 'No fair!'" Magie was confident that the more children were exposed to the game, the more effectively Henry George's "Single Tax" movement would be advanced. "Let the children once see clearly the gross injustice of our present land system and when they grow up, if they are allowed to develop naturally, the evil will soon be remedied."

Yet as early as 1902, two years before she received a patent on *The Landlord's Game*, Magie saw that it was a game "of amusement as well as instruction, and one which has attractions for both young and old." Decades later, Charles Darrow, a domestic heater salesman from Germantown, Pennsylvania, created a variant of *The Landlord's Game* based on street names in Atlantic City, New Jersey. While the fundamentals of Darrow's version of the game were essentially the same as Magie's, the intent was reversed: rather than caution impressionable youth against land-grabbing through a direct experience of its inequitable consequences, Darrow's version encouraged land-grabbing through a direct experience of its unique thrills.

So it was that *Monopoly* came into existence. For 80 years, fans of the game have been unwittingly taking a tutorial on "the gross injustice of our present land system."

IN AN 1887 essay titled "The Absence of Design in Nature: The Prodigality of Nature and the Niggardliness of Man," American nature writer Richard Jefferies described the propensity of living things to reproduce themselves at exponential rates. "There is no *enough* in nature," he writes. "It is one vast prodigality. It is a feast. There is no economy, no saving; no penury; a golden shower of good things forever descending . . . Contrast this with the material economy of our world, in which each individual is compelled, in order to exist, to labor, to save and to compete with other people for control and possession of scarce resources. This is the iron law of economics in our world: the superabundance of nature and the utter niggardliness of man.'"

Envisioning a similar future in which abundance displaces scarcity while also stressing the advance of code as a central driving factor, Marc Andreessen recently offered the following on Twitter: "Posit a world in which all material needs are provided free, by robots and material synthesizers. Imagine six, or 10, billion people doing nothing but arts and sciences, culture and exploring and learning . . . Technological progress is precisely what makes a strong, rigorous social safety net affordable."

Andreessen has good company in articulating such a view. John Stuart Mill predicted two centuries ago that human society ultimately would reach a stage in which a population that is no longer increasing earns high (relative) incomes and has a steadily improving state of well-being, all sustained by continued investment in what I have called the advance of code. John Maynard Keynes offered a similar vision in a 1930 essay titled "Economic Possibilities for our Grandchildren," in which he predicted that humanity was on a trajectory to solve the problem of economic scarcity within a matter of decades. Humanity's problem thereafter, according to Keynes, would be to solve the problem of leisure time, noting that "it is fearful for the ordinary person, with no special talents, to occupy himself, if he no longer has roots in the soil or in custom or in the beloved conventions of a traditional society."[1] In such a world, the promise of meaningful occupation ultimately would come to be valued above wealth.

Not everyone accepts this vision, of course (see Text Box 12.1). Among the first to see its flaws was Henry George, the economist whose ideas inspired the creation of *Monopoly.* Why was the land system unjust, according to George? And what relevance do George's views on injustice have to the code economy?

Much like his English contemporary Richard Jefferies, George saw man's natural state as being one of abundance rather than scarcity. "The present century has been marked by a prodigious increase in wealth-producing power," he wrote in *Progress and Poverty.* "The utilization of steam and electricity, the introduction of improved processes and labor-saving machinery, the greater subdivision and grander scale of production, the wonderful facilitation of exchanges, have multiplied enormously the effectiveness of labor. At the beginning of this marvelous era it was natural to expect, and it was expected, that labor-saving inventions would lighten the toil and improve the condition of the

Text Box 12.1 An End to (Important) Innovation?

At a retreat hosted by the Kauffman Foundation that I attended a year ago, Robert Gordon, a noted macroeconomist at Northwestern University, opened his talk with the following comment: "Bob Solow in 1957 taught us that the best way to talk about the importance of innovation is to examine the history of Total Factor Productivity (TFP). [Based on analysis of TFP data] I'm going to argue that the most important innovations happened a hundred years ago."

The facts as reported by Gordon are as follow: Measured TFP growth was high in the postwar era, slowed significantly in the 1970s and 1980s, and then picked up considerably from the mid-1990s to the mid-2000s. Since 2008, the average rate of productivity growth has been slower than it has been in a generation. Gordon's conclusion? "I see stasis everywhere I look."[2]

How do we reconcile this perspective with Marc Andreessen's claims not only that "software is eating the world" but also that "technological progress is precisely what makes a strong, rigorous social safety net affordable"?

It turns out that, as a measure of dividends to society from the advance of code, TFP has two categories of shortcomings: what it includes, and what it leaves out. The deficiencies of TFP as a measure call into question the entire narrative of "stasis" advanced by Gordon and others.

The calculation of TFP requires measures of aggregate output, capital, and labor. The measurement of each of these is inherently difficult, however (see Text Box 12.2). What is more, there is reason to believe that the inherent challenges involved in measuring output, capital, and labor are growing over time, rather than shrinking, as a direct consequence of the advance of code.

Take the Internet. The Internet is a platform that enabled the sharing of digitally encoded information and the use of digitally encoded tools. We use the Internet for . . . well, lots of things. We pay for some of the resources we access via the Internet, but many (if not most) we access without payment. What is the value of those services? By one estimate, for the United States alone, $100 billion.

That number will only grow as digital services continue to expand in dominant sectors of the economy such as education, health, and even energy. None of that is measured as output, and thus none is captured in TFP measures.[3]

This leads to what is arguably the most serious defect of TFP: that it is constructed from a method that all but excludes the two market structures arguably most clearly associated with the advance of code: open source on one side and monopolistic competition on the other.[4]

The actual business of firms in the economy is increasingly about differentiation—creating goods and services for which close substitutes do not exist. In other words, the point of business is increasingly about contradicting the assumptions that underlie the measurement of TFP. Consider just this astonishing fact, noted recently by economics blogger Justin Fox:

> The S&P 500 are five hundred big public firms listed on US exchanges. Imagine that you wanted to create a new firm to compete with one of these big established firms. So you wanted to duplicate that firm's products, employees, buildings, machines, land, trucks, etc. You'd hire away some key employees and copy their business process, at least as much as you could see and were legally allowed to copy.
>
> Forty years ago the cost to copy such a firm was about 5/6 of the total stock price of that firm. So 1/6 of that stock price represented the value of things you couldn't easily copy, like patents, customer goodwill, employee goodwill, regulator favoritism, and hard to see features of company methods and culture. Today it costs only 1/6 of the stock price to copy all a firm's visible items and features that you can legally copy. So today the other 5/6 of the stock price represents the value of all those things you can't copy.

Upon some reflection, we can see how this would be true. How much of the valuation of the world's two most highly valued companies at the moment, Apple and Alphabet, is attributable to the stock of land, buildings, and office equipment that these companies own?

The answer is: not much. Most of the value is intangible—in the company's business processes, proprietary knowledge, and powerful brand built on the cumulative experience of hundreds of millions of people using Apple and Google products. In other words, the value is not in capital, but in code.

Amar Bhidé, present at the same Kauffman Foundation retreat to which I alluded above, accurately sums up the conclusion: "It is not that there is a better way of aggregating productivity. There is a fundamental disconnect between measures of TFP which assume a monolithic, mechanistic process, that's fundamentally incompatible with the widespread exercise of individual imagination and agency. And there is simply no way around it."[5]

---

laborer; that the enormous increase in the power of producing wealth would make real poverty a thing of the past."[6]

To George, the natural outcome of progress is precisely consistent with the bounty of nature: shared prosperity and an end to poverty. Yet at the time George wrote, the actual outcome of progress had been—paradoxically and unnaturally, in his view—a reduction in the well-being of workers and increased inequality: "Where the conditions to which material progress everywhere tends are the most fully realized—that is to say, where population is densest, wealth greatest, and the machinery of production and exchange most highly developed—we find the deepest poverty, the sharpest struggle for existence, and the most enforced idleness."[7] Progress is in fact the cause of poverty, according to George, not its relief.

The reason? Anticipating theories of economic geography that would not gain prominence for another century, George observed that land values are driven fundamentally by the benefits people derive from proximity to other people: "The most valuable lands on the globe [are those] to which a surpassing utility has been given by the increase of population."[8] Given the rate at which land values have increased in major metropolitan areas around the world in the past three decades, this statement seems almost self-evident. However, it contrasted directly with the views of the classical economists who

dominated political economics in George's day. George continued: "The reason why, in spite of the increase of productive power,
wages constantly tend to a minimum which will give but a bare living,
is that, with increase in productive power, rent tends to even greater
increase, thus producing a constant tendency to the forcing down of
wages."[9]

George uses the terms "natural" and "unnatural" to break down into
two components the increase in rent associated with the agglomeration
of people and productive power in cities:

> We have seen that with material progress, as it is at present going
> on, there is a twofold tendency to the advance of rent. Both are to
> the increase of the proportion of the wealth produced which goes as
> rent, and to the decrease of the proportion which goes as wages and
> interest. But the first, or natural tendency, which results from the
> laws of social development, is to the increase of rent as a quantity,
> without the reduction of wages and interest as quantities, or even
> with their quantitative increase. The other tendency, which results
> from the unnatural appropriation of land to private ownership, is
> to the increase of rent as a quantity by the reduction of wages and
> interest as quantities.[10]

Just as one landlord in *Monopoly* inevitably ends up with all of the
money as a result of positive feedback built into the structure of that
toy economy, so do landlords in the real economy, according to George,
end up appropriating a vastly disproportionate share of the overall
wealth society produces. At the root of this dynamic is the power of
cities, noted by Jane Jacobs long ago, to act as a platform for the creation of wealth though the advance of code.

IN THE UNITED STATES, concern over inequality of income and wealth
began to grow following the 2008 recession, when awareness increased
of the longstanding gap between the growth of labor productivity and
that of real wages. It intensified in 2014 with the publication of *Capital
in the Twenty-First Century,* the massive, and massively influential,
volume by economist Thomas Piketty that detailed trends in income
and wealth inequality in advanced industrialized countries.

For all its length and technical complexity, the argument advanced in Piketty's book can be summarized simply: the natural functioning of markets doesn't reduce inequality, it creates inequality.

In the 1950s and 1960s, pioneering economist Simon Kuznets—the person most responsible for the development of national income accounts and the concept of gross domestic product (GDP)—undertook a thorough analysis of the relationship between economic growth and inequality in the United States. He found that, while inequality had increased as the U.S. economy grew rapidly in the first half of the twentieth century, the trend thereafter was reversed and inequality declined. The conjectured "upside-down-U-shaped" relationship between economic growth and inequality became known as the Kuznets curve. It supported a widespread view that, if government permitted the code-driven advance of the economy to proceed on its own terms, the problem of inequality would eventually be solved.

By undertaking a more comprehensive and current analysis of the type first undertaken by Kuznets, Piketty challenged the idea that economic growth eventually reduces inequality of income and wealth. Rather than converging toward egalitarianism and meritocracy, the gap between rich and poor in United States and other advanced industrialized countries is growing—as Piketty emphasizes, the gap is now approaching levels not seen since the 1920s. Piketty concludes: "Economic growth is quite simply incapable of satisfying this democratic and meritocratic hope [as conveyed by the Kuznets curve], but must create specific institutions for the purpose and not rely solely on market forces or technological progress."[11] To ensure that the advance of code does not lead to an increasingly inegalitarian society, Piketty asserts, government action is needed.

The trend of growing inequality in the United States over the past century as computed by Piketty and his coauthors is conveyed in figure 12.2, which indicates that, after diminishing sharply from the 1950s to the 1980s—the endpoint for the analyses undertaken by Kuznets—wealth inequality is back to levels not seen since the Gilded Age.[12]

A more careful look at the data presented in *Capital in the Twenty-First Century* reveals, however, that when considered in the sense of the productive assets of society—which, as I have argued throughout this book, overwhelmingly consist of code—"capital" as referred to in this

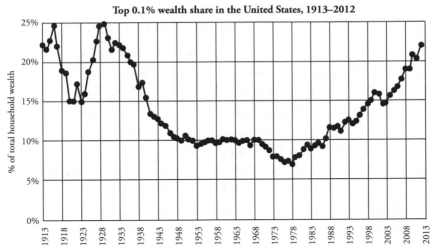

Top 0.1% wealth share in the United States, 1913–2012

This figure depicts the share of total household wealth held by the 0.1% richest families, as estimated by capitalizing income tax returns in 2012, the top 0.1% includes about 160,000 families with net wealth above $20.6 million.

FIGURE 12.2 Top 0.1% Wealth Share in the United States, 1913–2012. The figure plots wealth share owned by the top .1% richest families in the U.S. from 1913 to 2012. Wealth is total assets (including real estate and funded pension wealth) net of all debts. Wealth excludes the present value of future government transfers (such as Social Security or Medicare benefits).

Source: Saez, Emmanuel and Gabriel Zucman (2014). "Wealth Inequality in the United States since 1913: Evidence from Capitalized Income Tax Data", CEPR Discussion Paper 10227, October.

book is not really capital at all (see Text Box 12.2).[13] "Capital" as defined by Piketty is really just tradable wealth: stocks, bonds, jewelry, cash, and, very importantly, as we'll see now, real estate.

The much discussed increase in inequality since the 1970s that Piketty documents is primarily about one thing: the increasing value of real estate, an asset that is disproportionately held by the wealthy. Indeed, the most important lesson in Piketty's book is conveyed to us in a much more accessible form in Lizzie Magie's description in *The Single Tax Review* "of how the landlord gets his money and keeps it" in the game of *Monopoly*. Magie observed that "the quickest way to accumulate wealth and gain power is to get all the land they can get in the best localities and hold on to it." This simple observation sums up the core of the empirical content of *Capital in the Twenty-First Century*.

Referring to David Ricardo but sounding more like Henry George in the following passage, Piketty acknowledges the trend in real

Text Box 12.2 The Cambridge Capital Controversy

Just what is "capital"? More specifically, to what are economists actually referring when they employ the word "capital" in an aggregate sense, as does Piketty in *Capital in the Twenty-First Century*? To be sure, a plow is a plow, a loom is a loom, and an assembly line is an assembly line. We can without great difficulty sum all the plows used in an economy. But how does one compute the sum of a plow, a loom, and an assembly line? By their weight? Certainly that is not a good economic measure. By their cost? The productivity they enable? If the latter, how do we compare the different types of outputs machines produce? And how does one account for computers, much less code?

This turns out to be a difficult problem to solve. Indeed, long-standing debate exists over the use of both aggregate capital and aggregate production functions into which such capital measures are an input (see Text Box 5.2 on the Cobb-Douglas production function). The debate began when famed Cambridge University economist Joan Robinson wrote the following in 1953:

> The production function has been a powerful instrument of miseducation. The student of economic theory is taught to write $Q = F(L, K)$ where L is a quantity of labor, K a quantity of capital and Q a rate of output of commodities. He is instructed to assume all workers are alike, and to measure L in man-hours of labor ... and then he is hurried on to the next question, in the hope that he will forget to ask in what units K is measured. Before he ever does ask, he has become a professor, and so sloppy habits of thought are handed on from one generation to the next.[14]

With this paragraph as an opening salvo, Robinson set off a debate over the nature of capital that engaged leading economists for over a decade. Because the protagonists were concentrated in Cambridge, Massachusetts, and Cambridge, UK, it was dubbed the Cambridge Capital Controversy.

For a dozen years, from 1954 to 1966, claims and counterclaims regarding the conceptual coherence of "aggregate capital" flew back and forth across the Atlantic, encased within the bindings of the top economics journals. In addition to the fiery and charismatic Robinson, the protagonists from Cambridge, UK, included Piero Sraffa, a uniquely inventive scholar whose work on "the production of commodities by means of commodities"—while barely remembered and rarely taught—is increasingly relevant in today's algorithmic world. The protagonists from Cambridge, Massachusetts, included Paul Samuelson, one of the primary architects of neoclassical theory, the author of the world's bestselling economics textbook, and the recipient of the Nobel Prize in Economics in 1970. They also included Robert Solow.

Solow understood full well the difficulties inherent in measuring aggregate capital. In his 1957 paper, "Technical Change and the Aggregate Production Function," Solow stated that measuring aggregate capital was a task that "will really drive a purist mad." Referring to a correction he made to the data to account for the fact that the rates of capital utilization vary over time, he states, "This is undoubtedly wrong, but probably gets closer to the truth than making no correction at all."[15] Here and throughout the debate, Solow's defense of aggregate capital rests on pragmatic grounds, rather than theoretical ones. Elsewhere he quips, "If God had meant there to be more than two factors of production, he would have made it easier for us to draw three-dimensional diagrams."[16]

How did the two future Nobel Laureates from Cambridge, Massachusetts, fare in this debate against Robinson and her iconoclastic cohorts from Cambridge, UK? On the technical case, they actually lost—and rather badly. With characteristic intellectual integrity and graciousness, Samuelson offered this concession in a 1966 essay simply titled, "A Summing Up": "The conventional neoclassical version . . . is spelled out at length in my *Economics*. Unfortunately, until the [technical issues relating to the capital controversy] had alerted me to the complexity of the process, I had not realized that the conventional account represents only one of two possible outcomes."[17] Renowned general equilibrium theorist Frank Hahn was more direct, writing in 1972 that aggregate production functions "cannot be shown to follow from [general equilibrium] theory and in general [are] therefore open to severe logical objections."[18]

The debate revealed that "aggregate capital" is a coherent concept only under restrictive assumptions about the nature of production and technology. Yet that outcome did not prevent the formulation "*Output = F(Labor, Capital)*" in general, and the Cobb-Douglas production function in particular, from becoming the dominant frameworks for understanding and representing production in economics. Why? While the English Cantabrigians offered a potent critique of neoclassical production theory, they failed to offer something even more powerful: an alternative. Yes, as Solow clearly acknowledged in the 1957 paper, aggregate capital was almost impossible to measure with any accuracy. But some measure of aggregate capital—however imperfect—was essential to advancing work in empirical macroeconomics. And the world at large demanded answers to macroeconomic questions, not objections to the theoretical foundations on which such answers were based, however legitimate those objections might be.

estate values, and thus land rents, and alludes to their destabilizing impact: "Once both population and output begin to grow steadily, land tends to become increasingly scarce relative to other goods. The law of supply and demand then implies that the price of land will rise continuously, as will the rents paid to landlords. The landlords will therefore claim a growing share of national income, as the share available to the rest of the population decreases, thus upsetting the social equilibrium."[19]

Economic geography has taught us that the "best localities" will be the places where the returns to density are greatest—which is consistent with Henry George's assertion, backed by the Santa Fe team data that I discussed in chapter one, and completely contrary to the arguments of the Reverend Thomas Malthus and other classical economists. Land in "the best localities" increases in value because cities offer people tangible economic returns that derive from density and interconnection. The mechanism by which cities deliver on this promise is to convert code into infrastructure. The catch-22 is that cities' very success in generating concentrated abundance creates a new form of scarcity: proximity to that abundance.

In 2015, based on similar logic, former U.S. Office of Management and Budget head Peter Orszag stated in a column for *Bloomberg View* that, "in the lasting debate over Thomas Piketty's book on outsized returns on capital, a significant fact has been obscured: If you exclude land and housing, capital has not risen as a share of the U.S. economy." Orszag goes on to offer data that validate Henry George's conjecture: "Capital excluding land and housing has been roughly constant as a share of the economy since the mid-1950s, and is lower today than at the turn of the 20th century. What has skyrocketed over the past several decades is the value of land and housing." He concludes with an endorsement of a land tax of the variety backed by Lizzie Magie and her fellow Single Taxers: "Sometimes old ideas are good ideas. Henry George advocated forcefully for a land tax in his 1879 book, *Progress and Poverty*. More than 135 years later, perhaps its time is ripe."[20]

In chapter five I quoted the quip, "Buy land, they're not making it anymore." The value of land and housing has indeed grown dramatically in recent decades, but the reason is not because increasingly marginal lands have come under agricultural cultivation, as foreseen by classical economists. The growth has instead been due to increasing returns to density, as Henry George predicted. Cities continue to be humanity's greatest invention, but their very success as platforms for enabling the creation and sharing of code has increased the financial divide between those who own land and those who do not.

"GEOGRAPHY CONSTRAINS EVERYTHING humans do," wrote Cory Ondrejka in 2007 in the journal *Innovations,* which I founded and coedit with GrameenPhone founder Iqbal Quadir. "From our amazing abilities to navigate and model 3-dimensional space to the locations of multinational corporations' headquarters, physical and social evolution have been firmly shaped by geographic constraints. At the personal level, it impacts how we build memories, communicate, and collaborate. At the cultural level, geography defines how and where cities are built, impacts rates of technological development, and has been the cause for innumerable wars. Geography is an inescapable feature of all our lives."[21]

Ondrejka was writing with a unique perspective on geography: for the previous seven years he had been the chief technology officer for Linden Lab, which created *Second Life,* the first large-scale virtual world. Ondrejka's essay appeared at the peak of the platform's popularity, when *Second Life* had nearly seven million registered users and 50,000 human-driven "avatars" were interacting with one another on the platform at any given time. *Second Life* sustained an economy consisting of the production and exchange of virtual goods and services; it had a GDP equivalent to $500 million, benchmarked by $6 million per month of monetized trade with the real world.

Second Life was, and is, a platform on which people share experiences. Unlike games like *World of Warcraft* and *The Sims,* the entire *Second Life* experience is user created. "There is no manufactured conflict, no set objective [in *Second Life*]," Catherine Smith, Linden Lab's spokesperson, was quoted as saying around the time Ondrejka's essay appeared. "It's an entirely open-ended experience."[22] Ondrejka commented further: "Creation within Second Life is accomplished through the use of atomistic creation, an approach granting residents both great freedom to explore design space and an interface allowing multiple builders to create together, much as multiple construction workers collaborate simultaneously when building a home. In atomistic construction, simple geometric primitives are combined in a multitude of ways to build extremely complex creations and behaviors."[23]

Although launched before Facebook, Twitter, and *World of Warcraft* were created, and still in existence, *Second Life* never achieved a fraction of the participation of those better-known platforms. The interface for creating content in the game—a mouse and keyboard, as envisioned by Douglas Engelbart in his "Mother of all Demos"—ultimately proved too difficult for many people to master; in the words of the game's founder, it was "like learning to play the violin or something. I thought, 'We'll just figure out how to use a mouse to do this all.' But it was too hard."[24]

Yet, as Ondrejka communicated in his *Innovations* essay, *Second Life* represented something far more significant than was indicated by its number of users: it offered a fully digital community that signaled a fundamental shift in the nature of organizations and even governance.

Electric cars provide an analogy. The General Motors EV-1, the first all-electric car designed for mass production, was an early and famous failure. Nevertheless, it set the stage for later all-electric vehicles that have gradually shifted buyers' preferences and behaviors—the Tesla, the Chevy Volt, and the Nissan Leaf. The once-unimaginable shift away from internal combustion engines to electric vehicles is now only one small dimension of the more fundamental transformation of the transportation infrastructure that is clearly underway, with "parking assist" and other automated features signaling the arrival of driverless vehicles in the immediate future. Driverless vehicles will in turn interact with real-time spatial databases evolved from applications like Google Maps, which will navigate "real" three-dimensional space based on a code-based representation of geographical space that is located in cyberspace. In this way, virtual and real driving will converge.

The virtual and real worlds of entrepreneurship and work are converging in similar ways. In the pioneer world that was *Second Life,* as described by Ondrejka in 2007, Linden Lab implemented a change to the terms of service that dramatically lowered the cost of creating virtual goods and services and made it easier for users to collaborate: "As soon as tens or hundreds of U.S. dollars were sufficient to start a business in Second Life, thousands of people began to try. Compare this to the real world, where a primary source of funding for small businesses is a second mortgage ... These communities are all creating within a zero marginal cost environment, quite literally a post-scarcity economy. Although there are limits on the density of creation within Second Life, for the most part the only scarce resource is time, thus Second Life is a very pure example of an attention economy."[25]

Seven years later—a century in Internet time—*The Economist* published an article about entrepreneurial startups in the United States titled "The Cambrian Explosion," the title referring to the relatively brief interval about 540 million years ago during which most of the major animal phyla appeared. The article described how an array of new platforms had dramatically lowered the cost of launching and growing a real-world business: "One explanation for the Cambrian explosion of 540m years ago is that at that time the basic building blocks of life had just been perfected, allowing more complex organisms to be assembled more rapidly. Similarly, the basic building blocks for digital services and products—the 'technologies of startup production,' in the words of Josh Lerner of Harvard Business School—have become so evolved, cheap and ubiquitous that they can be easily combined and recombined."[26] The result is an environment that is a convergence of the virtual and real worlds.

What are these building blocks? "Some of these building blocks are snippets of code that can be copied free from the internet, along with easy-to-learn programming frameworks (such as Ruby on Rails)," Ondrejka explained. "Others are 'application programming interfaces' (APIs)" that are automated programs that allow one computer to communicate and share with another computer—enabling a car to draw traffic data easily from the Internet. There are the infrastructure platforms, "services that can host startups' offerings (Amazon's cloud computing), distribute them (Apple's App Store) and market them (Facebook, Twitter)." And, at the base of it all, "there is the Internet, the mother of all platforms, which is now fast, universal and wireless."[27]

As Ondrejka noted in his 2007 essay, the convergence of virtual and real platforms will extend to every dimension of work life and will have profound implications for governance and the organization of human society. "Virtual worlds will change the alignment of labor markets and the shapes of large organizations, including nation-states," Ondrejka wrote. "Changing the substrate for innovation necessitates rethinking common ideas about what constitutes a working group. When less connected individuals can still work together effectively, new possibilities exist for more focused and efficient collaboration requiring lower time commitments than conventional jobs. When a person is able to join multiple organizations, each only requiring a few hours per month, labor markets will adapt to utilize this transformation."[28]

Considering Ondrejka's observations in the context of Henry George's theories and Thomas Piketty's empirical findings, we are prompted to ask the following: If cities have been man's greatest invention, serving as platforms for the creation and evolution of code, what will happen as we create new digital cities—cities located not on land but in "the cloud" of cyberspace? How will the advent of these new platforms affect work, governance, prosperity, and equity? And what will all of this mean for us all as we seek to make our way through this new, rapidly changing world—to play *The Game of Life* according to ever-changing rules?

Code isn't only about advancing technology. It's also about expanding geography.

IF OUR ERA has a Henry George, it is not Thomas Piketty but Jaron Lanier. Like Vint Cerf, Lanier is an Internet pioneer (although of a more recent generation). He coined the term "virtual reality" and founded the first company to produce virtual reality goggles and gloves. In physical appearance, however, Lanier is Cerf's opposite. Cerf is lean, bald, wears three-piece suits, and drives a vintage Jaguar bearing the license plate "Cerf's Up." Lanier is corpulent, sports Medusa-esque dreadlocks, and, as a matter of sartorial principle, takes "low-key" to its black-T-shirt-and-jeans extreme. Yet Cerf and Lanier share many intellectual traits—extreme intelligence being the most obvious, but also a ready wit and a deep understanding of the social context within which code originates and evolves.

If Cerf's primary concern about the societal impact the advance of code will have is employment, then Lanier's is ownership. Like Cerf, Lanier has no doubt that the digital revolution will generate enormous value for society. The question is, how will that value be distributed?

Speaking about his book *Who Owns the Future?* at a 2013 Santa Fe Institute symposium on Big Data in which I participated, Lanier began by emphasizing that the machine-learning algorithms that dominate the field of artificial intelligence today—which simultaneously enhance human capabilities and displace human workers—are themselves just the aggregation of human intelligence. "Big data has to be understood as repackaging of human labor. It's not stand-alone automation, it's human-driven automation," Lanier reminded his audience. "The people are still valuable, they're just invisible."[29]

And yet, while a large number of people contribute to the value Big Data creates, a relatively small number captures most of the gains. Why is this?

The reason is the same as what Henry George discovered with regard to cities. The value people derive from living and working in cities itself derives directly from their proximity to others, and to the role cities play as platforms for the creation and evolution of code, which is also related to that proximity. In this sense, large numbers of people contribute to creating value in cities. However, over at least the past three decades, the financial rewards of the growth and development of cities have accrued disproportionately to one subset of the people associated with cities: the owners of real estate. Value creation is broadly based, while wealth accumulation is narrowly concentrated.

The same is true of digital platforms. Many people create value on these platforms, but the financial rewards of their growth and development have accrued disproportionately to one specific subset of the people associated with them: their owners.[30] Furthermore, in a manner analogous to the Santa Fe team's findings regarding the growth of cities, platforms have a "winner-take-all" quality to them, in that past success feeds future growth. This "positive feedback" that is common to cities and technology platforms concentrates the returns from value creation on both of these types of platforms.

Lanier reminds us that, as the boundaries between virtual worlds and the real world blur and shift, the definition of land and the meaning of monopoly are blurring and shifting as well. Digital platforms are the new land; will they also be the new *Monopoly?*

The answer depends largely on the evolution of a particularly important dimension of the advance of code: protocols for authentication and verification. Why? Physical land is yours if, and only if, you have both the right and the practical capacity to prevent other people from accessing it.[31] The same is true of digital land. The value of the moment of attention owned by a Facebook post or of the proprietary data and analytic resources owned by Google depends on the ability of Facebook to prevent others from using that space or of Google to prevent others from accessing their proprietary data and analytic resources. That capacity for exclusion—the source of all monetized value derived from digital exchange—depends on the existence of reliable protocols for authentication and verification. As Internet guru Tim O'Reilly has put it, "Open leads to value creation, it doesn't lead to value capture. To capture value you have to find something to close."[32]

The nineteenth- and twentieth-century economies evolved a set of systems for managing authentication verification that were all based to some extent on the same ancient concept: branding. A dollar bill is a branded piece of paper. A Mercedes-Benz is a branded assemblage of steel, plastic, and rubber. A Harvard graduate is a branded human being. Brands are the attempted institutionalization of a quality more fundamental than money and more enduring than markets: authenticity. Brands aggregate trust and in so doing mine value. Brands are the primary way human beings navigate complexity in today's advanced industrialized economy. They offer the promise of differentiating between what is "the real thing" and what isn't.

The value of brands is a direct reflection of the anonymity of the world that the advance of code has enabled over the past two centuries. In the village, the very concept of the "brand" is superfluous. Reputations are personal. Experience is immediate. Monitoring is direct. Memory is human. In the village, chieftains can be made, rights can be defined, witches can be burned, and shamans can be worshiped, without the need for any third-party intermediation. Not so in the city—which, as I have argued throughout this book, is the ultimate expression of and vehicle for the advance of code. Because cities are big, interactions among people in them are largely anonymous. People in cities reduce that anonymity to some degree through the evolution of laws, cultural conventions, and neighborhoods. What can't be managed through those mechanisms, the city manages through brands.

If you doubt the importance of brands, consider the penalties we impose on those who violate the boundaries of this most fundamental form of property. The never-ending battle of the State against currency counterfeiters is a good example. Recall that Isaac Newton, among the greatest geniuses in human history, spent a full 20 years of his life as Master of the Royal Mint in England, the prosecution of counterfeiters among his primary preoccupations. The U.S. Secret Service, now primarily known as the branch of government responsible for protecting the president, began as America's first federal police force, with the arrest and prosecution of counterfeiters its sole initial mandate. In eighteenth-century England and nineteenth-century United States, as in most other countries for as long as kings and nation-states have issued currency, counterfeiting was considered a form of treason, punishable by death.

The sanctions that accompany brand transgressions today are less severe but are nonetheless among the harshest we impose for social offenses. We routinely compel prominent people—from captains of industry to four-star generals—to leave privileged positions in shame for the offense of misrepresenting educational credentials, regardless of how little their alleged educational pedigree related to their later accomplishments. Product counterfeiters who produce copies of luxury goods that are sold at a fraction of the price of branded originals are labeled "pirates," and we legally pursue them as such: in the United States, individuals and companies that violate the Trademark Counterfeiting Act of 1984 are subject to fines of up to $5 million and prison sentences of up to 20 years.[33]

Yet just as the advance of code has created brands, code is now in the process of undoing them. How? By converting trust directly into code—into algorithmic systems of verification and authentication. Such systems have the power to hire people to do work, to cure the ill, to feed the hungry, to launch wars, and bring peace. They are doing so already.

The accelerated automation of trust has the potential to create abundant benefits for society but it also brings—as always with the advance of code—commensurate risks. Those risks come down to the integrity of systems of verification and authentication. Any system of trust that can be breached can also be controlled. If I can represent myself as the general of your army, I am the army. If I can represent myself as the administrator of your system, I am your system. I have assumed control . . . that is, until my own system is breached. This is the essence of the challenge of cyber-security, which is the newest version of a code-based category of human endeavor that has existed for millennia at the core of social organization.

"It has been said that 'he who enrolls, controls,'" observes, John Clippinger, a pioneer in natural language processing, the founder of four software companies, and the founder of The Law Lab at the Berkman Center for Internet & Society at Harvard University. "Any 'authoritative' party that defines and selectively confers 'credentials' to access valued resources, privileges and rights—e.g., a bank, state, religious body or social website—exercises enormous power, often with little democratic oversight."[34] To "enroll" users on a digital platform is exactly like issuing an ID card or validating a property claim in the physical world. It is a position of inherent power.

Indeed, a significant fraction of the institutions that dominate modern society—central banks and other large financial institutions,

universities, credit bureaus, and land-titling services among them—
exist in their current form due to the need for third-party authentication and validation in an anonymous, complex world. The advance of
code along this important frontier will determine not only how such
institutions will evolve in the twenty-first century, but also the extent
to which emerging digital platforms turn out to be nothing more than
the new *Monopoly*—or develop into something more.

13

Authenticity

Creating the Foundation for Reputation

It's the real thing.

—Coca-Cola advertisement

OVER THE SPAN of four days during the 2014 South by Southwest (SXSW) festival in Austin, Texas, a food truck manned by chefs from New York's Institute of Culinary Education (ICE) offered an eclectic mix of dishes: Vietnamese Apple Kebab, Caribbean Snapper Fish & Chips, Belgian Bacon Pudding, an Austrian Chocolate Burrito that featured lean ground beef and two ounces of dark chocolate, and, on the last day, Peruvian Potato Poutine. Aside from novelty, what these dishes had in common is that they all were created by a computer: IBM's Watson supercomputer, to be precise.

Nicolas Vanderveken, a Canadian digital strategist, organized a social media campaign to get poutine, a French fry and bean curd favorite of his native Quebec, on the menu for the SXSW Watson food truck. "I wanted to see how the system would work with a dish you've probably never heard of," said Vanderveken. Chef James Biscione responded before serving the Watson-created version, "I'm really nervous about this. I know that you've got some strong opinions about what poutine is, and that it is something near and dear to your heart, so I hope you're going to like what we've come up with here."[1]

IBM calls its food truck project Cognitive Cooking. The point of the experiment is to find out if computers can be creative. "The problem with making creative computers in the past was that computers could do novel things but there was no way to know if they were any good," observes Florian Pinel, the chef and IBM data scientist who leads the Cognitive Cooking project. "We chose cooking because this is something that everyone can refer to. The difference is that we have access to a lot of data and using Big Data we can predict the quality of the recipes. The computer can create something that tastes good, and it knows why it tastes good."[2]

How does Watson manage this? Employing machine-learning algorithms of the type I described in chapter six, it identifies ingredients that will combine well by mining large datasets. "The system doesn't look at ingredients the same way that chefs do," Pinel explains. "When a chef looks at an ingredient he thinks of the history of the ingredient and recipes where it's been used. The system does a little bit of the same, of course, but it also looks at the chemical composition of that ingredient. To understand why they go together, you have to look further at the compounds that are found in these ingredients."[3]

Steve Abrams, director of IBM Watson Life, of which Cognitive Cooking is a part, elaborates: "What you see is a system that was trained on 35,000 different recipes, as if it was digesting a giant cookbook. From reading that cookbook it has learned an awful lot about different cuisines and the ingredients that are often used in different cuisines, ingredients that are often paired together, and what it takes to make a particular dish—what it takes to make a burrito different from soup, or Japanese cuisine different from Tex-Mex."[4] To get to the combination of ingredients that resulted in Peruvian Potato Poutine and the other dishes served at SXSW, Watson tested more than a quintillion possible combinations. However, refining the most promising combinations and the template recipes produced by Watson into those actually used to prepare the dishes at the festival required the human talent of the highly trained ICE chefs.[5] This is the essence of cognitive computing: algorithmic support for human decision-making, and even human creativity.

Summarizing two centuries of the advance of code, from Jacquard-inspired punch-card (or "tabulated") machines to human-machine systems like the Watson Food Truck, including more than a century of IBM's own history, Abrams states, "Originally we had tabulated machines, then we went on to programmable systems, now we're in the era of cognitive systems." As I have emphasized throughout this book, the advance of code summarized by Abrams spans almost every domain of human creative activity.

As a further example, consider the fate of two films that premiered on the same night at the 2015 Sundance Film Festival, as recounted by Tim Wu of *The New Yorker* in a January 2015 article. One of these films, *What Happened, Miss Simone?* was a documentary about singer and civil rights icon Nina Simone. That film was funded by Netflix, whose corporate decision to back the film was based in part on insights algorithmically gleaned from the vast trove of data it has collected on users of its streaming video and movie rental services. The second film was a comedy titled *The Bronze,* which featured television star Melissa Rauch as a vulgar gymnast. *The Bronze* was produced by Duplass Brothers Productions and privately financed by "a few wealthy individuals" whose decision to back the film was presumably not based on complex impersonal algorithms but rather, as has been the Hollywood norm, on business intuition. At the Sundance screening of *The Bronze,* the festival's director, John Cooper, indicated that it was a personal selection of his.

You can, of course, guess the outcome. "While not a formal competition in any sense," Wu recounts, "the night seemed to be a clear victory for algorithms over instincts. 'Miss Simone' gained a standing ovation at its screening and has earned critical respect. 'The Bronze,' while garnering some laughs, currently sits at ten per cent on Rotten Tomatoes, where critics have called it 'a grueling experience to sit through' and 'a mean-spirited and largely witless satire.'"

Granted, the use of data and even algorithms to inform film and television programming decisions is nothing new. Television executives for decades have had their decisions guided by the Nielsen ratings, as film industry executives have been guided by the dissection of box office receipts. However, ratings and receipts are both retrospective measures—and simple ones at that. In contrast, Netflix used its vast data resources and complex algorithms to make forward-looking predictions about audience reactions, like IBM Watson with the cognitive computing project.

This is just one anecdote, of course, but the code-focused approach Netflix has taken to movie-moguling and TV producing has yielded broadly impressive results, including breakout hits like *House of Cards, Orange Is the New Black,* and *Unbreakable Kimmy Schmidt.* Due in large part to its industry-leading focus on data and algorithms, Netflix has gone from a company that was widely judged to be on the brink of failure after a pricing mistake four years ago that sparked large-scale user defection to one that is to the business of streaming media what Alibaba and Amazon are to electronic commerce. In 2015, after years of steady growth, Netflix accounted for almost 37 percent of all downstream Internet traffic in North America during peak evening hours.[6]

Does this mean that Netflix is a company run entirely by algorithms in which human intuition and insight play no part? "It is important to know which data to ignore," Netflix chief content officer Ted Sarandos noted to Wu. "In practice, it's probably a seventy-thirty mix, [where] seventy is the data, and thirty is judgment. But the thirty needs to be on top, if that makes sense."

When it comes to various jobs' susceptibility to automation, movie mogul would still have to rank close to the bottom. The combination of cultural sensibility, financial acumen, negotiating savvy, and personal charisma required for success as a film industry executive would be difficult to duplicate. Yet anyone who has used a driving app such as Google Maps to guide the process of urban navigation knows what Sarandos is talking about. Augmenting human decision-making with automated input—the advent of Big Data or what IBM calls cognitive computing—is not a future possibility but a present reality. Furthermore, it is limited neither to experts nor to narrowly technical domains and is being applied in a broad range of human endeavors, from cooking and film production to public health, urban planning, disaster response, and environmental management.

"Never before has it been possible to self-consciously design and test at scale new forms of social technologies with rapid iterations and innovation," John Clippinger wrote in his contribution to the informatively titled *From Bitcoin to Burning Man and Beyond: The Quest for Identity and Autonomy in a Digital Society,* a 2014 book he coedited with author/ activist David Bollier.[7] "The convergence of open platforms, social networking, Big Data and encryption innovations allows us to address many social and economic problems that simply could not be seen or addressed under the regnant system of authoritative institutions."[8]

Clippinger has been thinking and writing about human societies as cybernetic systems for 40 years. Most recently he started the Institute for Innovation & Data Driven Design, a nonprofit organization formed to develop, and to field test, legal- and software-based "trust frameworks" for data-driven services, infrastructures, and enterprises. Core to this work is the use of an authentication and verification system known as the Blockchain, which allows for the irreversible and open documentation of verified transactions of any type.

The era of cognitive computing is clearly upon us. Social systems are already man-machine systems. Whether this next stage in the advance of code is desirable is a less interesting question than how to make it as broadly beneficial as possible. Who does the work in the era of cognitive computing? Who gets the credit? Who earns the reward? Who owns the data . . .

. . . and, when all is said and done, who gets to decide if computer-generated poutine is *real* poutine?

THE COMITÉ INTERPROFESSIONNEL du vin de Champagne is an organization dedicated exclusively to ensuring the authenticity of wines sold under the name "champagne." For a bottle of sparkling wine to be so branded, it must be produced not only in the Champagne region of France but also according to a specific set of processes, including the choice of grape varietals, care of vines, and actual production of the champagne. Like Swiss watchmakers in their market, the producers of authentic champagnes comprise a relatively small share, about 13 percent, of the sparkling wines sold globally. However, with $2.4 billion in export sales in 2014, they constitute more than 50 percent of the global export market for sparkling wine.

Most French wines and an array of other agricultural products are produced in accordance with regulations established by the Institut National de l'Origine et de la Qualité, a government organization formed in 1935 that functions as a sort of modern-day guild.[9] The Institut National ensures quality and restricts output in order to maintain the integrity of brands and protect producers' livelihoods.

Many other countries have similar entities, each with its own methods of authenticating culinary products by ensuring compliance with production standards. In Thailand, the government has recently taken such work to a new level with its introduction of a tasting robot designed for a single task: authenticating Thai dishes. A box the size of an old-style television set, the "e-delicious" machine scans samples of supposed "Thai food" and compares the chemical composition of the samples against the known chemical signatures of authentic dishes. The government entity that created the machine, the Thai Delicious Committee, is taking additional action to ensure the authenticity of Thai food, including offering a logo that restaurants can affix to their menus if they use government-sanctioned recipes.

Given that sales of food and beverages constitute between one-sixth and one-fifth of global economic exchange, these attempts to ensure the authenticity of culinary code are of inherent importance in understanding the code economy in past, present, and (likely) future forms. However, they also underscore the fundamental relationship between algorithms of production and protocols for authentication and verification, such as Blockchain.

The analogy between monetary and culinary protocols for authentication and verification is illustrated further by considering the personal history of one of history's greatest creators of new concoctions: Sir Isaac Newton.

What do I mean by this? Well, Isaac Newton is renowned for his invention of calculus (simultaneously with Gottfried Leibniz). And, as I noted in chapter 12, Newton served for more than two decades as the Master of the Royal Mint, during which time he oversaw the introduction of common currency for the new Kingdom of Great Britain. However, during the course of Newton's lifetime, he also wrote over a million words of notes on alchemy, of which he published none. These notes detailed his extensive and exhaustive attempts to find a recipe for gold, using base metals as inputs. Newton's mentors and peers who shared his passion for alchemy included the great natural scientist Robert Boyle (known to chemistry students everywhere via Boyle's Law) and philosopher John Locke, whose essays on cognition and political freedom inspired Jean-Jacques Rousseau and helped spark the American Revolution.[10]

Acting like human versions of Watson in their search for a recipe for gold, Newton, Boyle, Locke, and a vast pan-European guild of alchemists tried thousands of different combinations of ingredients, subjected to a panoply of preparations, all the while taking scrupulous notes on the conjectured composition of the base metals they used as ingredients and the results they observed. Lacking any real understanding of chemistry, they could only observe raw correlations and seek patterns that seemed to promise a solution in machine-learning fashion.

True, Newton and his contemporaries failed utterly in their quest to create gold. However, they did contribute significantly to what has turned out to be a far greater project: the discovery of the algorithms of structured inquiry into the nature of the world that they termed "natural philosophy," which we refer to today simply as "science."[11]

ON OCTOBER 31, 2008, Satoshi Nakamoto—who may or may not exist—posted a nine-page paper to the "metzdowd.com" cryptography mailing list, which was titled "Bitcoin: A Peer-to-Peer Electronic Cash System." The paper proposed "a system for electronic transactions without relying on trust." Its publication was timely. Six weeks earlier, Lehman Brothers Holdings, Inc., the fourth-largest U.S. investment bank, had sought Chapter 11 protection, thus initiating the single biggest bankruptcy proceeding in U.S. history. Trust in the financial system was as low as it had been for decades, as experts and members of the general public alike asked, "How can the global financial system be made more transparent and less subject to systemic distortions?" By offering an architecture for the issuance of currency and the documentation of transactions that is based on code rather than individual discretion, Bitcoin provided at least one possibility.

Is Bitcoin really money? The best approach to answering this question begins with insights from William Stanley Jevons, cofounder of the neoclassical school in economics and pioneering inventor in the field of artificial intelligence, to whom I referred in chapter six. Jevons set forth the basic parameters for contemporary understanding of money in a monograph published in 1875, titled *Money and the Mechanism of Exchange*.

"To decide upon the best material for money is thus a problem of great complexity," Jevons wrote, "because we must take into account at once the relative importance of the several functions of money, the degree in which money is employed for each function, and the importance of each of the physical qualities of the substance with respect to each function."[12] Jevons organized the desirable properties of a material functioning as money along seven dimensions: "(1) Utility and value;

(2) Portability; (3) Indestructibility; (4) Homogeneity; (5) Divisibility; (6) Stability of value; (7) Cognizability." To validate his framework, Jevons used it to explain the historical dominance of gold as a medium of exchange. Gold has intrinsic appeal, Jevons noted; it is permanently lustrous and possesses "a rich and brilliant yellow colour, which can only be adequately described as golden." It is easy to carry, it can be subdivided without difficulty, it is scarce and thus relatively stable in value, and, perhaps most importantly, it can be readily recognized due to its exceptional density. Jevons stated that, for these reasons, when it comes to money gold is, well, the gold standard.

Given the supremacy of gold as a medium of exchange, it was only natural that, when national governments began to issue paper currency in the nineteenth century, they sought to tie the value of their currency to gold. The emergence of a gold standard—first in the Commonwealth countries and then in the United States and other leading European nations—contributed to the dramatic growth in global trade that occurred toward the end of the nineteenth and the beginning of the twentieth century. The outbreak of World War I brought that first era of globalization to a sudden halt, and with it the beginning of the end of the gold standard. For the past 40 years the world's currencies have been untethered from gold or any other metal. National "fiat" currencies are nothing more or less than tradable trust, whose function as currency is based entirely on government-enforced scarcity and verifiability not tethered to its intrinsic usefulness.

Bitcoin—a digital currency created and exchanged on the Blockchain platform—satisfies all the criteria for being "money" that William Stanley Jevons set forth more than a century ago, with one exception: intrinsic utility and value. That does not mean that that Bitcoin will grow in significance as a means of exchange, much less achieve any position of dominance. But with digital transactions via mobile phones—Apple Pay and the like—becoming ever more common and the concept of a digital currency not backed by any government gaining rapid acceptance, the prospect of one or another digital currency competing successfully with fiat currencies is not nearly as far-fetched today as it was even three years ago.

Sixty-four days after publication of the Bitcoin protocol, the system was operational. The first solution to the progressively more difficult algorithm described in Nakamoto's paper was discovered, which is the same as saying that Bitcoin number 1 had been "mined." In the six years that followed the creation of Bitcoin, it traced out the full trajectory of the Gartner Hype Cycle: from early obscurity to "the peak of inflated expectations" as the price of Bitcoin surged in 2011 and again in 2013, and subsequently to "the trough of disillusionment" as adoption remained slow.

Through these stages, some bullish pundits proclaimed Bitcoin's ascendancy as a global currency imminent and the displacement of the world's central banks correspondingly inevitable. Others decried Bitcoin as being suited only to money laundering and the facilitation of illicit transactions and argued that it would never develop into a viable commercial platform. Yet while the volatile public discussion of Bitcoin has focused on the viability and desirability of a digital currency not backed by any government, a bigger story has been hidden in plain sight all along: the creation of "a system for electronic transactions without relying on trust" that the person (or persons) named Satoshi Nakamoto described in a technical note published one Halloween night more than seven years ago. That system is the Blockchain.

TO UNDERSTAND THE Blockchain, consider anew the image of Bob Cratchit laboring over his desk in *A Christmas Carol,* making calculations and entering them into a ledger. That ledger constituted the authoritative record of the business of Ebenezer Scrooge and Company. Each transaction fit into a horizontal block—a row in the ledger—and the entire ledger thus constituted a chain of such blocks, each one dependent on the accuracy of the one before. In other words, a ledger is a block chain.

The Blockchain that underlies Bitcoin is also a ledger. However, it is a ledger with two special properties. First, it is a "distributed" ledger. Rather than being validated by a lone "Bob Cratchit" working in obscurity—or, in more contemporary form, an army of auditors from PriceWaterhouseCoopers—the Blockchain is a ledger that is validated by thousands of strangers, all of whom perform their own calculations to ensure that a given block in the chain is accurate and authentic. What Wikipedia has accomplished for knowledge, Blockchain thus promises to accomplish for transactions: returning validation authority to users. And just as Wikipedia put an end to the dominance of *Encyclopaedia*

Brittanica, Blockchain has the potential to put an end to the dominance of central banks, university registrars, land title companies, and any other third-party validators of transactions, credentials, or claims.

The second special property of the Blockchain, which follows directly from the first, is that once a block in the Blockchain has been validated, it stays validated forever. In other words, unlike physical ledgers that can be doctored or altered, the Blockchain is immutable. How? Simply because—due to its digital rather than paper-based nature—the Blockchain exists in many places at once. Any attempt to tamper with one copy of the Blockchain would be invalidated by the abundance of copies that collectively affirmed the authoritative version. To attempt to tamper with blocks in the Blockchain is a task of comparable (or, for technical reasons, even greater) difficulty than trying to get the world to accept as legitimate a new version of *Hamlet* or a modified version of the Beatles song "Yesterday." So many authoritative copies exist that a fraud is easily unmasked.

Thus the Blockchain is not just any ledger. It is an example of a distributed, immutable ledger.

The very existence of the Blockchain brings to the foreground an essential dimension of code economics that I have only briefly alluded to: authenticity and verification. We judge the authenticity of a coin from the imprint it bears, from its weight, and (with some work) from its physical composition. We judge the authenticity of paper currency from the engraving it bears, including difficult-to-reproduce watermarks and microprinted characters. But how do we judge the authenticity of a digital payment—be it a digital dollar bill or a Bitcoin? Or, in a complex anonymized world, of a bottle of wine? A work of art? Even an experience?

The problem the Blockchain solves is as old as monetized exchange: how to verify that that a person, an object, or a claim is what it represents itself to be. Without such verification, it is impossible to establish rights over property and rules over contracts; without rights over property and rules over contracts, it is impossible to structure a market system of exchange.

Nearly all economic analysis takes the existence of rights over property and rules over contracts as a given and focuses on the nature and consequences of market exchange. The advent of the Blockchain (subsuming within it the applications of Blockchain code such as Bitcoin) surfaces the fact that markets depend on platforms for exchange, which in turn rely on protocols of authentication and verification.

It turns out that the immutability of the Blockchain makes it a powerful tool for authentication and verification—and, potentially, a next phase in the advance of code.

SO FAR, THE Blockchain applications that have drawn the greatest attention have been in financial services—taking a cue from, though going well beyond, the precedent set by Bitcoin. However, the applications of Blockchain that ultimately may have the greatest direct impact on the human experience are likely to be those related to the (self-)governance of peer-to-peer networks.

By their very structure, peer-to-peer platforms start out being distributed. The challenge is how to organize all of the energy contained in such networks so that people are rewarded fairly for their contributions. This is a problem that in the past has been solved either by impersonal markets (which do a bad job of keeping track of reputation) and centralized administrative authority (which does a bad job of rewarding contribution). Blockchain-based systems for governing peer-to-peer networks hold the promise—so far unrealized—of incorporating the best features of markets when it comes to rewarding contributions, and of organizations when it comes to keeping track of reputations.

If designed as Robin Chase, Lisa Gansky, John Clippinger, and others believe they can be, peer-to-peer systems have the potential to scale-out the value created on peer-to-peer platforms to reach the tens of thousands, even hundreds of thousands, of people who contribute to them. Moreover, they will create new and enticing invitations to latent producers within the economy to employ their individual assets and talents to create new economic value. Dynamically negotiated "smart contracts" on the Blockchain and other peer-to-peer innovations hold the promise of realizing Jevons' long-ago articulated vision of "a more useful and beneficial form of organization" based on profit-sharing, which I discussed in chapter 6.

The significance of peer-to-peer business models thus is not effectively measured by adding up the current share of GDP they represent in terms of monetized transactions. These innovations in work are rushing in at the fringes of the advanced economies to fill the void left behind as large corporations continue to "lean up"—that is, to shrink their pay-rolls by employing algorithms and machines to perform routine tasks previously performed by people. Steven Straus, former managing direc-tor of the Center for Economic Transformation at the New York City Economic Development Corporation, looks at the same phenomenon from the standpoint of job seekers: "We currently have about three job seekers for every available job and 11 million people looking for work—so the growth of the sharing economy isn't surprising."[13]

In the coming decades, the United States and other advanced in-dustrialized economies will no sooner return to the routinized manufacturing-centric economy of the twentieth century than to the agrarian economy that preceded it. The issue is not whether new liveli-hoods based on peer-to-peer business models are better or worse than the Industrial Age jobs that are disappearing from large corporations, but whether, when jobs are eliminated in the process of digital dis-ruption, they will be coming back in their old form—or not. As that happens, we humans have no choice but to fall back on our most fun-damental social skills: creating and sharing with one another. There is, however, one big difference: unlike our isolated ancestors of millennia past, Americans and people everywhere in this century are empowered by architectures of collaboration that allow for the creation of new and diverse livelihoods at an unprecedented rate.

In her book *Peers Inc.,* Robin Chase draws from well-considered analysis, as well as her own personal experience as the cofounder of the car-sharing company Zipcar, to differentiate between the "Peers" and "Inc."—the crowd that creates value, and the platforms on which that value creation takes place. In a chapter fitingly titled "Who Has the Gold?" she makes the following observation: "Peers Inc. thrives when peers are motivated to contribute. Platforms that do not adequately reward peers, value their contribution, and invest in their potential, will fail in the long term."[14]

Therein lies the potential of today's peer-to-peer economy. However, the existence of peer-to-peer networks alone is not sufficient to ensure inclusion and equity. Because "he who enrolls, controls," another re-quirement for inclusion and equity may be that the networks are based on systems of trust and verification that are not wholly owned by dis-interested third parties.

"MAN IS BORN FREE and everywhere he is in chains." This powerful opening sentence from Jean-Jacques Rousseau's *The Social Contract* encapsulates the fundamental paradox of the advance of code, and the progress of human society.

Echoing Rousseau, I noted at the outset of this book that the advance of code over the past four or five centuries has involved the collective willingness of human beings to cede to other people, and to code itself, authority and autonomy that we for millennia kept unto ourselves and our immediate tribal groups. This individual autonomy has allowed humanity's greatest inventions to emerge and propagate: cities, global trade, the rule of law, science, and democracy. That these greatest inventions are all social inventions is not surprising, for humans are deeply social beings. Progress in human society can be thought of as the evolution of chains, from those of subjugation and servitude to those of collaboration and interconnection. At every stage, the process has been enabled by the advance of code.

Earlier in the book I alluded to the significant advances in democracy, science, and financial systems that occurred simultaneously during the interval of history during which Rousseau, the Genevan watchmaker's son, wrote his great works of political and natural philosophy: the Age of Enlightenment. That systems of governance, inquiry, and economics should have advanced all at the same time—fueled by coffeehouse discussions in just a handful of cities—is no coincidence at all. Each of these foundational developments in human social evolution is, at its core, an algorithm for authentication and verification. The scientific method, democratic processes, and financial system protocols all serve to reduce the arbitrary power of single individuals—whether to rule, to establish facts, or to validate transactions—while simultaneously enhancing the collective capacity of groups. Each is an instance of an underlying phenomenon, which is the advance of code.

That political, scientific, and economic manifestations of the advance of code are fundamentally linked is reflected in the simple historical fact that many of the same people were responsible for parallel and linked advances in modern democratic forms of government, scientific methods, and the architecture of modern financial systems. As I mentioned, Newton, Leibniz, Locke, Boyle, Rousseau, and an array of colleagues whose names are now mostly lost to history, each contributed substantially to the conceptualization and in some cases the implementation of some of the institutional innovations that have shaped the modern world.

The patterns connecting systems of authentication and verification in politics, science, and economics continued into the nineteenth century, as embodied in figures as diverse as David Ricardo, Lord Byron, Charles Babbage, Ada Lovelace, Henry George, and William Jevons.

It is only because of the disciplinary fragmentation of inquiry that has occurred in the past century that we do not immediately perceive in the evolved historical record the patterns connecting systems of authentication and verification in politics, science, and economics as they have jointly evolved. Those patterns exist, but it takes some work to find them. Illuminating those patterns has been the point of this book.

The underlying unity of the advance of code along multiple frontiers is evident today in the work and writings of Jim Bessen, Robin Chase, John Clippinger, Vint Cerf, Lisa Gansky, Jaron Lanier, Tim O'Reilly, David Nordfors, and many others whose perspectives on the code economy I have shared in this book, or who have in other ways informed the patterns I have sought to illuminate. A significant number in this group considers self-governing protocols for authentication and verification to be an essential element of an inclusive and democratic digital future. The conviction these well-informed observers share regarding the importance of building self-governance into the architecture of the code economy is based in part on their concern about the potentially negative consequences of the concentration of data and the centralization of third-party powers of authentication and verification.

However, the development of new institutional mechanisms for ensuring authenticity does not preclude the use of old ones. If 40,000 years of the history of code is any indication, algorithmic improvements will shift the domains in which human judgment will be valuable but will not diminish its importance. What each of us believes to be authentic will determine what each of us believes to be valuable. These decentralized, individual determinations of value will shape the evolution of the economy and, to a significant extent, the development of human society.[15]

14

Purpose

The Promised Sand

No idea can substitute for immediate experience.

—Burning Man Principle No. 10

ON A RECENT September evening, a traffic jam of epic proportions formed on a dry lakebed in the Nevada desert. Cars, vans, motorcycles, campers, mechanical Mastodons, cruise-ships-on-wheels, and vehicles of a variety not present anywhere else on the planet formed a line five lanes wide and ten miles long. This procession crawled forward along the flat, cracked clay at a speed barely exceeding two miles per hour.

Just a day earlier, the vehicles' occupants had comprised the citizenry of a city of 70,000 people—the fourth largest in the State of Nevada. A bike repair shop had buzzed with activity as eager apprentices worked alongside experienced mechanics. Kids had played putt-putt golf. Impromptu restaurants had dispensed grilled-cheese sandwiches, waffles, and beignets by the hundreds. The city had literally pulsed with music, dance, and art for the full seven days of its existence.

Yet for all the evident energy and creativity of its citizens, the city had been an abject failure from the standpoint of conventional economic metrics. With an economy based on gifts rather than monetized trade, its contribution to gross domestic product was close to zero. Its endowment of natural resources was similarly nonexistent. According to standard definitions, unemployment was close to 100 percent.

Black Rock City, as this place was known, had been as rich in experiences and as poor in natural resources as any other. When its time came to an end, its citizens dispersed throughout the long night in ritual solemnity.

THE ESPLANADE IS to Black Rock City what the Bund is to Shanghai or the Quai d'Orsay to Paris: where you stand to gaze out at the illuminated tableau of an urban landscape. However, unlike these other famed front-ages, the Esplanade does not offer views of cathedrals, castles, or bridges. Instead it offers a view of a black expanse traversed by moving lights and bursts of flame so intense and numerous that they merge almost seam-lessly into the starscape above. Over the entire scene presides The Man: a colossal wooden stick figure situated at dead center of the semicircular grid of streets that comprise the layout of Black Rock City (see figure 14.1).

FIGURE 14.1 Map of Black Rock City. Satellite image of Black Rock City, taken from NASA World Wind. Personal creation from NASA World Wind program, zoomed in and centered on Black Rock City. Whole "city" represented to avoid confusion.
Source: NASA.

This is Burning Man: a temporary city with a population of 70,000—about the size of the Mesopotamian city of Uruk that I discussed in chapter 2—that exists in the Nevada desert for one week every year.

"I've always been very interested in scenes, particularly avant-garde scenes," said Larry Harvey, the founder of Burning Man, when we spoke at Black Rock City in September 2015. Avant-garde scenes, he said, act as "a crossroads for people doing radical things seeming unrelated to one another. People start to meet one another, and bounce off one another, and share ideas with one another. That could be the Beats in America. That could be the Bloomsbury Group in London. It could be older scenes even before that, around folks going back since forever. We are that." Harvey then paused, not for effect but for reflection. "Except we're the first organization, I believe, that turned a Bohemian scene into a city," he continued. "I don't think anyone's ever done that. So now it's a scene with 70,000 people. Usually scenes don't do that."

Like any city, Black Rock City has cultural norms and expectations. What is distinct about Black Rock City is that it offers those experiences on a platform that is, by design, as minimal as possible. Rather than a "festival" in any standard sense of the word, it is an ongoing social experiment in which a petri dish the size of downtown San Francisco is treated with a microbial growth medium that comes in the form of 10 principles and a semicircular urban plan (see Text Box 14.1). A functioning city emerges: Artists experiment. Engineers create. (The light design in the basement of the National Gallery of Art in Washington, D.C., is one of a number of Burning Man experiments that has found its way into the world at large.)

But it didn't start out this way. "One day in 1986 I called a friend and said, let's build a man and burn him on the beach," Harvey recalled in one of the countless talks and interviews he has given on the origins of the city. "I did this on impulse. There was really nothing on my mind. I've thought about it over the years, because [people] keep asking, and the best I can say is that some passionate prompting, some immediate vision just had to be embodied in the world." The original burning of The Man on Baker Beach in San Francisco was more of an elaborate and inspired prank than it was a conscious effort to launch a social movement—much less to create a city. "We built our man from scraps of wood, then called some friends and took it to the beach. We

Text Box 14.1 Ten Principles of Burning Man

Burning Man cofounder Larry Harvey wrote these Ten Principles in 2004 as guidelines for the regional network that the organization was forming at that time. They are described by the Burning Man organization as having been "crafted not as a dictate of how people should be and act, but as a reflection of the community's ethos and culture as it had organically developed since the event's inception" in 1986.[1]

Radical Inclusion

Anyone may be a part of Burning Man. We welcome and respect the stranger. No prerequisites exist for participation in our community.

Gifting

Burning Man is devoted to acts of gift giving. The value of a gift is unconditional. Gifting does not contemplate a return or an exchange for something of equal value.

Decommodification

In order to preserve the spirit of gifting, our community seeks to create social environments that are unmediated by commercial sponsorships, transactions, or advertising. We stand ready to protect our culture from such exploitation. We resist the substitution of consumption for participatory experience.

Radical Self-reliance

Burning Man encourages the individual to discover, exercise, and rely on his or her inner resources.

Radical Self-expression

Radical self-expression arises from the unique gifts of the individual. No one other than the individual or a collaborating group can determine its content. It is offered as a gift to others. In this spirit, the giver should respect the rights and liberties of the recipient.

Communal Effort

Our community values creative cooperation and collaboration. We strive to produce, promote, and protect social networks, public spaces, works of art, and methods of communication that support such interaction.

Civic Responsibility

We value civil society. Community members who organize events should assume responsibility for public welfare and endeavor to communicate civic responsibilities to participants. They must also assume responsibility for conducting events in accordance with local, state, and federal laws.

Leaving No Trace

Our community respects the environment. We are committed to leaving no physical trace of our activities wherever we gather. We clean up after ourselves and endeavor, whenever possible, to leave such places in a better state than we found them.

Participation

Our community is committed to a radically participatory ethic. We believe that transformative change, whether in the individual or in society, can occur only through the medium of deeply personal participation. We achieve being through doing. Everyone is invited to work. Everyone is invited to play. We make the world real through actions that open the heart.

Immediacy

Immediate experience is, in many ways, the most important touchstone of value in our culture. We seek to overcome barriers that stand between us and a recognition of our inner selves, the reality of those around us, participation in society, and contact with a natural world exceeding human powers. No idea can substitute for this experience.

saturated it with gasoline and put a match to it, and within minutes our numbers doubled. That's actually when Burning Man began as an institution. We were so moved by that, we knew we had to do it again."

After four years at Baker Beach, the gathering began to run into the sort of problems to be expected when a large-scale outpouring of anarchic expression takes place in a major metropolitan area. So Larry Harvey and a group of cofounders who by then had taken responsibility for the gathering decided to find another location.

They settled on the Black Rock Desert, an arid expanse whose utter desolation is accounted for accurately by the U.S. Interior Department's Bureau of Land Management: "The environment . . . contains no true soils; surface or ground water; vegetation; wildlife; threatened or endangered species; wild horses; paleontology; solid or hazardous waste materials; wilderness; or cultural resources . . . In addition, the following critical resources are not present: Areas of Critical Environmental Concern, prime or unique farmland, floodplain, wetlands, or noxious weed."[2] It is an environment that can only be described satisfactorily in the negative—by what it does not contain for the 51 weeks per year it is not home to Black Rock City.

For its first six years, according to one early participant, Burning Man consisted of "a few thousand jackasses going [crazy] across the desert floor . . . People were driving around shooting guns out of moving cars while dragging their friends from the bumper on tarps." In 1992 the event became ticketed, with the price of admission set at $25. (In 2016 it was $390.) The city's volunteer patrol, the Black Rock Rangers, came into existence the same year. That era of unrepressed and ungoverned mayhem flamed out in 1996, when one reveler drove through an occupied tent in the middle of the night, severely injuring all inside. The same year another participant on a motorcycle lost a game of chicken with a pickup truck, with fatal consequences. "We decided to build a vessel to contain the community. We realized we had to create a real city."

When Burners (as Burning Man participants call themselves) returned the following year, they found a city plan had been imposed. All tents and RVs were confined to a semicircular grid of streets on which speed limits would be carefully enforced. Black Rock City thus was born.

Like everything about Black Rock City, the layout is the product of both planning and evolution.[3] Cities are what physicists refer to as dissipative structures: highly complex organisms whose existence depends on a constant throughput of energy. If you were to close down all bridges and tunnels into New York City or similarly cut off any other city, grocery stores would have only a three-day supply of food.[4] The same is generally true of a city's other energy requirements. All cities are temporary, and they survive only because we feed them.

In that sense, the explicitly—indeed, contractually—temporary nature of Black Rock City reveals a fundamental truth about all cities. The evolution of Black Rock is for urbanists what a real-life Jurassic Park would be for a paleontologist. We really have no idea what the experience of living in humanity's first cities might have been—whether Uruk in Mesopotamia or Çatalhöyük in Anatolia. And yet all cities also have elements of planning. Where Black Rock City has its Larry Harvey, London had its Robert Hooke and Washington, D.C., had its Pierre L'Enfant. Each had a notion of how to bound a space, build symmetry and flow, and in so doing provide a platform where the human experience can unfold.

"Human culture—as distinct from social institutions that surround it—is a pure phenomenon of nature. Social institutions have the power to protect it and sustain it, much as any vessel—a petri dish or ceramic pot—might help or hinder the growth of any living thing," Harvey has observed. "But the innate vitality of culture belongs to the world of nature; it occurs spontaneously, it is without a plan, and when it is allowed to grow it has a power to affect our world in ways that dwarf our normal estimate of our resources."[5]

To the denizens of Black Rock City, all that lies outside the city walls (actually, the trash fence that defines the perimeter of the space where Burning Man takes place) is known as "default world." In default world's getaway destinations—hotels and motels—the two items one can count on getting for free are ice and coffee. At Black Rock City, the exact opposite holds: the only two items available for purchase are ice and coffee. The irony is instructive, as the economy of Black Rock City is more or less the exact inverse of the default world economy.

"We allow no vending, no advertising, no buying or selling of anything," says Harvey. "We discourage bartering because even bartering is a commodity transaction. Instead, we've originated both an ethos and an economic system that is devoted to the giving of gifts. This is a radical departure from the marketplace that we're accustomed to, because, of course, the marketplace invades every crack and corner of our lives today. A gift economy is founded on principles that are diametrically different from those that dominate our consumer culture."[6]

Yet Harvey draws an important distinction between what occurs within the "container" that is Black Rock City and the manner in which the city interacts with the environment outside. "There's this notion that this is a moneyless utopia," he observed to a group of journalists gathered at Black Rock City in 2015. "Where did all this stuff come from? It was purchased in the marketplace. Where did this tent come from? It wasn't cobbled together in this environment that furnishes no material resources whatsoever ... Most people didn't knit their tent from wool, from shearing sheep." This is the throughput of energy that allows Black Rock City—like any city—to survive.

What differentiates Black Rock City is its all-pervasive culture of participation. If Burning Man has a rule, it is "no spectators." As Harvey says of the resources participants transport, at great cost and difficulty, to the Nevada desert: "The crucial question is what happens when they cross the city boundaries and decide what to do with those resources. The meaning isn't stamped into the goods at the factory or something. The meaning derives from what they do with those goods and how they use those goods to connect with everybody here. That's the curious nature of the economy at Burning Man."

Yet even with the singular nature of Black Rock City's participatory culture, this aspect of the city also generalizes. All cities are fed with resources from the outside, and meaning derives from what citizens do with those goods they draw from the outside—including how they use those goods to connect with others around them.

IN PART THREE of this book I have focused a lot on games and invented worlds. Given the weighty nature of the questions I am addressing, this may have seemed an odd approach. Are *Monopoly* and *Second Life* and Burning Man really the best narrative vehicles for exploring the advance of code? Wouldn't real-world examples be more illustrative than a focus on games?

Perhaps. But note this: games themselves are code. The purpose of games, as code, is to make the world intelligible by practicing how to exist within it. In this way, the best games represent the models of the world that actually dominate and function effectively at any point in time. Such games are not more real than reality, but they are the ideal lens for understanding how a particular society makes sense of reality. The games people play at a particular point in time represent a pure form of applied economics (see Text Box 14.2). Indeed, generations of economists know the great physicist John von Neumann (see chapter

Text Box 14.2 Yin-Yang

Some years after publishing "De arte combinatoria," Gottfried Leibniz came across the *I Ching*, also known as the "Book of Changes." The *I Ching* is a book of divination in which fundamental modes of being are structured into 64 hexagrams. Each hexagram is a figure composed of six stacked horizontal lines (爻 *yáo*), where each line is either Yin (a broken line with a gap in the center) or Yang (an unbroken or solid line). Yin and Yang represent masculine and feminine elements in both Taoism and Confucianism. Expressing Yin as "0" and Yang as "1" naturally leads to a binary representation, where three digits, each valued at either zero or one, generate the 64 possibilities in the hexagram.[7]

Leibniz found some support for his concept of "the Universal Character," the first notion of a programming language, in the *I Ching's* representation of the universe in terms of dualities: a series of yes-no possibilities that could combine to express life and consciousness in its full complexity. Boosted by this insight, Leibniz resumed work on the binary system. More than a century later, George Boole picked up this line of work. The result is the Boolean logic that is the foundation of all digital computing languages today.

Deeply embedded in the binary world is the juxtaposition of Yin (|) and Yang (二) that inspired Leibniz three centuries ago. When combined in much the same manner Leibniz envisioned, the characters for Yin and Yang form a new character: | 二.

Its meaning? Humanity.[8] Within Confucianism, this character, written in modern Chinese as 仁 and in Hanyu Pinyin as *rén*, has a meaning that extends well beyond the character that might be translated as "humankind." It conveys a person's outward orientation or altruism. Lacking a precise analogue in English, it is variously translated as "benevolence," "virtue," and "goodness." Yet none of those words captures the functional aspect of rén within Confucianism, which is intended not only as a sentiment but as the origin of ritual—in short, the code of social order.

As noted above, I have used the stories of *Monopoly* and Burning Man to describe the code economy, including both how to help us understand the code economy as it is now and how it is evolving.

Yet these two models are almost exact opposites: Atlantic City in its heyday—the inspiration for *Monopoly*—is nothing like Black Rock City, and vice versa.

Properly understood, *Monopoly* and Burning Man represent a binary pair—a Yin and a Yang of worldviews.

In *Monopoly* the winner takes all; at Burning Man there is no winner because there is no winning. In *Monopoly* the value of land increases with proximity to the water. At Burning Man ... well, it's the desert. In *Monopoly* every exchange is monetized and accumulating wealth is the goal. At Burning Man no exchange is monetized and sharing experiences is the goal.

Yet *Monopoly* and Burning Man have some things in common. Both are designed spaces in which people can learn about each other's aspirations and motivations. Both exist for a finite period of time, then repeat, following the same rules. Both have inspired the creation of ritual.

Monopoly was designed to expose the fundamentally competitive essence of human beings—our desire to own, control, and extract. Burning Man was designed to provide space for the fundamentally collaborative essence of human beings—our desire to share, give, and build together. Yet upon further examination we realize that each contains the other.

The views of human nature and of the dynamics of society that Henry George articulated in *Progress and Poverty*, the inspiration for *Monopoly*, harmonize remarkably well with that of his contemporary, Richard Jefferies, who in turn inspired Burning Man founder Larry Harvey. In the "Absence of Design in Nature," Jefferies wrote, "I say that the entire laboring population—some skilled trades excepted as not really laboring—is miserably underpaid, not because there is pressure or scarcity, a trouble, a famine, but from pure selfishness ... Thrift, economy, accumulation of wealth, are inventions. They are not nature."[9] According to Jefferies, nature is fundamentally abundant and human society is an extension of nature. Human society is in turn enriched by the productive power of people.

Humanity is selfish, and it is altruistic. The advance of code reduces individual power and autonomy while it increases individual capabilities and freedom.

three) only as the coauthor, with economist Oskar Morgenstern, of *The Theory of Games and Economic Behavior.* They have no knowledge of his role as leader of the project that developed the first digital computer. Much of today's behavioral and experimental economics traces back to fundamental insights first introduced by von Neumann and Morgenstern in that book on the theory of games.

When it comes to the specific games that convey the core point of this book, perhaps the best example—or, really, counterexample—is *The Game of Life,* which I discussed at the start of chapter 11. As I noted there, much as *Monopoly* encodes the political philosophy of Henry George, *The Game of Life* encodes a fundamental theory in economics known as the "permanent income hypothesis," which was introduced by Milton Friedman in 1957.

In reality, the premise on which the permanent income hypothesis was based began to fail almost as soon as it was encoded in *The Game of Life.* In 1966, Paul Armer, a senior scientist at the RAND Corporation, authored a report to the White House titled "Computer Aspects of Technological Change, Automation, and Economic Progress." The report was a comprehensive study of the relationship between the advance of code and the evolution of work:

> Increases in human productivity are to be expected, although the improvement will not be uniform. The overall impact of computers and technological change should result in an even higher rate of growth in productivity than the economy has enjoyed in recent years. Some types of jobs will disappear, many will change, and new ones will be created. Education, government, industry, unions, and individuals must expect and plan for continuing change, which will become an increasingly important factor in life. Many individuals will have to learn and perform two, three, or more different types of work in their lifetime, and education must be accepted as a continuing, lifelong process. This will be especially true for people in professional and technical occupations. Those who are unable to adapt to change will find life difficult.[10]

Writing fully a half-century ago, Armer observed, "It used to be that a man could go to school, take a job in a profession or in an industry, move up in the organization, and do his job well until retirement, drawing upon what he was taught in school and on what he learned through experience. In many fields, including business, this is becoming more and more difficult."[11]

Armer had an advantage in writing about the advance of code: one scientist whose research contracts he was responsible for monitoring was Herbert Simon, who has appeared frequently in the preceding pages. Having worked closely with Simon and his collaborator Allen Newell, Paul Armer had come to understand and appreciate the deeply transformative power of this new mode of creating and evolving code. He understood as clearly as anyone—even Simon himself—the challenges this transformation would pose to the people in adapting to a rapidly changing world.

Is the answer to the challenges facing workers today to offer more and better education? What would *The Game of Life,* updated to the twenty-first century, look like?

IN MOST OF this book I have focused on the "how" of production and work. But what of the "why?" After all, as John Stuart Mill and John Maynard Keynes foresaw long ago, a solid majority of people on earth today have been liberated from the Malthusian trap of a bare subsistence existence—and that fraction continues to grow rapidly, for reasons I described in my previous book, *The Coming Prosperity.*[12] In 1990, a staggeringly high 43 percent of people in the "developing world," approximately 1.9 billion people, lived in extreme poverty. By 2010 that number had fallen to 21 percent, or 1.2 billion.[13] Progress has continued since.

For the past two centuries, the vehicle for that progress has been the continual capacity of economies to generate more and better jobs. Jim Clifton, the CEO of the global polling firm Gallup, is a passionate and well-informed advocate for the need to keep that process going. "Gallup has discovered that having a good job is now the great global dream; it's the number one social value for everyone," Clifton wrote in 2011. "This is one of our most powerful findings ever. 'A good job' is more important than having a family, more compelling than democracy and freedom, religion, peace and so on . . . Stimulating job growth is the new currency of all leaders because if you don't deliver on it you will experience instability, brain drain, sometimes revolution—all of the worst outcomes of failed leadership."

This is all quite persuasive, and in accordance with the reflexes of politicians around the world. Yet, as another Gallup study released in 2013 indicates, there is more to the story. That study, titled "The State of the Global Workplace," found that only 13% of employees worldwide are "engaged" at work, while nearly twice that total (26%) are "actively disengaged." That means that twice as many people globally find their actual jobs to be alienating as find their jobs to be rewarding.

Putting these two Gallup findings together, we appear to be led to the following conclusion: What people around the world desire more than anything—"family . . . religion, peace, and so on"—is stable work that makes them miserable. When it comes to the idea conveyed by politicians almost everywhere that creating "jobs" is society's number one objective, an observer is tempted to recall the words of Inigo Montoya in the movie *The Princess Bride:* "You keep using that word. I do not think it means what you think it means."

So why are so many of the growing majority of people who have escaped the Malthusian trap dissatisfied with their jobs? What are we seeking from our work that "jobs" are, according to Gallup's results, largely failing to deliver?

According to researcher Mihaly Csikszentmihalyi, the answer is contained in one word: flow.

As used by Csikszentmihalyi, "flow" describes an experience of complete, intensely focused concentration on the present moment. To experience flow is to experience total immersion and a sense of purpose.

Think of a rock climber scaling the most challenging cliff she has ever encountered. Or a parent fully engaged in playing in a park with their two-year-old child. Or a writer at work in a cafe, when ideas that have swirled around incoherently in his brain for months suddenly seem to appear on the page, as if by their own volition. These are, according to Csikszentmihalyi, experiences of flow.[14]

To arrive at this definition, Csikszentmihalyi asked hundreds of people to do the following: reflect on an experience that made you truly happy. In that moment, he asked, were you distracted and thinking about other things, or were you intensely focused on the present moment? Did you feel at once fully in control and unselfconsciously out of control? Did time seem to slow down or speed up? Did you feel that what you were doing had a purpose?

Csikszentmihalyi's theory of flow has yet to be validated with hard, neuro-scientific evidence. Indeed, the scientific study of happiness is only in its infancy and we can say little about it with any certainty. But Csikszentmihalyi's theory has two things going for it. First, it is based on research as solid as any in the scholarly literature on happiness. Second, based on the enduring popularity of Csikszentmihalyi's work, it appears to resonate with people.

Once we start looking for flow, we find it in many places. Take spices, for example. Eating spicy food can be painful for the uninitiated and can upset digestion. Spices have little nutritional value and are expensive—indeed, for centuries spices were among the most valuable traded commodities. So why do we eat spices to begin with, much less value them as highly as we do?

Research on this topic suggests that there are at least two evolutionary reasons for humans to consume spices and to value them highly. The first is that spices seem to have a preservative effect on foods, particularly when employed in combination. Thus the evolutionary value of developing a taste for spices from this standpoint is evident: spices keep us safe.[15]

The second is very different: using spices provides us with a controlled experiment in pain and danger. Much like roller coasters and horror movies, the experience of eating spicy food challenges our body and helps us remain resilient.[16]

Evidence for this second interpretation comes from work by Paul Rozin, a professor of psychology at the University of Pennsylvania, who for more than four decades has been trying to understand why people like spicy food. In one study, Rozin compared the tolerance of a group of Mexican villagers who were accustomed to spicy food with that of a group of Americans accustomed to a relatively bland diet. After feeding each group corn snacks flavored with increasing degrees of chili powder, he asked the research subjects to rank when the taste was optimally enjoyable and when it became unbearable.

Not surprisingly, the Mexicans were more tolerant of the spicy food than the Americans. However, for both groups, a very narrow margin separated "just right" and "ouch." Rozin summarized his findings for the *Wall Street Journal:* "The hotness level they [the two groups] liked the most was just below the level of unbearable pain. So that led me to think that the pain itself was involved: They were pushing the limits, and that was part of the phenomenon."[17] Pushing the limits is an essential part of flow, and jobs are generally not designed to push the limits. A job may be "nourishing," but it is not spicy. When work is routine and without challenge, it is not only boring, it is deadening.

Iconoclastic financier turned social theorist Nicholas Taleb, author of *Fooled by Randomness* and *The Black Swan,* takes this point further, arguing that performing the same job year after year is not only boring but unhealthy: "The expression in everyday life is: The dose makes the poison. Meaning in a small dose it's good for you; in a large dose it could kill you or will kill you. We see it constantly. The discoveries about the benefits of alcohol; obviously in small doses it appears wine is good for your heart. In large doses it destroys you."[18] The same, according to Taleb, is true of risk in work. Job security comes at a price, which is the cost of adjustment when the job comes to an end—as it inevitably will. In small amounts it is beneficial. In large amounts it can be deadly.

Whatever one's preference may be a priori for a long-held secure job, the issue raised by Taleb is, what happens when that long-held secure job is lost? Strong evidence suggests that few experiences are as devastating as unemployment following a long period of stable full-time employment.[19] Simply put, the longer a person has the same job in the same environment, the less resilient he or she may be when faced with the loss of that job. Like an organism hyperadapted to a particular environment, long-time employees become unable to cope with a dramatic change in their circumstances.

Shifting metaphors, to seek security and avoid risk in one's work life is like managing a forest to avoid brush fires. The ultimate result is much more devastating than it would have been to allow a small series of brush fires—in other words, the short-term experience of unemployment or other exposure to volatility in the labor market. "The brush starts to build up—in the natural case—and then when the fire does come, it's the fire of all fires. It is incredibly destructive."[20] Unintentionally but inevitably, seeking stability ultimately invites catastrophe. Instead of occurring a little at a time, damage occurs all at once.

As Jane Jacobs observed decades ago, what holds for people and forests in this regard also holds for cities. She offers an example of the hazards of efficiency and specialization in the following description of Manchester and Birmingham in the nineteenth century: "Let us begin by examining city inefficiency from the point of view of two English manufacturing cities: Manchester and Birmingham. Back in 1844, a character in one of Disraeli's novels said 'Certainly Manchester is the most wonderful city of modern times . . . Birmingham was just the kind of city that seemed to have been outmoded by Manchester."[21] Just as mid-twentieth-century Detroit specialized in the production of cars and Akron in the production of tires, so mid-nineteenth-century Manchester specialized in the production of textiles. Then along came the American textile industry, and Manchester eventually lost its core industry while its citizens lost their once secure jobs. The result was a devastation from which it took decades to recover. "Manchester's efficient specialization [in the production of textiles] portended stagnation and a profoundly obsolescent city. For the 'immensity of its future' proved to consist of immense losses as other people in other places learned how to spin and weave cotton efficiently too."[22] In contrast, Birmingham's relatively diverse economy proved much more resilient over time. The result, according to Jacobs, was that "Birmingham's economy has remained alive."

The same balance between specialization and adaptability that we found to be a necessity for species and industries (see chapter eight) also turns out to be necessary for cities.

LIKE ALL PLATFORMS in the economy, cities are at once organic and designed, natural and artificial. Understanding how cities resolve the duality between unconscious evolution and planning gets us one step closer to understanding how the economy may have not only structure but purpose.

What economists call capital is really the accumulated artifacts that surround modern humans. Each of these artifacts encodes an intended purpose. Some of these we call infrastructure, others tools, and still others toys. Also among them are computers. Code is always operative, whether in a recipe or in the stove used to prepare it. Each in its own way encodes an idea that enables us to be producers. Thus we are surrounded by the realized imaginings of people who came before us.

As Henry George understood clearly nearly a century ago, platforms that draw people to collaborate, share, and experience together are singularly powerful vehicles for the creation of value in society. The question is now, as it was when George wrote *Progress and Poverty*, how will that value be shared?

George's solution was a single tax on land. As economist Peter Orszag has noted, an increased tax on real estate has some logic to it from an equity standpoint. Such a tax could be used to fund the institutionalization of a society-wide guaranteed minimum income—an idea generally considered entirely impractical only a few years ago that now has a growing number of adherents.

But redistribution constitutes only half of any real solution to the challenges posed by the advance of code—if that. As I have argued throughout this book, we humans are producers at least as much as we are consumers. Due to that fact, it is at least plausible to state that what we seek is not only a guaranteed minimum income but also, and perhaps more importantly, a guaranteed minimum purpose—where by "purpose" I specifically mean the opportunity to connect with others and contribute meaningfully through our work.

In the next round of digital disruption, tasks that can be automated (the "high-volume, low-price" option resulting from ongoing code-driven bifurcations to which I referred in chapter 10) will yield only small dividends for most people. The exception is the relatively small number of people who will maintain the platforms on which such tasks are performed, whose role will be comparable to that of utilities employees and other infrastructure companies in the economy of the twentieth century.

The promising pathway for inclusive well-being is humanized work (the "low-volume, high-price" pathway resulting from ongoing code-driven bifurcations to which I also referred in chapter 10). This pathway includes everything about value creation that is differentiated, personal, and human. It encompasses value created through farm-to-table restaurants, home healthcare services, peer-to-peer coaching, live performances—in short, every task in which there is a human advantage. It will be more about shared experiences then impersonal services. If organized on a distributed, immutable, reputation-rich platform such as the Blockchain, there is every reason to believe that this pathway can provide a broad majority of the population with both guaranteed minimum income and guaranteed minimum purpose.

For such activities to reliably create opportunity for people in the future, three conditions must hold:

- There must be no limit to the potential creation and cocreation of discernibly new experiences.
- There always must be some cost to fully automating new experiences.
- It must be easier to create new computers than to create new people.

Combining these conditions allows work to bifurcate endlessly and new processes (which is to say, new work) to persistently earn a profit consistent with a living wage.

The transition to the digital economy is, above all, defined by a shift from the "what" of human productive activity to its "how" and "why." Many if not most of the greatest opportunities for new work enabled by the advance of digitally enabled code will likely be those most distant from digitally enabled code (see Text Box 14.2).

Jobs that consist of unchanging roles in fixed algorithms within large corporations are disappearing. By economic default as well as by human choice, the future economy is overwhelmingly likely to be dominated not by work that consists of performing routinized tasks but by the capacity to continuously improvise new forms of value—creating for others at the same time we grow our own capacities, and finding new recipes along the way.

Whereas both the classical and neoclassical schools of economics have, for over two centuries, focused on consumption and material scarcity, the actual economy is increasingly driven by production and algorithmic abundance. Why? We human beings do not create only in order to consume. We also create in order to see our potential realized in the world. We create in order to share and connect with others. The history of code is thus also the history of humanity's cumulative progress in advancing our collective capacity to create.

It turns out that the primary question facing human societies in the face of digital disruption is not whether opportunities for meaningful work will exist in the future. It is not even how such opportunities for meaningful work will be compensated. The question is more fundamental: It is about the nature of human productive activity and how we value what we create and share. In other words, it is about what it means to be human.

CONCLUSION

Identity

A Copernican Moment

At rest, however, in the middle of everything is the sun.

Nicolaus Copernicus, *De revolutionibus orbium coelestium*, 1543

NEANDERTHALS HAD BIGGER brains than *Homo sapiens,* but the two species were related closely enough that they interbred during the several thousand years that they coexisted during modern-day Europe's Upper Paleolithic Era.[1] As a result, about 1 percent of the DNA of every living human today derives from our Neanderthal forebears, rather than from our direct *Homo sapiens* ancestors. From recent sequencing of the Neanderthal genome, we know that Neanderthals had the FOX2 gene, which is associated with language ability, notably including a particular code sequence they uniquely shared with *Homo sapiens.*[2] Yet despite their evolutionary proximity and the advantage of a larger brain, Neanderthals became extinct roughly 40,000 years ago, probably at least in part due to competition with *Homo sapiens.*

Something other than brain size alone seems to have conferred an advantage on our *Homo sapiens* ancestors. So what was it?

"Perhaps the most interesting thing about [the Neanderthals] is not what they were but what they failed to become," observes biologist E. O. Wilson, whose work I cited in chapter one. "Virtually no progress occurred in their technology or culture during their two hundred millennia of existence. No tinkering with tool manufacture, no art, and no personal decoration—at least none exists in the archaeological evidence we have so far."[3] In contrast, during the exact interval in which Neanderthal and *Homo sapiens* overlapped, our direct ancestors proved themselves to be irrepressible tinkerers.

"What catapulted *Homo sapiens* to this level?" Wilson asks, referring to the birth of code during the Late Paleolithic era, as evidenced by advanced techniques for producing obsidian axes and spear tips, as well as elegant representational cave art, the corralling of animals using controlled burns, and the development of complex social rituals indicated by the advent of costumed shamans. "Experts on the subject agree that increased long-term memory, especially that put into working memory, and with it an ability to construct scenarios and plan strategy in brief periods of time, played the key role in Europe and elsewhere."[4] Humans were dramatically better than Neanderthals at creating, storing, modifying, and, importantly, sharing code.

Shifting to the present tense, Wilson sums up the human advantage: "Humans, it appears, are successful not because of an elevated general intelligence that addresses all challenges but because they are born to be specialists in social skills. By cooperating through the communication and the reading of intention, groups accomplish far more than the effort of any one solitary person."

In the introduction to this book I suggested that the answer to the question, "Is there anything humans can do better than digital computers?" turns out to be fairly simple: humans are better at being human. What does this mean? To be human is to think critically. To collaborate. To communicate. To be creative. What we call "the economy" is one extension of these activities. It is the domain in which we develop and advance code.

While focused on the essential qualities that have differentiated the human species over the long term, E. O. Wilson's observations are valuable not only in helping us understand our distant past, but also in putting into context our present and immediate future. Consider, for example, the current emphasis among educators on the importance of developing competency in the "4 C's" that are argued to define twenty-first-century skills: critical thinking, communication, collaboration, and creativity. These skills are precisely the same ones that E. O. Wilson argues were essential for the success of *Homo sapiens* in our contest with the Neanderthals.

"Political Economy or Economics is a study of mankind in the ordinary business of life; it examines that part of individual and social action which is most closely connected with the attainment and with the use of the material requisites of wellbeing," Alfred Marshall writes at the start of his 1910 masterwork, *Principles of Economics,* stating the premise that would become the theoretical cornerstone of neoclassical economic theory. But then he goes on to say, "Thus [political economy] is on the one side a study of wealth; and on the other, and more important side, a part of the study of man. For man's character has been moulded by his every-day work, and the material resources which he thereby procures, more than by any other influence unless it be that of his religious ideals."[5]

It is an axiom of the human condition, clearly understood by Alfred Marshall, that we are shaped at least as much by what we create and share in the world—"our every-day work"—as we are by what we consume.

It is for this very reason that the continued advance of code is of such fundamental importance. As Herbert Simon observed in 1965, the year I was born, "The developing capacity of computers to simulate man . . . will change man's conception of his own identity as a species."[6] A wave of change that Simon was able to see coming from afar a half-century ago has traversed the open ocean of history and hit human societies with force.

How will we respond? Simon's own answer is indicated in his belief in the human spirit: "I am confident that man will, as he has in the past, find a new way of describing his place in the universe—a way that will satisfy his needs for dignity and for purpose . . . But it will be a way as different from the present one as was the Copernican from the Ptolemaic."[7] A previous human generation had to contend with the realization that our planet does not reside at the center of the solar system, much less the universe—the shift from the Ptolemaic to the Copernican worldview to which Simon refers. Generations alive today must contend with a parallel concern: We are not at the center of our cognitive universe. Our own creations are eclipsing us.

For each of us, redefining work requires nothing less than redefining identity. This is because production is not something human beings do just to consume. In fact, the opposite is true. We are living beings. We consume in order to produce. Production is our purpose.

The chains Rousseau referred to constrain us, but they also connect us. They are made of code. Forty-thousand years of human history shaped those bonds. They will not soon slip away.

ACKNOWLEDGMENTS

On Tuesday, February 19, 2013, I met Scott Parris, then a senior economics editor at Cambridge University Press, for lunch at the Arte Café in Manhattan's Upper West Side. I had been connected to Scott via a colleague of his and a former editor of mine, John Berger. Over lunch I described to Scott an idea I had for a short monograph in which I would develop some of my longstanding work on production recipes—the "how" of production in economics, as opposed to the "what"—in the context of broader ideas of the evolution of the economy. Scott was interested in the idea, but encouraged me to develop the concept for the book further, with a focus on the application of these evolutionary themes to current trends in the economy.

A few weeks later I received an invitation from Vint Cerf and David Nordfors to participate in the first Innovation for Jobs (I4J) Summit. The agenda for the Summit, which took place at SRI International in Silicon Valley, stated: "Information technology is the new industrial revolution. As the world continues to move ever faster into the innovation economy, economies are struggling with adapting labor markets. Jobs are evolving faster than educational and employment systems can adapt. Economies now need innovation for jobs, not innovation or jobs." The topic resonated with me immediately. I had opened my prior book, *The Coming Prosperity*, with an anecdote about Norbert

Wiener, the father of robotics, highlighting his anticipation of current concerns over robots displacing human workers. That was only a beginning. I was eager to explore the topic further.

Soon thereafter I received a second invitation, this one from my former collaborator, José Lobo, to join a meeting that he and his colleague Deborah Strumsky were organizing that summer at the Santa Fe Institute. The meeting, titled "Getting Inside the Black Box: Technological Evolution and Economic Growth," was focusing on themes that José and I had first begun exploring at the Santa Fe Institute (SFI) exactly 20 years earlier as SFI summer school students, first with the evolutionary biologist Stuart Kauffman, and later with the macroeconomist and economic theorist Karl Shell: the microeconomic structure of production as an evolutionary process.

With Scott Parris' prompt in mind and these two gatherings providing ample opportunities to test and share initial ideals, I began to consider how a better understanding of the "how" of production could be a contribution to the literature on the disruption of work due to the advance of digital technologies—already rapidly growing at that time. When Scott fortuitously moved to Oxford University Press, my able agent, Jessica Papin, was able to conclude a contract, and I began work on this book.

To a greater extent than any previous writing project of mine, this book has been shaped by input I received over the nearly two years during which I was working actively on the manuscript. That process began with input from Scott and Jessica, to whom I am deeply grateful. I also must thank three anonymous referees, whose thoughtful consideration of an early version of the manuscript enabled considerable further development.

In addition to the anonymous reviewers, a few people read the book carefully and offered detailed feedback. Among them, I have to acknowledge in particular Dane Stangler and Steve Bunney, who went above and beyond what any author might ask of an early reader, offering substantive input that helped shape the book. Robert Axtell, Lokesh Dani, Bethany Edwards, Jane Hegeler, Amisha Miller, Lesa Mitchell, Dwight Read, Jim Spohrer, and John Zysman similarly offered invaluable comments at various stages. Nadine Romero contributed much of the research supporting the section on Sumerian writing with which I opened chapter 4.

I will not undertake to single out particular individuals among the participants in the SFI "Getting Inside the Black Box" meeting in August 2013 or members in the I4J network, beyond those I have specifically named in the book. Suffice it to say that I owe a great deal to both the SFI and I4J communities. Many of us are seeing, and seeking to communicate, similar trends and ideas. Yet at the same time, we come to our discussions with distinct perspectives. The interactions over the past three years have been very rich. Published work by I4J members Robin Chase and John Clippinger, as well as by James Bessen, Nicholas Bloom, Erik Brynjolfsson and Adrew McAfee, Tyler Cowen, Ricardo Hausmann, Paul Romer, and Sidney Winter, have been particularly significant inspirations.

I owe a special debt of gratitude to another dynamic intellectual community to which I have the privilege of belonging: the Kauffman Foundation in Kansas City. I have benefited enormously from the interactions that my role as an advisor to the Foundation have afforded me during the time I have worked on this book. In this context I again thank Dane Stangler and Amisha Miller, as well as Alex Krause, Arnobio Morellix, Yasuyuki Motoyama, Derek Ozkal, and Jonathan Robinson.

I further thank Bob Litan and Bo Cutter for inviting me to offer initial presentations on the book to audiences at the Council on Foreign Relations and the Roosevelt Institute, respectively. The insights of participants at those events helped me bring my work on the book to a close.

In the last phase of the project, Dody Riggs performed her customary editorial magic on the manuscript. Dody has been a valued contributor in so many aspects of my work that I am delighted to have the opportunity to thank her here for her unfailing professionalism and her wonderful spirit.

Additionally, I would like to acknowledge Lissa Muscatine and Bradley Graham, the co-owners of Politics & Prose bookstore, where I composed a significant fraction of the text in this book. Our communities are greatly enriched by "third places," including independent bookstores and coffeehouses, and Politics & Prose is an exceptional example of both.

Along similar lines I must thank my Dream Society campmates at Burning Man for having welcomed me into their community, and Cori Lathan, for her initial invitation.

Finally, I must thank my three daughters, Cecelia, Helena, and Isabel, and my wife, Katje, for their patience as I immersed myself in the writing of this book. The incursion of purchased books and printed papers into every space in our home may not have come to an end permanently with the conclusion of this project. I do pledge a pause in the onslaught, however . . . at least until I start the next book.

NOTES

Introduction

1. These correspond to the modes that Kahneman, 2011, refers to as "thinking fast" and "thinking slow."

2. The word "logic" also derives from *logos,* which in turn derives from *legō* (λέγω), meaning "to count, tell, say, speak"—an interesting coincidence with the name of the children's toy to which I allude later in my discussion of the combinatorial nature of technological evolution.

3. It did so by breaking starch molecules into digestible fragments and denaturing proteins so that digestive enzymes could go to work on them. Wrangham, 2009.

4. Zink and Lieberman, 2016, p. 1: "The origins of the genus Homo are murky, but by H. erectus, bigger brains and bodies had evolved that, along with larger foraging ranges, would have increased the daily energetic requirements of hominins. Yet H. erectus differs from earlier hominins in having relatively smaller teeth, reduced chewing muscles, weaker maximum bite force capabilities, and a relatively smaller gut. This paradoxical combination of increased energy demands along with decreased masticatory and digestive capacities is hypothesized to have been made possible by adding meat to the diet, by mechanically processing food using stone tools or by cooking. Cooking, however, was apparently uncommon until 500,000 years ago, and the effects of carnivory and Palaeolithic processing techniques on mastication are unknown. We find that . . . although cooking has important benefits, it appears that selection for smaller masticatory features in Homo would have been initially made possible by the combination of using stone tools and eating meat."

5. Rifkin, 1995, p. xvi.
6. Rifkin, 1995, p. 106.
7. Kurzweil, 2006, p. 371.
8. Kurzweil, 2006, p. 20.
9. Cowen, 2013; Frey and Osborne, 2013; Brynjolfsson and McAfee, 2014.
10. The best recent work in economics has expanded understanding of human decision-making in a social context, primarily in the context of consumer choice. This includes Kahneman, 2013, and other works of "behavioral economics." Separately, default practices in the measurement of human well-being have for decades focused on consumption metrics; a notable exception is Sen, 1985, 1999, who received the Bank of Sweden Prize in Honor of Alfred Nobel (generally known as the Nobel Prize in Economics) for his work emphasizing the realization of freedoms and the expansion of capabilities as the goals of human development, rather than consumption for its own sake.

Chapter 1

1. "Artifact" is word that originated in the early nineteenth century as a combination of the Latin words *arte,* "by or using art," and *factum,* "something made." By "artifact" I mean a physical manifestation of a production process. An artifact is analogous to a phenotype in biology, where the code that created the artifact corresponds to DNA.
2. Read (2008); Read and van der Leeuw, 2015, pp. 33–38.
3. Wilson, 2012, p. 92, describes the process: "Axes and adzes invented in the Neolithic were made by a series of steps. Each blade was first flaked out to the right shape from a block of fine-grained rock. Then it was shaped more finely by chipping out progressively smaller flakes. Lastly, rough spots on the surface were removed by precise chisel work or grinding. The final product was a blade with a smooth surface, sharp-edged, and flattened or rounded to the form needed."
4. Wilson, 2012, p. 91. Wilson refers to this phenomenon more broadly as the discovery of eusocial behavior. The word "eusocial" is a combination of the Greek prefix "eu," which signifies "good/real" and the word "social." Eusociality thus refers to the highest level of insect or animal social behavior, involving cooperation and collaboration. Following Wilson, I say humans "discovered" rather than "invented" eusocial behavior because it characterizes ants and other social insects as well as humans, and other social mammals, such as the naked mole rat. Wilson situates the date far earlier in human history than I do here. I choose 50,000 years because my focus is on the economy. It is clear that an epochal change in society occurred roughly 10,000 years BCE, when humans invented agriculture in six parts of the world simultaneously. The fact of this simultaneity directly suggests the advance of code represented by the invention of agriculture was part of a forward movement of code that started much earlier.

5. Bessen, 2015, p. 41.
6. Read (2008); Read and van der Leeuw, 2015, pp. 33–28.
7. Read and van der Leeuw, 2008.
8. Wilson, 2012, p. 226, states: "The primary and crucial difference between human cognition and that of other animal species, including our closest genetic relatives, the chimpanzees, is the ability to collaborate for the purpose of achieving shared goals and intentions. The human specialty is intentionality, fashioned from an extremely large working memory. We have become the experts at mind reading, and the world champions at inventing culture. We not only interact intensely with one another, as do other animals with advanced social organizations, but to a unique degree we have added the urge to collaborate."
9. Wilson, 2012, p. 91.
10. Sander van der Leeuw, personal communication.
11. Aristotle, in *Politics* (book I, part II), characterizes the origin of villages as arising from the union of multiple households: "The family is the association established by nature for the supply of men's everyday wants, and the members of it are called by Charondas 'companions of the cupboard,' and by Epimenides the Cretan, 'companions of the manger.' But when several families are united, and the association aims at something more than the supply of daily needs, the first society to be formed is the village."
12. Hobbes, 1689.
13. From *Documents Relating to the Revels at Court in The Time of King Edward VI and Queen Mary* (the Loseley manuscripts). Accessible at https://archive.org/stream/documentsrelatin00greauoft#page/n5/mode/2up.
14. Hofstadter, 1955, offers a critical perspective on Spencer's legacy, of which *The Stanford Encyclopedia of Philosophy* offers the following assessment: "Richard Hofstadter (1955) devoted an entire chapter of *Social Darwinism in American Thought* to Spencer, arguing that Spencer's unfortunate vogue in late nineteenth-century America inspired Andrew Carnegie and William Graham Sumner's visions of unbridled and unrepentant capitalism. For Hofstadter, Spencer was an 'ultra-conservative' for whom the poor were so much unfit detritus. His social philosophy 'walked hand in hand' with reaction, making it little more than a 'biological apology for laissez-faire' (Hofstadter, 1955: 41 and 46). But just because Carnegie interpreted Spencer's social theory as justifying merciless economic competition, we shouldn't automatically attribute such justificatory ambitions to Spencer. Otherwise, we risk uncritically reading the fact that Spencer happened to influence popularizers of social Darwinism into our interpretation of him." Accessible at http://plato.stanford.edu/entries/spencer/.
15. Schumpeter, 1954, p. 258.
16. Statutes of the Realm, 1810, pp. i, 307. Additionally, the Ordinance stipulated that "all victuallers [sellers of food] must sell their wares for 'reasonable' prices."

17. The early history of the production of watches in Switzerland, to which I'll allude in chapter 10, provides one example of the shift from self-contained workshops to complex supply chains constructed around highly specialized tasks. See also Auerswald, 2012, ch. 8.
18. Smith, 1776.
19. Hamilton, 1791.
20. Glaeser, 2011.
21. Wilson, 2012.
22. This observation is an extension of the ideas first introduced into economics by Sen, 1985.

Chapter 2

1. Steinkeller and Postgate, 1992, and Steinkeller, 2002.
2. Viscato, 2000.
3. The number of Sumerian symbols decreased over the millennia as well. In the early third millennium BCE, Sumerian writing included twelve hundred pictograms. By the end of the second millennium BCE, Mesopotamians had reduced the number of economic symbols in use to only six hundred by establishing language rules and clustering signs into various spatial orders.
4. Literary epics appeared by 2220 BCE, and by 1700 BCE literature had become more commonplace and abundant. Encoding with cuneiform symbols grew from simple pictograms into 8,000-line "creation myths."
5. Knuth, 1972.
6. Bauer, Englund, and Krebernick, 1998, p. 3.
7. A woman with an undergraduate degree in general studies operating in a world dominated entirely by male professors and businessmen, Jacobs was derided by those she criticized as a "housewife" and a "crazy dame." Gratz, 2011.
8. Jacobs, 1969.
9. Jacobs, 1969.
10. Jacobs, 1969.
11. Lobo is a coauthor on my own earliest papers related to production recipes.
12. Bettencourt et al., 2007.
13. Kleiber, 1932.
14. Bettencourt et al., 2007.
15. Whitehead, 1911, p. 61.
16. Gleick, 2011, p. 47.
17. Gleick, 2011, p. 48.
18. Gleick, 2011, p. 50.

Chapter 3

1. Samuel Rolle thinks "the burning of London, by means of that obscure lane, was like the killing of that great Giant Goliath by a pebble stone flung from

the sling and arm of little David." From "A True and Faithful Account of the Several Informations Exhibited to the Honorable Committee Appointed by the Parliament to Inquire into the Late Dreadful Burning of the City of London, 1667," pp. 7–8, quoted in Rietveld, 2012, Kindle Locations 424–427.

2. Beely, 2003.
3. Leibniz, 1666.
4. Grattan-Guinness, 1990, pp. 177–178.
5. Grattan-Guinness, 1990, p. 179.
6. Simon, 1965, p. 2, observes: "If computers, regarded as factors of production, are to be classified with capital, they are capital with a difference." He continues, "To be sure, there are precursors, such as the Jacquard loom, which was as truly programmed as the most modern solid state machine. But the software component is so prominent in comparison with anything that went before that we must treat the difference as having qualitative significance." Simon's comment not only articulates a fundamental distinction between computer code and what is conventionally considered "capital," but also, with his reference to the Jacquard loom, helps us to map the advance of code.
7. The first exhibition was held in 1798. The official title was "L'Exposition publique des produits de l'industrie française." Danvers, 1867, pp. 488–499.
8. Stanford, 1912.
9. Quoted in Rodgers, 1974, p. 53; cited in Saval, 2014, p. 47.
10. Taylor, 1911, p. 64.
11. Saval, 2014, p. 59.
12. Saval, 2014, p. 60.
13. Essinger, 2004, p. 19.
14. By some accounts, by the time the Luddites were following their Lyonnaise counterparts in smashing mechanized looms in Nottinghamshire, over 10,000 Jacquard looms were operating in France. See also chapter five.
15. The influence of the Jacquard loom extends directly into the digital age: the father of renowned mathematician John von Neumann brought home punch cards from Jacquard looms, which he had inspected in the course of his work. Dyson, 2012, p. 61.
16. See http://www.computerhistory.org/babbage/charlesbabbage/.
17. Simon, 1978.
18. The Difference Engine also inspired the 1990 novel by William Gibson and Bruce Sterling with the same name, which is credited with having established the steampunk genre.
19. From Burroughs, 1910, p. 25: "For several years Babbage labored incessantly in the work-shops which he had built in the grounds of his home near London, but from the first the most stupendous obstacles were met, and the work came to a halt in 1833 with the engine only half completed. Over £17,000 of government money had now been spent,

and, so Babbage claimed, nearly as much more from his own private resources. He went to Lord Derby, who had succeeded Peel as Premier, and proposed that a new appropriation be made to proceed with his work. Derby took the matter up with Disraeli, then chancellor of the Exchequer, but the novelist-statesman pooh-poohed the idea, saying that since so much money had been spent with no apparent result, it was impossible to see the end of the possible expenditure, and, in short, 'turned it down flat.' Babbage's means had all gone into his invention and the net result of the whole business was the half-finished engine of differences, which the government offered to present to Babbage, but which he refused. It was then turned over to the Museum of King's College, where it still remains, a ponderous mass of mechanism as big as a barrel, mutely testifying to the first real step in the development of the practical calculating machine."

20. Simon, 1991, p. 206.
21. Simon, 1991, pp. 206–207.
22. A century later, in 1950, Turing generalized of this principle as the Turing Test for artificial intelligence.

Chapter 4

1. Taub, 2003, from the review of this book by Hine, 2005: "'Meteorology,' like the names of various other branches of knowledge, has changed its meaning since antiquity. To modern ears it indicates primarily weather forecasting, or more widely the study of weather and climate, but Greek *meteorologia* (the study of the things above) embraced not only what we call meteorological or atmospheric phenomena, but also certain astronomical phenomena, including comets and shooting stars (hence our use of 'meteor' and 'meteorite'), and terrestrial phenomena such as rivers, seas, and earthquakes, which were thought to have causes similar to those of the other meteorological phenomena. This meteorologia was normally the province of philosophers and technical writers. But there was also a tradition of weather-forecasting lore, of which our earliest representative is Hesiod, and which for the most part was preserved by different writers from those who dealt with meteorologia."
2. Knuth, 1972.
3. Halloran, 2006.
4. Taub, 2003.
5. Richardson, 1922, p. vii.
6. Richardson, 1922, p. 219.
7. Richardson, 1922, p. 219. For context, see Lynch, 2008.
8. Turing, 1950, p. 436.
9. Turing, 1950, p. 426.
10. Dyson, 2012, p. 69.
11. As Dyson, 2012, pp. 69–70, reports in his comprehensive history of the origins of digital computing, "A human computer working with a

desk calculator took about twelve hours to calculate a single [ballistic] trajectory . . . To compete a single firing table required about a month of uninterrupted work."

12. Dyson, 2012, p. 70.
13. Goldstine did not know that von Neumann was part of another secret military team that was working in the New Mexico desert on the design of the atomic bomb.
14. Platzman, 1979, p. 308.
15. Dyson, 2012, p. 75.
16. Dyson, 2012, p. 167.
17. Dyson, 2012, p. 167; Charney, 1955, p. 800.
18. By 1958, numerical forecasts were running neck-and-neck with manual ones, and by 1960 they had pulled ahead. Dyson, 2012, p. 169.
19. Dyson, 2012, p. 3.
20. With a byte it is possible to specify a character in the American Standard Code for Information Interchange (ACSII) character set, with one bit to spare. Other commonly used measures of quantities of data are all defined in terms of the byte: a kilobyte (KB) is one thousand bytes; a megabyte (MB) is one million bytes; a gigabyte (GB) is one billion bytes; a terabyte (TB) is one trillion bytes; a petabyte (PB) is one quadrillion bytes.
21. Indeed, the entire chocolate chip cookie recipe in chapter 1 of this book can be encoded in the following precise binary sequence comprising 404 bits:

    OIOOIOOI OIOOIIIO OIOOOIII OIOIOOIO OIOOOIOI OIOOOIOO OIOOIOOI
    OIOOOIOI OIOOIIIO OIOIOIOO OIOIOOII OOOOIOIO OOOOIOIO OOIIOOIO
    OOIOOOOO OOIIOOOI OOIOIIII OOIIOIOO OOIOOOOO OIIOOOII OIIIOIOI
    OIIIOOOO OIIIOOII OOIOOOOO OIIOOOOI OIIOIIOO OIIOIIOO OOIOIIOI
    OIIIOOOO OIIIOIOI OIIIOOIO OIIIOOOO OIIOIIII OIIIOOII OIIOOIOI
    OOIOOOOO OIIOOIIO OIIOIIOO OIIOIIII OIIIOIOI OIIIOOIO OOOOIOIO
    OOIIOOOI OOIOOOOO OIIIOIOO

    If you "google" "binary to text decoder," you will find a tool that enables you to recover the Toll House recipe written in the English language from this sequence of 0s and 1s.

22. Moore, 1965.
23. Grace, 2013, p. i.
24. A 2013 article by Dylan McClain in the *New York Times* reads as follows: "A high-profile player has been caught up in the growing number of cheating scandals. The player, Jens Kotainy, a German international master, was disqualified at the Sparkassen Chess Meeting's open section before the last round this month after tournament officials questioned how he was using his cellphone . . . The tournament's director, Christian Goldschmidt, said in a note posted online that when he asked to see the cellphone, Kotainy pulled it out of his pocket and said it was turned off, as required by the rules. But Goldschmidt said that while he was holding it, the phone started

giving off vibrations that resembled Morse code . . . Goldschmidt had been suspicious of Kotainy because several experts—including Kenneth W. Regan, a computer science professor in Buffalo who is working on a program to detect cheating—found that Kotainy's moves had matched the choices of a leading computer program almost exactly."

Chapter 5

1. See Kelly, 2015.
2. R.U.R. stands for *Rosumovi Univerzální Roboti* (Rossum's Universal Robots). Also notable is *Player Piano,* the first novel by author Kurt Vonnegut, published in 1952.
3. Hanson, 2016, offers a research-based imagining of a world in which human-emulating robots have taken over most work, intriguingly written from the standpoint of the "artificial aliens" to which Kevin Kelly refers.
4. Andreessen, 2011.
5. This story is a later account by Ricardo's brother.
6. This was the first of many instances in which Ricardo argued as a matter of principle for a position that was adverse to his own self-interest. Sraffa, 1951, p. 13, cited in King, 2013.
7. Ricardo, 1821, para. 5.9: "Capital is that part of the wealth of a country which is employed in production, and consists of food, clothing, tools, raw materials, machinery, &c. necessary to give effect to labour."
8. Ricardo, 1821, para. 5.1: "The natural price of labour is that price which is necessary to enable the labourers, one with another, to subsist and to perpetuate their race, without either increase or diminution." Accessible at http://www.econlib.org/library/Ricardo/ricP2.html#Ch.5,%20Of%20 Wages.
9. As Adam Smith wrote in *The Wealth of Nations* (book I, chapter 8, paragraph 38):

> In civilized society it is only among the inferior ranks of people that the scantiness of subsistence can set limits to the further multiplication of the human species . . . by destroying a great part of the children which their fruitful marriages produce. The liberal reward of labour, by enabling them to provide better for their children, and consequently to bring up a greater number, naturally tends to widen and extend those limits . . . The liberal reward of labour, therefore, as it is the effect of increasing wealth, so it is the cause of increasing population. To complain of it, is to lament over the necessary effect and cause of the greatest public prosperity.

10. David Ricardo wrote similarly in *On the Principles of Political Economy and Taxation:*

> It is when the market price of labour exceeds its natural price, that the condition of the labourer is flourishing and happy, that he has

it in his power to command a greater proportion of the necessaries and enjoyments of life, and therefore to rear a healthy and numerous family. When, however, by the encouragement which high wages give to the increase of population, the number of labourers is increased, wages again fall to their natural price, and indeed from a re-action sometimes fall below it. (pp. 5–6)

11. The legislation instituting the Poor Laws includes the following passage summarizing the wage fund theory:

    What number of persons can be employed in labour must depend absolutely upon the amount of the funds which alone are applicable to the maintenance of labour. In whatever way these funds may be applied or expended, the quantity of labour maintained by them, in the first instance, would be very nearly the same ... Whatever portion is applied, under the provisions of the law, would have been applied to some other object, had the money been left to the distribution of the original owner; whoever therefore is maintained by the law as a labouring pauper, is maintained only instead of some other individual, who would otherwise have earned by his own industry, the money bestowed on the pauper.

12. Ricardo, 1821, chap. 5, para. 5.9.
13. Nicholas and Steckel, 1991.
14. Barton, 1817, p. 24: "A rise of wages then does not always increase population; I question whether of itself it ever does so—For every rise of wages tends to decrease the effectual demand for labour,—it induces the manufacturer and the farmer to lessen their circulating and enlarge their fixed capitals.—Suppose that by a general agreement among farmers the rate of agricultural wages were raised from 12 shillings to 24 shillings per week;—I cannot imagine any circumstance calculated more effectually to discourage marriage. For it would immediately become a most important object to cultivate with as few hands as possible; wherever the use of machinery, or the employment of horses could be substituted for manual labour, it would be done; and a considerable proportion of the existing labourers would be thrown out of work. If, indeed, a young man could step at once into a place, with 24s. per week, he would marry without scruple: but the probability is that the older labourers would obtain a preference in finding employment, and that the younger ones would be unable to earn any wages at all."
15. Barton, 1817, pp. 17–18: "Let us then enquire why a given increase in wealth does not always create an equal demand for labor ... It is the proportion which the wages of labor at any particular point in time bear to the whole produce of that labour, which appears to me to determine the appropriation of capital in one way or the other ... Dr. Smith's opinion that the rate of profit is measured by the greatness of the national wealth, may perhaps

be thus reconciled with Mr. Ricardo's doctrine that profit is exclusively regulated by wages. Of the annual savings of the community, while the value of money remains unaltered, the greater part is added to the fixed capital, but a certain portion goes to increase circulating capital, which portion of course augments the demand for labour, and raises wages. Now an extension of the demand for labour can not produce an enlargement of the supply for at least fifteen or sixteen years. During the whole of that period wages must necessarily stand above their former level, and a new generation growing up in the mean time, habituated to such improvement of circumstances, the advanced price of labour comes to be regarded by this new race of workmen as indispensable. Thus the accumulation of capital depresses profits by raising wages." See also discussion in Schumpeter, 1954, pp. 650–655.

16. Ricardo, 1821.
17. Ricardo, 1821.
18. George, 1868.
19. George, 1904, p. 210. See also George, 1898, p. 163.
20. George, 1879, p. 114. As an anonymous reviewer of this book brought to my attention, the idea that population density can lead to prosperity goes back further in economics. In a work completed in 1676 and published posthumously in 1690, William Petty responded to the economic dominance at the time of Holland—where population was concentrated in a small area—by suggesting that the pathway to prosperity for England lay in mass population relocation to cities from outlying areas. Petty, 1676.
21. George, 1879.
22. George, 1879, p. 191.
23. Tabarrok, 2003.
24. Summers, 2014.
25. Douglas, 1926.
26. Bradsherjan, 2013.
27. Kauffman, 1993.
28. The intuition of constant returns to scale is straightforward. Suppose you have a factory that employs 100 people using 10 machines, which together produce 500 widgets per day. It stands to reason that one should be able to construct a second factory, also employing 100 people and 10 machines that also would produce 500 widgets. The combined production output of the 200 people and 20 machines would be 1,000 widgets. Doubling all inputs leads to a doubling of output—the definition of "constant returns to scale." Extending this logic of "replication" of an existing economic activity to the entire economy, it follows naturally that an aggregate production function should exhibit constant returns to scale. The assumptions that underlie a constant returns to scale production function fit relatively well with the characteristics of the manufacturing economy in the United States during the years 1899–1922: many small manufacturing firms had more or

less been using the same technologies and were producing similar products. The companies competed with each another on the basis of price, thereby keeping any one of them from cornering their respective markets.

29. Simon and Newell, 1958, p. 3.

30. Simon, 1950, p. 4, cited in Simon, 1991, pp. 198–199.

31. The circumstances were as follows: Lord Byron and Anne Isabelle Milbanke, the parents of Ada Lovelace, were married on January 2, 1815. Ada was born eleven months later, on December 10, 1815. She was the only child of Byron's to be born in wedlock. As Essinger, 2004, recounts: "Ada was only a few weeks old when Annabella, sick of Byron's unstable moods, debts, and infidelities, took the child and fled from her husband's London house in the middle of the night" (p. 124). On April 25, 1816, Byron went abroad. He never returned to England, dying of swamp fever at Missolonghi, Greece, on April 19, 1824. Apparently determined that Ada not develop her father's poetic inclinations, Lady Byron, Ada's mother, insisted that her daughter focus her studies on mathematics, which Ada did throughout her youth.

Chapter 6

1. A fundamental difference exists between machine learning and the aspirations of the early proponents of artificial intelligence. Early AI aspired to create programs that mimic processes of human reasoning, and even creativity, which Herbert Simon termed "heuristic programs." Simon, 1960, offers a definition: "Computer programs that handle non-numerical tasks, use humanoid problem-solving techniques, and sometimes include learning process, are called 'heuristic programs.'" Such programs "do not merely substitute machine brute force for human cunning. Increasingly they imitate—and in some cases improve upon—human cunning." In contrast, machine learning is precisely about harnessing what Simon somewhat derisively termed "machine brute force" to arrive at "learned" solutions.

2. Valiant later recalled: "The main problem, as I saw it, was to specify what needs to be achieved if a learning algorithm is to be declared effective. It was clear that this definition would need to be quantitative if it was to mean anything, since with infinite data and computation there is no real problem. Existing statistical notions, such as Bayesian inference, did not seem enough because they did not distinguish quantitatively between what is learnable in practice and what is not." Hoffmann, 2011, p. 128.

3. Rothkopf, 2015.

4. Levitt, 2015. Accessible at https://www.youtube.com/watch?v=r5jATFtKtI8.

5. Simon, 1978.

6. Simon, 1978.

7. Simon, 1978.

8. Simon, 1978.

9. Early in his career, Jevons also formulated a view of human nature that would govern his later theoretical work and prove influential in the field

of economics: "I regard man in reality as essentially selfish, that is as doing everything with a view to gain enjoyment or avoid pain." Peart, 1996, p. 3. For Jevons, as for most economists since, work was to be endured only for the income it provided. There was no inherent joy or value in the process of being productive. Consequently, human decision-making in a market economy was reduced to balancing the need to endure pain in order to earn an income against the desire to avoid work in order to seek enjoyment.

10. Jevons, 1866.
11. A song popular in the city prior to abolition expressed the general sentiment:

If the slave trade had gone, there's an end to our lives,
Beggars all we must be, children and wives,
No ships from our ports, their proud sails e'er would spread,
And our streets grown with grass, where the cows might be.

Lamb and Smallpage, 1935, p. 34.

12. Jevons, 1870, p 125.
13. Jevons, 1870, p. 123.
14. Peart, 1996, p. 147.
15. Jevons, 1870, p. 148, emphasis in original.
16. Jevons, 1870, p. 134.
17. For publication it was retitled "Reliable Circuits Using Less Reliable Relays."
18. Gleick, 2011, p. 222.
19. Gleick, 2011, p. 299.
20. Marshall, 1910.
21. Schumpeter, 1912, famously wrote, "The carrying out of new combinations we call 'enterprise' [and] the individuals whose function it is to carry them out we call 'entrepreneurs.'" Chisholm, 2015, offers a practical implementation of this idea.
22. Other important contributions in this domain include Roy Radner on firms as information processors; Richard Nelson and Sidney Winter on evolutionary economics; Oliver Williamson on the theory of the firm; and Tom Schelling on non-cooperative games. Daniel Kahneman and Amos Tversky also focus on information acquisition and processing, although in a different direction.

Chapter 7
1. Child and Prud'homme, 2006, p. 19.
2. Child and Prud'homme, 2006, p. 89.
3. Frost, 1923, "The Road Not Taken."
4. See http://www.handsomeatlas.com/us-census-statistical-atlas-1870.

5. Walker begins by conjecturing the existence of exactly the world neoclassical production theory posits as the default: one where a large number of employers of identical ability compete against one another in overseeing the production of one or more interchangeable outputs. In this world, any employer's innovation in production is immediately, and perfectly, copied by all the other employers. Competition among the employers drives profits down to the point where employers as a group do no better than they would in their next-best alternative occupation—which is to say, earning wages as employees in businesses run by others. At that point the employers are managers who inertly oversee the highly routinized operation of fundamentally unprofitable businesses.

6. Walker, 1887, p. 276.

7. Walker, 1887, p. 275. As Walker states directly, large profitable firms also may have distorted the competitive environment through political manipulation or coercion. They also may have access to basic inputs at lower prices than the unprofitable firms (for example, due to economies of scale), or to a lower-cost labor force, or to markets from which others are precluded. However, if firms derived their advantages uniquely, or even primarily, through such noncompetitive actions, we would expect to see an inverse correlation (or no correlation at all) between the extent of market dominance and customer satisfaction, as well as close to zero turnover at dominant firms. While a small number of market-dominant firms may be able to get away with consistently providing customers with poor service, most companies can't. Consequently, we can reasonably assume that a particularly successful employee—or, if you prefer, entrepreneur—is able to grow his/her firm initially, and potentially stay dominant after the firm has grown, simply because they are able to arrive at a combination of managerial actions that solves a difficult problem in a relatively effective manner.

8. This is the core thesis of Wilson, 2012.

9. Bessen, 2015, p. 3.

10. Harold Ickes served as U.S. Secretary of the Interior for 13 years, from 1933 to 1946.

11. Owing to parallel increases in operational scale and in the efficient use of inputs, the average assembly time per "Liberty Ship" was reduced from 186 days at the start of the U.S. war effort to as few as 19 days by the end.

12. Moore and Davis, 2001, p. 6.

13. Moore and Davis, 2001, pp. 4–5.

14. Moore provides two examples of the central role (imperfect) imitation of best practices plays in the process of new firm creation: first, the decision by the "traitorous eight"—the term Moore uses to refer to the eight engineers, including himself, who left Shockley Semiconductor to found Fairchild— to hire Ed Baldwin, an experienced manager from the leading incumbent firm, to guide the creation of Fairchild; and second, Baldwin's subsequent departure from Fairchild, along with a cadre of the firm's engineers, to

form a competing spinoff firm. Linking both examples to the concept of a (broadly conceived, firm-wide) production recipe, we can describe one core strategy of spinoff firms as the attempt to copy the production recipe of a successful incumbent firm. The extent to which such copying can be successful is constrained by a number factors, including but not limited to the underlying complexity of the production process, the strength and enforceability of trade secret laws, and the relative importance tacit knowledge plays in the production process. The complexity of production thus limits a new firm's ability to copy the practices of an incumbent firm.

In the terms favored by academic economists, tacit knowledge dominates, information asymmetries are the norm, and transactions costs are significant. Important early work by Mansfield, 1961, 1963, on the subject of technological change related to one firm's imitation of the production methods of another. This work advanced the studies by Griliches, 1957, on technological adoption. Where Griliches had used published data to study the adoption of essentially modular agricultural technologies, Mansfield, 1961, used questionnaires and interviews to study the adoption of new production techniques by large firms in four industries.

15. In a later section of the same narrative, Moore refers to a fundamental decision made early in Intel's history "to avoid [the] split between [R&D] and manufacturing. We'd be willing to accept less efficient manufacturing for a more efficient transfer process. We made the R&D people actually do their development work right in the production facility and we have continued that (with some variation) ever since" (Moore and Davis, 2001, p. 14). These statements together suggest that the conventional distinction between discontinuous technical change that occurs as the result of explicit investment (R&D) and incremental shop-floor learning by doing may, at least in this case, be exaggerated. This section is drawn from Auerswald, 2010.

16. Pioneering growth theorist Robert Solow, also a Nobel Laureate, delivered a sequence of lectures at Stanford University in 1996 in which he reflected on the insights for the field of economics of this body of work. "There appear to be two processes at work [in technological change]," he states. "The more obvious one is the occurrence of discrete innovations, some major, some minor, whose development changes the nature of the products or the production process in existing industries, or may even lead to the creation of new industries. The less obvious process is usually described as 'continuous improvement' of products and processes. It consists of an ongoing series of minor improvements in the design and manufacture of standard products" (Solow, 1996, p. 20). Solow's conclusion is that the second of these—continuous improvement, or learning by doing—is more important to economic progress in the long term than the first—the more celebrated processes of discrete, discontinuous technological change.

17. Bloom et al., 2013, p. 1.

18. Marshall continued: "Organization aids knowledge; it has many forms, e.g., that of a single business, that of various businesses in the same trade, that of various trades relatively to one another, and that of the State providing security for all and help for many. The distinction between public and private property in knowledge and organization is of great and growing importance: in some respects of more importance than that between public and private property in material things; and partly for that reason it seems best sometimes to reckon Organization apart as a distinct agent of production" (Marshall, 1910, book IV, chap. 1, para. 2.).
19. Goldfarb and Yang, 2009.
20. Drucker 1974, p. 1.
21. Jacob, 1977, p. 1163.
22. I am paraphrasing Bateson, 1979, p. 52.
23. Bateson, 1979.

Chapter 8
1. Wyman, 2014, p. 23.
2. Winter, 1968, p. 9.
3. Gleick, 2011, p. 299.
4. A third brother, Percy Wright, was a noted political scientist.
5. In comparison, single-point mutations scale linearly.
6. Wright, 1932, p. 356: "There is no reasonable chance that any two individuals have exactly the same genetic constitution in a species of millions of millions of individuals persisting over millions of generations. There is no difficulty accounting for the probable genetic uniqueness of each human being or other organism which is the production of bi-parental reproduction."
7. Wright, 1932, p. 359.
8. Wright, 1932, p. 360. Inbreeding also leads to greater risk of generically caused disease, as well as diminished resilience of the phenotype.
9. *Entrepreneur,* 2008.
10. Young, 2007.
11. Kroc continues:

> Art Bender, my first franchisee, says he's sometimes asked why he doesn't just start his own restaurant instead of paying a percentage of his gross to McDonald's. After all, he helped teach Ray Kroc the business; he could make it on his own easily.
> "I might have a successful restaurant," Art says, "but I'd have to think what it would cost me as an individual to buy the services I get from the corporation." Kroc, 1987, p. 178.

12. Kroc, 1987, p. 178.

13. The original quote from Wiener is as follows: "We are swimming upstream against a great torrent of disorganization, which tends to reduce everything to heat death of disequilibrium and sameness . . . This heat death in physics has a counterpart in the ethics of Kierkegaard, who pointed out that we live in a chaotic moral universe. In this, our main obligation is to establish arbitrary enclaves of order and system . . . Like the Red Queen, we cannot stay where we are without running as fast as we can" (Gleick, 2011, p. 32).
14. Schrödinger, 1944.
15. Schrödinger, 1944.
16. Watson, 1968.
17. Watson and Crick, 1953.
18. Watson and Crick shared the Nobel Prize with Maurice Hugh Frederick Wilkins. Rosalind Franklin merited being a joint recipient for her fundamental contributions to the discovery of the structure of DNA, but she had died by the time the Nobel Prize was awarded.
19. Specifically: the traveling salesman problem and spin glasses.
20. Jacob, 1977, p. 1163.
21. Jacob. 1977, p. 1164.
22. Jacob, 1977, p. 1163.
23. Kauffman and Levin, 1987, p. 29: "We considered Boolean model genetic networks with N binary genes, either active or inactive, each receiving K-2 regulatory inputs from 2 genes chosen at random among the N. We assigned at random to each gene one of the 16 possible Boolean functions specifying the activity of that gene as a function of the activities of its two input genes the moment before. For example, a gene might be active if either or both of its inputs were active before, hence the OR function, or active only if both were active, hence the AND function, etc. Such a network is a deterministic dynamical system, sampled at random from the ensemble of NK Boolean networks. With N genes, a network admits 2 N possible combinations of gene activities, each a state of the network. At each clocked instant, each gene assesses the activities of its inputs, and, according to its own Boolean function, assumes the proper next activity value; hence the network passes from a state to a unique successor state. There are a finite number of states, and hence eventually the network arrives at a state visited previously. Our simulations confirm the above theory of long jump adaptation."

Chapter 9

1. In other words, far-from-equilibrium thermodynamic systems. See Prigogine and Stengers, 1984.
2. Auerswald and Kim, 1995.
3. Porter, 1998, p. 86.
4. Kash and Rycroft, 1999.

5. In other words, the physical manifestations of complexity (e.g., the number of parts in a part and the intricacy of their assembly) are directly linked to the organizational requirements of production. Increasing technological complexity may also be understood as the extent to which new market innovations require the efforts of teams incorporating multiple distinct technological fields; the average size and/or diversity of teams involved in the creation of new technological innovations; or, from a human capital standpoint, as the average investment required by an individual in order to reach the technological frontier.

6. Remarks at the Santa Fe Institute, "Inside the Black Box" workshop, August 7, 2013.

7. Before their work on the structure of economic complexity, macroeconomists tended to be satisfied with one of two approaches to explaining highly uneven patterns of specialization among economies. The first of these focused on the magnitude of undifferentiated "capital" accumulation as the key determinant of observed patterns of specialization: we expect that workers paired with more capital will not only earn more than workers paired with less capital, but also that they will produce higher quality output. The second approach emphasized fundamental technological differences, but did so in a fairly linear manner; one commonly used approach represents technologies as rungs on a "quality ladder" that countries must climb in order to reach higher levels of development. These approaches at the level of the macroeconomy directly parallel default neoclassical approaches to patterns of specialization at the microeconomic level, the firm level.

8. Hidalgo and Hausmann, 2009, p. 10570.

9. Adam Smith also stated that "it is the maxim of every prudent master of a family, never to attempt to make at home what it will cost him more to make than to buy . . . What is prudence in the conduct of every private family, can scarce be folly in that of a great kingdom." This is a simpler version of the theory of comparative advantage later articulated by David Ricardo. Smith, 1776, book IV, chap. 2, paras. 11–12.

10. Hidalgo and Hausmann, 2009, p. 10570.

11. Bloom et al., 2007; Bloom and Van Reenen, 2010.

12. Remarks at the Santa Fe Institute, "Inside the the Black Box" workshop, August 7, 2013.

13. Quoted in Murphy and Yates, 2009, p. 7.

14. Note that standardization to enable the interoperability of recipes as subroutines is different from the standardization of firm-level recipes themselves. In the food service industry, standardized recipes and production processes have constituted the basis of the success of franchise-based firms like McDonald's and KFC. As I noted in the last chapter, such firms have contributed to evolution of the code economy. Baldwin and Clark, 2000.

15. Smith, 1776.
16. As an anonymous reviewer of this manuscript notes, Marx predicted that precisely this combination of complexity and interdependence would have the effect of leading the capitalist system to inevitable collapse. In the words of that reviewer, with which I concur, "Marx's failure to anticipate Code evolution is a bit parallel to Malthus's failure to anticipate the effects of birth control and technological advance in agriculture."
17. As Hezekiah Agwara, Brian Higginbotham, and I have argued, "In contrast with the traditional multinational assembly of subsidiaries, the global enterprise is a flexible assembly of firms around the world, with skills and capacity that can be drawn upon for the most efficient combination of business processes. The rapid globalization and economic integration witnessed in recent years has, in this manner, created the need for standardization of management systems, which are essentially the interface layer between production subroutines." Agwara, Auerswald, and Higginbotham, 2013, p. 394.

    As then-CEO of IBM Palmisano wrote in 2006:

    > Starting in the early 1970s, the revolution in information technology (IT) improved the quality and cut the cost of global communications and business operations by several orders of magnitude. Most important, it standardized technologies and business operations all over the world, interlinking and facilitating work both within and among companies. This combination of shared technologies and shared business standards, all built on top of a global IT and communications infrastructure, changed the sorts of globalization that companies found possible. (Palmisano, 2006, p. 130)

18. Whitehead, 1911, p. 61.
19. Smith, 1776, pp. 12–13.
20. Bush, 1945, p. 113.
21. Bush, 1945, 124.
22. Engelbart, 1962.
23. Licklider, 1960, p. 4.
24. Licklider, 1963.
25. Licklider, 1963.

Chapter 10

1. Bearaknov, 2014.
2. Miller, 1956, and Baddeley, 1992.
3. Moore, 2016.
4. Although there is strong consensus among historians that the term "Huguenots" was originally intended derisively, its precise origin is disputed.
5. A website hosted by the University of Maryland that is dedicated to the study of Romantic literature and culture offers this elaboration of the

inspiration behind the Frankenstein story: "During the 1816 summer, Byron and Shelley undertook a boat tour of the northern shore of Lake Geneva with the particular aim of visiting locations associated with Rousseau and his writings. Although Mary [Shelley] remained behind, she would have shared their enthusiasm for this last great figure of the French Enlightenment. It could not have been absent from her mind that to begin a first-person narrative account, 'I am by birth a Genevese' (1.1.1) would automatically remind readers of Rousseau's *Confessions*, the fourth paragraph of which begins in a similar manner. Rousseau's spirit, indeed, might be said to hover over the entire novel, from its emphasis on a new 'noble savage' to its concern with education, particularly in the formation of the Creature, to its antiestablishment political undertones." Fraistat and Jones, 2015.

6. Hartley, 1983.
7. Moore, 2016.
8. Auerswald, 2015a.
9. Organisation for Economic Co-operation and Development, 2010.
10. Reasons for this are described by Baumol and Bowen, 1966, and Spence, 2011.
11. Simon, 1960.
12. Simon, 1960, p. 35.
13. Simon, 1960, p. 23.
14. Simon, 1960, p. 24.
15. Autor, Levy, and Murnane, 2003. Gabe, Florida, and Mellander, 2012, observe along similar lines: "The economic crisis contributed to sharp increases in U.S. unemployment rates for all three of the major socio-economic classes. Results from regression models using individual-level data from the 2006–2011 U.S. Current Population Surveys indicate that members of the Creative Class had a lower probability of being unemployed over this period than individuals in the Service and Working Classes, and that the impact of having a creative occupation became more beneficial in the two years following the recession. These patterns, if they continue, are suggestive of a structural change occurring in the U.S. economy—one that favors knowledge-based creative activities."
16. Autor, 2014, p. 1.
17. Fox News, 2011, and *Economist,* 2011.
18. Bessen, 2013.
19. Bessen, 2013.
20. Frey and Osborne, 2013.

Chapter 11

1. Case and Deaton, 2015.
2. Goldin and Katz, 2008, p. 122: "Technology-skill complementarity emerged in manufacturing early in the twentieth century as particular technologies, known as batch and continuous-process methods of production, spread.

The switch to electricity from steam and water-power energy sources was reinforcing because it reduced the demand for unskilled manual work in many hauling, conveying, and assembly tasks."

3. Bessen, 2015, pp. 40–41: "Typically, new technologies demand that a large number of variables be properly controlled. Henry Bessemer's simple principle of refining molten iron with a blast of oxygen works properly only at the right temperatures, in the right size vessel, with the right sort of vessel refractory lining, the right volume and temperature of air, and the right ores. Even very old and simple technologies, such as machines for spinning yarn out of cotton fiber, require the control of a large number of parameters. Yarn can break as it is wound onto the spindle of a spinning machine." Furthermore, the products of these factories were really ones that, in the United States, previously had been created at home, not by craftsmen: "In the de-skilling narrative, technology allowed unskilled factory workers to replace skilled artisans. This narrative is a bit misleading for two reasons: first, the guild system and traditional artisan apprenticeships were in decline well before the advent of large-scale mechanization. Prior to mechanization, the artisan workshop had been substantially replaced by nonmechanized 'manufactories' where workers, many with little or no apprenticeship training, performed narrow tasks. Second, most early factories in the United States produced goods that had formerly been made at home, not in workshops. That is, the factory did not so much replace the artisan workshop as it replaced household work, at least for many decades" (pp. 23–24).

4. Bessen, 2015, p. 75. He elaborates: "A standard growth accounting using capital and labor as factors of production would attribute 43 percent of the growth to capital accumulation, based on a growth rate of output per worker of 3.72 percent, a growth rate of capital per worker of 2.89 percent, and capital share of output averaging 55 percent between the beginning and ending periods. This calculation is, however, based on some strong assumptions that don't apply, including one that technical change is neutral when it was actually labor saving. Given the importance of textiles to overall productivity growth during the Industrial Revolution, this finding suggests that standard multifactor productivity growth estimates understate the role of technology and overstate the role of capital accumulation" (p. 238).

5. Bessen, 2015, p. 75.

6. Bessen, 2015, p. 21.

7. Bessen, 2015, p. 18.

8. Bessen, 2015, pp. 41–42. Referring to the role of start-up firms in this process, he states: "Early-stage technologies—those with relatively little standardized knowledge—tend to be used at a smaller scale; activity is localized; personal training and direct knowledge sharing are important; and labor markets do not compensate workers for their new skills. Mature technologies—with greater standardized knowledge—operate at large

scale and globally, market permitting; formalized training and knowledge exchange are more common; and robust labor markets encourage workers to develop their own skills" (p. 68). The intensity of interactions that occur in cities is also important in this phase: "During the early stages, when formalized instruction is limited, person-to-person exchange is especially important for spreading knowledge" (p. 21).

9. Bessen, 2015, p. 3.
10. Bessen, 2015, p. 14.
11. Licklider, 1963: "There is an analogous problem, and probably a more difficult one, in the matter of language for the control of a network of computers. Consider the situation in which several different centers are netted together, each center being highly individualistic and having its own special language and its own special way of doing things. Is it not desirable, or even necessary for all the centers to agree upon some language or, at least, upon some conventions for asking such questions as 'What language do you speak?' At this extreme, the problem is essentially the one discussed by science fiction writers: 'how do you get communications started among totally uncorrelated "sapient" beings?'' But, I should not like to make an extreme assumption about the uncorrelatedness. (I am willing to make an extreme assumption about the sapience.) The more practical set of questions is: Is the network control language the same?"
12. Aeppel, 2015.
13. Shiller, 2015.
14. Chase, 2015, p. 249.
15. Hall and Krueger, 2015, provide what they describe as "the first comprehensive analysis of Uber's driver-partners, based on both survey data and anonymized, aggregated administrative data." They find that, "although it is difficult to compare the after-tax net hourly earnings of Uber's driver-partners and taxi drivers and chauffeurs taking account of all costs, it appears that Uber driver-partners earn at least as much as taxi drivers and chauffeurs, and in many cases more than taxi drivers and chauffeurs."
16. Dyson, 2012.
17. See also Shirky, 2010.

Chapter 12
1. Keynes, 1930.
2. To Gordon and those who share his perspective, nothing about present-day advances in code matches the power of the platform technologies that emerged at the end of the nineteenth century to enable urbanization in the United States: electrification, motorized transportation, and indoor plumbing. Gordon, 2012, states further: "The profound boost that [inventions between 1875 and 1900] gave to economic growth would be difficult to repeat . . . New inventions always introduce new modes of growth, and history provides many examples of doubters who questioned

future benefits. But I am not forecasting an end to innovation, just a decline in the usefulness of future inventions in comparison with the great inventions of the past" (Gordon, 2014). This argument is advanced in full in Gordon, 2016.

3. More broadly, even if we accept that growth in TFP is an accurate measure of the advance of the technological frontier, the anomaly to be explained in the data covering the past forty years isn't the current productivity "slowdown" but rather the interval of exceptionally rapid growth in productivity that took place from the mid-1990s to the mid-2000s, compared with which the current "slowdown" is directly defined. The most rigorous breakdowns of these data reveal that the much-discussed surge in TFP growth from 1996–2004 took place almost entirely in emerging areas of work relating to digital computing. What we may have seen in the past decade is a shift from modes of digitally enabled value creation that were predominantly priced and monetized to ones that are predominantly free. If so, the data as currently measured are capturing a shift in business models from closed to open—not a decrease in productivity. TFP thus remains a far better tool for measuring the gradual exit of twentieth-century modes of work than the arrival of those of the twenty-first century.

   As Harvard's Dale Jorgenson has demonstrated in work spanning fifty years, it is indeed possible to account for novelty in a measurement system based on changes in index numbers over time. With Jorgenson in the lead, economists have devoted considerable effort to better measuring capital and labor; the development of "constant quality" labor indices and hedonic (that is, characteristics-based) pricing for output goods have both improved TFP measures. However, TFP still systematically fails to capture new versus old, software versus hardware, and shared versus exchanged goods and services. Since the economy is increasingly dominated by new software to enable the sharing of goods and services, this is a problem.

4. As Joan Robinson demonstrated long ago, market-based competition is consistent with the existence over time of an entire array of localized monopolies; Robinson termed this state of affairs in the economy "monopolistic competition." To illustrate this point, consider the fact that the monopolies that feature most prominently in the game *Monopoly* are not the railroads, "Electric Company," or "Water Works"; they are simple landowners. The bit of game trivia reminds us that every piece of land constitutes monopoly of the provision of services in that precise place. This is why economists talk about land generating rents: land exists in an essentially fixed quantity. We can use physical (as opposed to virtual) land more or less efficiently, but we can't create more of it.

   As Jorgenson, 1995, states in the preface to the first volume of the compendium of his research on this topic: "The defining characteristic of productivity as a source of economic growth is that the incomes generated by higher productivity are external to the economic activities that generate growth" (p. xvii). In this way, productivity differs from "investment." Productivity gains do not occur as a consequence of firms consciously seeking to improve their own goods and services, in ways that they can capture in the marketplace. They occur, instead, as a positive byproduct of productive activity, known to economists as a positive "externality." Investments by monopolistically competitive companies in goods and services that they are uniquely well placed to sell do not fall into this category.

5. Amar Bhidé, remarks at Cato Institute conference on "The Future of U.S. Economic Growth, December 4, 2014. Accessible at http://www.cato.org/events/future-us-economic-growth.

6. George, 1879, Introduction, p. 3.

7. George, 1879, Introduction, pp. 5–6.

8. George, 1879, Introduction, p. 184.

9. George, 1879, Introduction, p. 218.

10. George, 1879, Introduction, p. 341.

11. Piketty, 2014, p. 96.

12. This leads to an obvious question, to which Piketty provides a clear and compelling answer: How did wealth inequality get so low in the 1950–1980s? On page 15 of *Capital in the Twenty-First Century*, Piketty states flatly, "The sharp reduction in income inequality that we observe in almost all the rich countries between 1914 and 1945 was due above all to the world wars and the violent economic and political shocks they entailed (especially for people with large fortunes)." He continues: "The two world wars, and the public policies that followed from them, played a central role in reducing inequalities in the twentieth century. There was nothing natural or spontaneous about this process" (p. 237). While mentioning public policy, he leaves out the 1918–1919 Spanish Flu epidemic (which, by plausible estimates, killed more Americans than World War I and World War II combined) and the Great Depression (which also had a considerable effect on accumulated wealth in the United States). As Piketty states, there was "nothing natural or spontaneous" about the process of getting to the 1950–1980s level of inequality in the United States—an era that he, for much of the book, holds up as the desirable point of reference for the economy going forward.

By Piketty's own analysis, then, the relatively egalitarian distribution of wealth and income that the United States enjoyed in the decades following World War II was directly attributable to the death of more than one hundred million people due to war, tyranny, or influenza and a global economic depression, which all occurred between 1915 and 1950—the interval during which the documented decline in inequality took place. "It is quite difficult to say where this trajectory would have led without the major economic and political shocks initiated by the war," Piketty states (p. 8). "With the aid of historical analysis and a little perspective, we can now see those shocks as the only forces since the Industrial Revolution powerful enough to reduce inequality." These events had the beneficial side effect of reducing inequality in the advanced industrialized countries for an interval of about 30 years. But since 1980, inequality has come back.

13. McCloskey, 2015, makes a related point pertaining to the omission of human capital from Piketty's analysis: "Piketty's definition of wealth does not include human capital, owned by the workers, which has grown in rich countries to be the main source of income, when it is combined with the immense accumulation since 1800 of capital in knowledge and social habits, owned by everyone with access to them. Once upon a time, Piketty's world without human capital was approximately our world, that of Ricardo and Marx, with workers owning only their hands and backs, and the bosses and landlords owning all the other means of production. But since 1848 the world has been transformed by what sits between the workers' ears. The only reason in the book to exclude human capital from capital appears to be to force the conclusion Piketty wants to achieve. One of the headings in Chapter 7 declares that 'capital [is] always more unequally distributed than labor.' No it isn't. If human capital is included—the ordinary factory worker's literacy, the nurse's educated skill, the professional manager's command of complex systems, the economist's understanding of supply responses—the workers themselves, in the correct accounting, own most of the nation's capital—and Piketty's drama falls to the ground."

14. Robinson, 1953, p. 81.

15. Solow, 1957, p. 314.

16. Solow, 1955, p. 101.

17. Samuelson, 1966, p. 579.

18. Hahn, 1972, p. 8.

19. Piketty, 2013.

20. Orszag, 2015.

21. Ondrejka, 2007.

22. Kalning, 2007.

23. Ondrejka, 2007.

24. Demmitt, 2015.

25. Ondrejka, 2007.

26. *The Economist*, 2014.

27. See http://www.economist.com/news/special-report/21593580-cheap-and-ubiquitous-building- blocks-digital-products-and-services-have-caused.

28. Ondrejka, 2007.

29. Lanier, 2013, p. 15: "Digital information is really just people in disguise."

30. Metcalfe's law states that the value of a telecommunications network is proportional to the square of the number of connected users of the system (n^2).

31. Whether you choose to enforce that right is another matter; you can only choose to open to others what is truly yours to begin with.

32. O'Reilly. Remarks at TechAtState, November 4, 2010.
33. Summary from the National Association of Wholesale Distributors, accessible at https://www.naw.org/govrelations/advisory.php?articleid=563.
34. Bollier and Clippinger, 2014.

Chapter 13

1. The interview with James Biscione is accessible at http://www.ibm.com/smarterplanet/us/en/cognitivecooking/truck.html and https://www.youtube.com/watch?v=R4ssoD_P0Vc.
2. The interview with Florian Pinel is accessible at http://www.ibm.com/smarterplanet/us/en/cognitivecooking/truck.html and https://www.youtube.com/watch?v=Vp9z9vEZ7_s.
3. The interview with Florian Pinel is accessible at http://www.ibm.com/smarterplanet/us/en/cognitivecooking/truck.html and https://www.youtube.com/watch?v=MNg5R6Hy_z8.
4. The interview with Steve Abrams is accessible at http://www.ibm.com/smarterplanet/us/en/cognitivecooking/truck.html and https://www.youtube.com/watch?v=DX0601vQDqw.
5. Dewey, 2015.
6. Luckerson, 2015.
7. Bollier and Clippinger, 2014.
8. Bollier and Clippinger, 2014.
9. The National Institute of Origins and Quality, better known by its former name, the Institut National des Appellations d'Origine, or National Institute of Names of Origin.
10. Bosveld, 2010.
11. Bosveld, 2010, recounts: "Further evidence of their seriousness emerged after Boyle's death in 1691. In life, Boyle had guarded his recipe for red earth as if it were the most precious thing in the world. But upon his death, his executor, the philosopher John Locke, also an alchemist, was more generous, sending Newton the recipe along with a sample that Boyle had made before his death. No one knows what Newton did with the red earth. [Lawrence] Principe [a chemist and historian of science at Johns Hopkins University] notes that Newton suffered a mental breakdown a year after Boyle's death and wonders if that episode might have been brought on by mercury poisoning. After all, the first steps in making red earth require repeatedly heating and cooling mercury. 'Shortly after he would have gotten copies of this recipe, he was distilling mercury,' Principe says."
12. Jevons, 1875.
13. Strauss, 2013.
14. Chase, 2015, p. 199.
15. As for the authentication and the verification of the algorithmically inspired poutine served at SXSW, in the absence of an e-delicious machine tuned to

the tastes of the Quebecois, the task was left to poutine enthusiast Nicolas Vanderveken. "It's really good," he mumbles between bites in an IBM-produced video documenting the exploits of the Watson Food Truck. "I love it."

Chapter 14

1. See http://burningman.org/culture/philosophical-center/10-principles/.
2. Doherty, 2006, p. 52.
3. The model for Harvey, 2014, is explicitly and deliberately biological: "The design of Black Rock City is guided above all by the principle of bilateral symmetry . . . Bilateral symmetry centers everything along the spine. That's universal, cross-cultural. There has to be something primal to that. And that's true of sacred architecture too—that it has this very powerful centering effect and tends to reach transcendentally above people . . . The human body is bilaterally symmetric, therefore so is The Man. The Man stands at the center of the open semi-circle that is Black Rock City. The bilateral symmetry of the City follows directly from The Man. The initial act that marks the creation of Black Rock City every year is not the cutting of the ribbon, but rather the planting of a spike. The planting of the spike and the definition of the radial axis splits the desert. Urban mitosis follows."
4. Writer Alfred Henry Lewis famously wrote in a March 1906 issue of *Cosmopolitan* magazine that "there are only nine meals between mankind and anarchy." For more recent quantitative assessment, see Mahanta, 2013.
5. Harvey, 2014.
6. Harvey, 2014.
7. The number 64 continues to be important in computer architecture. Marc Andreessen's first computer, the Commodore 64, had that name because it shipped with 64 kilobytes of memory. For the reasons described above, memory in a binary computer always expresses itself as a power of two.
8. Later 仁.
9. Jefferies, 1885, p. 349
10. Armer, 1965, p. I-239.
11. Armer, 1965, p. I-239.
12. Auerswald, 2012.
13. *The Economist,* 2013.
14. Csikszentmihalyi, 1990.
15. Brody, 1998.
16. McQuaid, 2014.
17. McQuaid, 2014.
18. Roberts, 2012.
19. Young, 2012; McArdle, 2014; and Kroft, Lange, and Notowidigdo, 2012.
20. Roberts, 2012.
21. Jacobs, 1969, pp. 86–87.
22. Jacobs, 1969, p. 88.

Conclusion

1. Higham et al., 2014.
2. Wilson, 2012.
3. Wilson, 2012.
4. Wilson, 2012.
5. Marshall, 1910.
6. Simon, 1965, p. 52.
7. Simon, 1965, p. 62. Hanson, 2016, offers a start toward imagining this reality.

REFERENCES

Acemoglu, Daron, and James Robinson (2012). *Why Nations Fail: The Origins of Power, Prosperity, and Poverty.* New York: Crown Business.

Acs, Z. J. (2013). *Why Philanthropy Matters: How the Wealthy Give, and What It Means for Our Economic Well-Being.* Princeton, NJ: Princeton University Press.

Aeppel, Timothy (2015). "Silicon Valley Doesn't Believe U.S. Productivity Is Down." *Wall Street Journal,* July 16. Accessible at http://www.wsj.com/articles/silicon-valley-doesnt- believe-u-s-productivity-is-down-1437100700.

Agwara, H., Auerswald, P., and Higginbotham, B. (2013). "Algorithms and the Changing Frontier." In *The Changing Frontier: Rethinking Science and Innovation Policy.* Chicago, IL: University of Chicago Press, pp. 371–410.

Andersson, Claes (2011). "Paleolithic Punctuations and Equilibria: Did Retention Rather Than Invention Limit Technological Evolution?" *Paleo Anthropology*: 243–259.

Andreessen, Marc (2011). "Why Software Is Eating the World." *The Wall Street Journal,* August 20. Accessible at http://www.wsj.com/articles/SB10001424053 111903480904576512250915629460.

Armer, Paul (1965). "Computer Aspects of Technological Change, Automation, and Economic Progress." Report prepared by the RAND Corporation for the National Commission on Technology, Automation, and Economic Progress.

Auerswald, Philip (2010). "Entry and Schumpeterian Profits: How Technological Complexity Affects Industry Evolution." *Journal of Evolutionary Economics,* 20(4): 553–582.

Auerswald, Philip (2014). "The Power of Connection: Peer-to-Peer Businesses." Testimony before the U.S. House of Representatives Committee on Small Business, January 15.

Auerswald, Philip E. (2015a). "A Doctor in the House." *The American Interest*, 10(6): 62–69.

Auerswald, Philip E. (2015b). "Enabling Entrepreneurial Ecosystems." In D. B. Audretsch, A. N. Link, and M. L. Walshok, *The Oxford Handbook of Local Competitiveness* (pp. 54–83). New York: Oxford University Press.

Auerswald, Philip, and Jan Tai Tsung Kim (1995). "Transitional Dynamics in a Model of Economic Geography." In L. Nadel and D. Stein, eds., *1993 Lectures in Complex Systems*. Santa Fe Institute Studies in the Sciences of Complexity, Lecture Volume VI, Addison-Wesley.

Auerswald, Philip E., Stuart Kauffman, Jose Lobo, and Karl Shell (2000). "The Production Recipes Approach to Modeling Technological Innovation: An Application to Learning by Doing." *Journal of Economic Dynamics and Control*, 24: 389–450.

Autor, David (2014). "Polanyi's Paradox and the Shape of Employment Growth," NBER Working Paper No. 20485, September.

Autor, David H., Frank Levy, & Richard J. Murnane (2003). "The Skill Content of Recent Technological Change: An Empirical Exploration." *The Quarterly Journal of Economics*, 118 (4): 1279–1333.

Baddeley, Alan (1992). "Working Memory." *Science*, New Series, 255(5044), January 31: 556–559.

Baldwin, Carliss, and Kim Clark (2000). *Design Rules: Volume 1*. Cambridge, MA: MIT Press.

Barton, John (1817). *Observations on the Circumstances Which May Affect the Labouring Classes*. London: Printed for John and Arthur Arch, Cornhill, by W. Mason, Chichester.

Bateson, Gregory (1979). *Mind and Nature: A Necessary Unity*. New York: Bantam Books.

Bauer, Josef, R. K. Englund, and M. Krebernick (1998). *Mesopotamien: Späturuk-Zeit und Frühdynastische Zeit*. Orbis Biblicus et Orientalis 160/1, Freiburg: Universitätsverlag and Göttingen: Vandenhoeck & Ruprecht.

Baumol, William, and William Bowen (1966). *Performing Arts, the Economic Dilemma: A Study of Problems Common to Theater, Opera, Music, and Dance*. New York: Twentieth Century Fund.

Bearaknov, Max (2014). "Master of Memory Credits Meditation for His Brainy Feats." *New York Times*, November 18, p. A4.

Beeley, Philip (2003). "Leibniz on the Limits of Human Knowledge, with a Critical Edition of 'Sur la calculabilité du nombre de toutes les connaissances possibles.'" *The Leibniz Review*, Volume 13 (December): 83–91.

Bessen, James (2013). "Don't Blame Technology for Persistent Unemployment," Slate.com, September 30. Accessible at http://www.slate.com/blogs/future_tense/2013/09/30/ technology_isn_t_taking_all_of_our_jobs.html.

Bessen, James (2015). *Learning by Doing: The Real Connection between Innovation, Wages, and Wealth*. New Haven, CT: Yale University Press.

Bloom, Nicholas, and John Van Reenen (2010). "Why Do Management Practices Differ across Firms and Countries?" *Journal of Economic Perspectives*, 24(1): 203–204

Bloom, Nicholas, Benn Eifert, Aprajit Mahajan, David McKenzie, and John Roberts (2013). "Does Management Matter? Evidence from India." *The Quarterly Journal of Economics*, 128(1): 1–51.

Bollier, David, and John Clippinger, eds. (2014). *From Bitcoin to Burning Man and Beyond: The Quest for Identity and Autonomy in a Digital Society.* Cambridge, MA: ID3 in cooperation with Off the Common Books.

Bosveld, Jane (2010). "Isaac Newton, World's Most Famous Alchemist." *Discover Magazine.* July/August. http://discovermagazine.com/2010/jul-aug/05-isaac-newton-worlds-most-famous-alchemist.

Bradsherjan, Keith (2013). "Chinese Graduates Say No Thanks to Factory Jobs." *New York Times,* January 24. Accessible at http://www.nytimes.com/2013/01/25/business/as-graduates-rise-in-china-office-jobs-fail-to-keep-up.html.

Brandes Gratz, Roberta (2011). "Jane Jacobs and the Power of Women Planners." *The Atlantic:* CityLab, November 16.

Brody, Jane E. (1998). "Adding Cumin to the Curry: A Matter of Life and Death." *New York Times,* March 3. Accessible at http://www.nytimes.com/1998/03/03/science/adding-cumin-to-the-curry-a-matter-of-life-and-death.html.

Brynjolfsson, Erik, and Andrew McAfee (2014). *The Second Machine Age: Work, Progress, and Prosperity in a Time of Brilliant Technologies.* New York: W. W. Norton & Company.

Burroughs Corporation (1910), *A Better Day's Work at a Less Cost of Time, Work, and Worry to the Man at the Desk.* Detroit, MI: Burroughs Adding Machine Company.

Bush, Vannevar. (1945). "As We May Think." *The Atlantic,* pp. 112–124. Retrieved from http://www.theatlantic.com/magazine/archive/1945/07/as-we-may-think/303881/.

Byron, George Noël Gordon [Lord Byron] (1831). *The Complete Works of Lord Byron including His Lordship's Suppressed Poems with Others Never before Published*, Volume 1. Paris: Galignani.

Case, Anne, and Angus Deaton (2015). "Rising Morbidity and Mortality in Midlife among White non-Hispanic Americans in the 21st Century." *Proceedings of the National Academy of Sciences*, 112(49), December 8: 15078–15083.

Charney, Jule G. (1955). "Numerical Methods in Dynamical Meteorology." *Proceedings of the National Academy of Sciences*, 41(11): 798–802.

Chase, Robin (2015). *Peers Inc: How People and Platforms Are Inventing the Collaborative Economy and Reinventing Capitalism.* New York: PublicAffairs.

Child, Julia and Alex Prud'homme (2006). *My Life in France.* New York: Alfred A. Knopf.

Chisholm, J. (2015). *Unleash Your Inner Company: Use Passion and Perseverance to Build Your Ideal Business.* Austin, TX: Greenleaf Book Group Press.

Cowen, Tyler (2013). *Average Is Over: Powering America Beyond the Age of the Great Stagnation.* New York: Dutton.

Csikszentmihalyi, Mihaly (1990). *Flow: The Psychology of Optimal Experience.* New York: Harper & Row.

Demmitt, Jacob (2015). "Third Life? Second Life Founder Holds Out Hope for a VR Revival." GeekWire.com, October 28. http://www.geekwire.com/2015/third-life- second-life-founder-holds-out-hope-for-a-virtual-reality-revival/.

Dewey, Caitlin (2015). "Meet Chef Watson, IBM's Futuristic Foodie Robot." *The Washington Post*, May 12. https://www.washingtonpost.com/lifestyle/food/could-ibms-watson-eventually- replace-creative-chefs-not-at-this-rate/2015/05/11/82a0a3ca-f29f-11e4-b2f3-af5479e6bbdd_story.html.

Doherty, Brian (2006). *This Is Burning Man: The Rise of a New American Underground.* Dallas, TX: BenBella Books.

Douglas, Paul H. (1926). "The Movement of Real Wages and Its Economic Significance." *The American Economic Review*, 16(1), March, Supplement—Papers and Proceedings of the Thirty-eighth Annual Meeting of the American Economic Association: 17–53.

Dyson, Esther (2012). *The Rise of the Attention Economy.* Prague: Project Syndicate.

Dyson, George (2012). *Turing's Cathedral: The Origins of the Digital Universe.* New York: Pantheon.

The Economist (2011). "Are ATMs Stealing Jobs?" June 15. Accessible at http://www.economist .com/blogs/democracyinamerica/2011/06/technology-and-unemployment.

The Economist (2013). "Not Always with Us," June 1. Accessible at http://www.economist.com/news/briefing/21578643-world-has-astonishing-chance-take-billion-people-out-extreme-poverty-2030-not.

The Economist (2014). "A Cambrian Moment," January 16. Accessible at http://www.economist .com/news/special-report/21593580-cheap-and-ubiquitous-building-blocks-digital-products-and-services-have-caused.

Engelbart, Douglas C. (1962). *Augmenting Human Intellect.* Washington, DC: Air Force Office of Scientific Research, Summary Report AFOSR-3233 (October).

Entrepreneur Magazine (2008). "Ray Kroc: Burger Baron." *Entrepreneur,* October 9. Accessible at http://www.entrepreneur.com/article/197544.

Essinger, James (2004). *Jacquard's Web: How a Hand-loom Led to the Birth of the Information Age.* Oxford and New York: Oxford University Press.

Fox News (2011). "Obama Blames ATMs for High Unemployment." June 14. Accessible at http://nation.foxnews.com/president-obama/2011/06/14/obama-blames-atms-high-unemployment.

Fraistat, Neil, and Steven E. Jones (2015). "Notes: Geneva." In Neil Fraistat and Steven E. Jones, eds., *Romantic Libraries.* Romantic Circles. Accessible at https://www.rc.umd.edu/editions/frankenstein/V1notes/geneva.

Frey, Carl Benedikt, and Michael A. Osborne (2013). "The Future of Employment: How Susceptible Are Jobs to Computerisation?" Unpublished manuscript, Oxford Martin School.

Gabe, Todd, Richard Florida, and Charlotta Mellander (2012). "The Creative Class and the Crisis." Martin Prosperity Research Working Paper Series.

George, Henry (1879). *Progress and Poverty: An Inquiry into the Cause of Industrial Depressions and of Increase of Want with Increase of Wealth: The Remedy*. Garden City, NY: Doubleday, Page & Co.

George, Henry (1898). *The Science of Political Economy*. New York: Doubleday & McClure, Co.

George, Henry, Jr. (1904) *The Life of Henry George: First and Second Periods*. Garden City, NY: Doubleday Page & Co.

Glaeser, Edward L. (2011). *Triumph of the City: How Our Greatest Invention Makes Us Richer, Smarter, Greener, Healthier, and Happier*. New York: Penguin Press.

Gleick, James (2011). *The Information: A History, a Theory, a Flood*. New York: Random House.

Goldfarb, Avi, and Botao Yang (2009). "Are All Managers Created Equal?" *Journal of Marketing Research*, 46(5): 612–22.

Goldin, Claudia, and Lawrence F. Katz (2008). *The Race between Education and Technology*. Cambridge, MA: Belknap Press.

Gordon, Robert J. (2016). *The Rise and Fall of American Growth: The U.S. Standard of Living since the Civil War*. Princeton, NJ: Princeton University Press.

Grattan-Guinness, I. (1990). "Work for the Hairdressers: The Production of de Prony's Logarithmic and Trigonometric Tables." *Annals of the History of Computing*, 12(3): 177–85.

Griliches, Z. (1957). "Hybrid Corn: An Exploration in the Economics of Technological Change." *Econometrica*, 25(4): 501–22.

Hahn, Frank H. (1972). *The Share of Wages in the National Income*. London: Weidenfeld and Nicolson.

Hall, Jonathan, and Alan Krueger (2015). "An Analysis of the Labor Market for Uber's Driver-Partners in the United States." Unpublished manuscript.

Halloran, John (2006). *Sumerian Lexicon: A Dictionary Guide to the Ancient Sumerian Language*. Los Angeles: Logogram Publishing. Accessible at http://www.sumerian.org/sumerlex.htm.

Hanson, Robin (2016). *The Age of Em: Work, Love and Life when Robots Rule the Earth*. Oxford, UK and New York: Oxford University Press.

Hartley, John (1983). "Robots Start to Assemble Watches." *Assembly Automation*, 3(3): 169–70.

Harvey, Larry (2014). "Why The Man Keeps Burning." Talk at the Long Now Foundation, October 20. Accessible at http://longnow.org/seminars/02014/oct/20/why-man-keeps-burning/.

Hidalgo, César A., B. Klinger, A. Barabasi, and R. Hausman (2007). "The Product Space Conditions and the Development of Nations." *Science*, 317: 482–487.

Hidalgo, César A., and Ricardo Hausmann (2009). "The Building Blocks of Economic Complexity." *PNAS*, 106(26): 10,570–10,575.

Higham, Tom, Katerina Douka, Rachel Wood, Christopher Bronk Ramsey, and Fiona Brock, et al. (2014). "The Timing and Spatiotemporal Patterning of Neanderthal Disappearance." *Nature*, 512: 306–309.

Hine, Harry (2005). "Reviewed Work: *Ancient Meteorology* by Liba Taub." *Classical Philology*, 100(1): 83–88.

Hoffmann, Leah (2011). "Q&A: A Lifelong Learner: Leslie Valiant Discusses Machine Learning, Parallel Computing, and Computational Neuroscience." *Communications of the ACM*, 54 (6), June; pp. 128ff.

Hofstadter, Richard (1955). *Social Darwinism in American Thought, 1860–1915*. Boston: Beacon Press.

Jacob, François (1977). "Evolution and Tinkering." *Science*, New Series, 196(4295), June 10; pp. 1161–1166.

Jacobs, Jane (1969). *The Economy of Cities*. New York: Random House.

Jefferies, Richard (1885 [1990]). "The Absence of Design in Nature." In *The Norton Book of Nature Writing*, Robert Finch and John Elder, eds., New York: W. W. Norton & Company, pp. 338–49.

Jevons, William Stanley (1875). *Money and the Mechanism of Exchange*. New York: D. Appleton and Co.

Jorgenson (1995). *Productivity: Postwar U.S. Economic Growth, Volume 1*. Cambridge, MA: MIT Press.

Kahneman, Daniel (2011). *Thinking, Fast and Slow*. New York: Farrar, Straus & Giroux.

Kalning, Kristin (2007). "If Second Life Isn't a Game, What Is It?" NBCNews. com. Accessible at http://www.nbcnews.com/id/17538999/ns/technology_and_science-games/t/if-second-life-isnt-game-what-it/#.Vu8zmoRhiE6.

Kash, Don E., and Robert Rycroft (1999). *The Complexity Challenge: Technological Innovation for the 21st Century*. London: Thomson Learning.

Katz, Lawrence F., and Robert A. Margo (2013). "Technical Change and the Relative Demand for Skilled Labor: The United States in Historical Perspective." NBER Working Paper No. 18752, February.

Kauffman, Stuart (1993). *Origins of Order: Self-Organization and Selection in Evolution*. New York and Oxford, UK: Oxford University Press.

Kauffman, Stuart, and Simon Levin (1987). "Toward a General Theory of Adaptive Walks on Rugged Landscapes." *Journal of Theoretical Biology*, 128: 11–45.

Kelly, Kevin (2015). "Call Them Artificial Aliens." TheEdge.org. Accessible at https://www.edge.org/response-detail/26097.

King, John E. (2013). *David Ricardo*. London: Palgrave Macmillan UK.

Kleiber, Max (1932). "Body Size and Metabolism." *Hilgardia*, 6: 315–51.

Kroc, Ray (1987). *Grinding It Out*. New York: St. Martin's Paperbacks.

Kroft, Kory, Fabian Lange, and Matthew J. Notowidigdo (2012). "Duration Dependence and Labor Market Conditions: Theory and Evidence from a

Field Experiment." National Bureau of Economic Research (NBER) Working Paper No. 18387, September.

Kurzweil, Ray (2006). *The Singularity Is Near: When Humans Transcend Biology.* New York: The Viking Press.

Lamb, C. L., and E. Smallpage (1935). *The Story of Liverpool.* Liverpool, U.K.: Daily Post Printers.

Lanier, Jaron (2013). "Who Owns the Future?" New York: Simon & Schuster.

Levitt, Steven (2015). "Thinking Differently about Big Data." Remarks delivered at the National Academy of Sciences, Sackler Colloquium, "Drawing Causal Inference from Big Data," Washington, D.C., March 26. Accessible at https://www.youtube.com/watch?v=r5jATFtKtI8.

Licklider, J. C. R. (1960). "Man-Computer Symbiosis." *IRE Transactions on Human Factors in Electronics,* October; pp. 4–10.

Licklider, J. C. R. (1963). "For Members and Affiliates of the Intergalactic Computer Network." Unpublished memorandum, Advanced Research Projects Agency, April 23. Accessible at http://www.dod.mil/pubs/foi/Reading_Room/DARPA/977.pdf.

Luckerson, Victor (2015). "Netflix Accounts for More Than a Third of All Internet Traffic." Time.com, May 29. http://time.com/3901378/netflix-internet-traffic/.

Lynch, Peter (2008). "The Origins of Computer Weather Prediction and Climate Modeling." *Journal of Computational Physics,* 227: 3431–3444.

Marshall, Alfred (1910). *Principles of Economics.* London: Macmillan.

Mansfield, E. (1961). "Technical Change and the Rate of Imitation." *Econometrica,* 29: 741–766.

Mansfield, Edwin (1963). "The Speed of Response of Firms to New Techniques." *The Quarterly Journal of Economics,* 77 (2): 290–311.

McArdle, Megan (2014). "Unemployment: A Fate Worse Than Death." Time.com, February 19. Accessible at http://time.com/9009/unemployment-is-worse-than-death/.

McClain, Dylan Loeb (2013). "A Master Is Disqualified over Suspicions of Cheating." *New York Times,* August 17.

McCloskey, Deirdre N. (2015). "How Piketty Misses the Point." *Cato Policy Report,* July/August. Accessible at http://www.cato.org/policy-report/julyaugust-2015/how-piketty-misses-point.

McQuaid, John (2014). "Why We Love the Pain of Spicy Food." *Wall Street Journal,* December 31. http://www.wsj.com/articles/why-we-love-the-pain-of-spicy-food-1420053009.

Melvin, Harold (1922). "The Standard Reference Work, for the Home, School, and Library, Volume 4." Minneapolis, MN: Standard Education Society.

Mahanta, Siddhartha (2013). "New York's Looming Food Disaster: Hurricane Sandy Exposed Striking Vulnerabilities in the City's Supply Chains." TheAtlantic.com, October 21. http://www.citylab.com/politics/2013/10/new-yorks-looming-food-disaster/7294/.

Miller, George A. (1956). "The Magical Number Seven, Plus or Minus Two: Some Limits on Our Capacity for Processing Information." *Psychological Review*, 63: 81–97.

Monod, Jacques (1972). *Chance and Necessity: An Essay on the Natural Philosophy of Modern Biology*. New York: Vintage Books.

Moore, Geoffrey (2016). "Developing Middle Class Jobs in the Digital Economy." In David Nordfors, Vint Cerf, and Max Senges (eds.), *Disrupting Unemployment: Reflection on a Sustainable, Middle Class Economic Recovery.* Kansas City, MO: The Ewing Marion Kauffman Foundation.

Moore, Gordon, and K. Davis (2001). "Learning the Silicon Valley Way." Working Paper 00-45, Stanford Institute for Economic Policy Research.

Moore, Gordon E. (1965). "Cramming More Components onto Integrated Circuits." *Electronics*, April 19, pp. 114–117, April 19.

Murphy, Craig N., and Joanne Yates (2009). *The International Organization for Standardization (ISO): Global Governance through Voluntary Consensus.* London; New York: Routledge.

Nicholas, Stephen, and Richard H. Steckel (1991). "Heights and Living Standards of English Workers during the Early Years of Industrialization, 1770–1815." *The Journal of Economic History*, 51 (4): 937–57.

Ondrejka, Cory (2007). "Collapsing Geography: *Second Life*, Innovation, and the Future of National Power." *Innovations: Technology, Governance, Globalization*, 2(3): 27–54.

Organisation for Economic Co-operation and Development (2010). "OECD Health Data." Paris: OECD Health Statistics.

Orszag, Peter R. (2015). "To Fight Inequality, Tax Land." *BloombergView*, March 3. Accessible at https://www.bloomberg.com/view/articles/2015-03-03/to-fight-inequality-tax-land.

Palmisano, Samuel J. (2006). "The Globally Integrated Enterprise." *Foreign Affairs*, 85(3): 127–36.

Peart, Sandra (1996). *The Economics of W. S. Jevons*. London: Routledge.

Petty, William (1676 [1690]). *Political Arithmetick*. London. Accessible at http://oll.libertyfund.org/titles/petty-the-economic-writings-of-sir-william-petty-vol-1.

Piketty, Thomas (2014). *Capital in the Twenty-First Century*. Cambridge, MA: Harvard University Press.

Platzman, G. W. (1979). "The ENIAC Computations of 1950: Gateway to Numerical Weather Prediction." *Bulletin of the American Meteorological Society*, 60(4): 302–12.

Porter, Michael (1998). "Clusters and the New Economics of Competition." *Harvard Business Review*, 76(6): 77–90.

Read, Dwight W., and Sander E. van der Leeuw (2008). "Biology Is Only Part of the Story . . . " *Philosophical Transactions of the Royal Society B* 363: 1959–1968.

Read, Dwight W., and Sander E. van der Leeuw (2015). "The Extension of Social Relations in Time and Space during the Palaeolithic and Beyond." In Fiona

Coward et al., eds., *Settlement, Society and Cognition in Human Evolution*. New York: Cambridge University Press, pp. 31–53.

Ricardo, David (1821). *On the Principles of Political Economy and Taxation*, 3rd edition. London: John Murray.

Richardson, Lewis F. (1922). *Weather Prediction by Numerical Process*. Cambridge, UK: Cambridge University Press.

Rietveld, James D. (2012). *London in Flames: Apocalypse 1666*. Dallas: Highland Loch Press, Kindle Edition.

Rifkin, Jeremy (1995). *The End of Work: The Decline of the Global Labor Force and the Dawn of the Post-Market Era*. New York: G. P. Putnam's Sons.

Roberts, Russ (2012). "Taleb on Antifragility." EconTalk Episode with Nassim Nicholas Taleb, January 16. Accessible at http://www.econtalk.org/archives/2012/01/taleb_on_antifr.html.

Rodgers, Daniel (1974). *The Work Ethic in Industrial America, 1850–1920*, Chicago, IL: University of Chicago Press.

Romer, Paul M. (1986). "Increasing Returns and Long-run Growth." *Journal of Political Economy*, 94(5): 1002–37.

Romer, Paul M. (1990). "Endogenous Technological Change." *Journal of Political Economy*, 98(5): S71–S102.

Rothkopf, David (2015). "Requiem for the Macrosaurus: The Beginning of the End of the Jurassic Period of Economics." *Foreign Policy*, July 27. Accessible at http://foreignpolicy.com/2015/07/27/requiem-for-the-macrosaurus-economics-big-data/.

Saez, Emmanuel, and Gabriel Zucman (2014). "Wealth Inequality in the United States since 1913: Evidence from Capitalized Income Tax Data." CEPR Discussion Paper 10227, October.

Samuelson, Paul A. (1966). "A Summing Up." *Quarterly Journal of Economics* 80(4): 568–83.

Saval, Nikil (2014). *Cubed: A Secret History of the Workplace*. New York: Doubleday.

Schawbel, Dan (2011). "Gallup's Jim Clifton on the Coming Jobs War." Forbes. com, October 26. Accessed at http://www.forbes.com/sites/danschawbel/2011/10/26/gallups-jim-clifton-on-the-coming-jobs-war/#1032216e599c.

Schrödinger, Erwin (1944). *What Is Life?* Cambridge, MA: Cambridge University Press.

Schumpeter, Joseph A. (1912). *Theorie der wirtschaftlichen Entwicklung*. Leipzig: Duncker & Humblot. Revised English translation (1934) by Redvers Opie, *The Theory of Economic Development*, Oxford: Oxford University Press.

Schumpeter, Joseph A. (1954). *History of Economic Analysis*. London, UK: Allen & Unwin (Publishers) Ltd.

Scraffa, Piero (1951). *The Works and Correspondence of David Ricardo: Vol. 10, Biographical Miscellany*. Cambridge, UK: Cambridge University Press.

Sen, Amartya (1985). *Commodities and Capabilities*. New York: North-Holland.

Sen, Amartya (1999). *Development as Freedom*. Oxford, UK: Oxford University Press.

Shiller, Robert J. (2015). "What to Learn in College to Stay One Step Ahead of Computers." *New York Times,* May 22.

Shirky, Clay (2010). *Cognitive Surplus: How Technology Makes Consumers into Collaborators.* New York: Penguin Books.

Simon, Herbert (1960). "The Corporation: Will It Be Managed by Machines?" In *Management and the Corporations* (M. L. Anshen and G. L. Bach eds.). New York: McGraw Hill: 17–55.

Simon, Herbert A. (1965). *The Shape of Automation for Men and Management.* New York: Harper & Row.

Simon, Herbert A. (1967). "Programs as Factors of Production." *Proceedings of the Nineteenth Annual Winter Meeting Industrial Relations Research Association, San Francisco.*

Simon, Herbert A. (1991). *Models of My Life.* New York: Basic Books.

Simon, Herbert A., and Allen Newell (1958). "Heuristic Problem Solving: The Next Advance in Operations Research." *Operations Research,* 6(1): 1–10.

Simon, Herbert A., A. J. Smith, and C. B. Thompson (1950). "Modern Organization Theories." *Advanced Management,* 15(10): 2–4.

Smith, Adam (1776 [1904]). *An Inquiry into the Nature and Causes of the Wealth of Nations.* London: Methuen & Co., Ltd. Accessible at http://www.econlib. org/library/Smith/smWN.html.

Solow, Robert M. (1955–1956). "The Production Function and the Theory of Capital." *Review of Economic Studies,* 23: 101–108.

Solow, Robert M. (1997). *Learning from 'Learning by Doing': Lessons for Economic Growth.* Palo Alto, CA: Stanford University Press.

Spence, Michael (2011). "Globalization and Unemployment: The Downside of Integrating Markets." *Foreign Affairs,* July/August.

Stanford, Harold Melvin (1912). *The Standard Reference Work, for the Home, School, and Library, Volume 4.* Minneapolis, MN, and Chicago, IL: The Standard Education Society.

Steinkeller, Piotr (2002). "Money-Lending Practices in Ur III Babylonia: The Issue of Economic Motivation." In Michael Hudson (ed.), *Debt and Economic Renewal in the Ancient Near East,* Bethesda, MD: CDL Press / Capital Decisions Limited, 2002; pp. 109–37.

Steinkeller, Piotr, and J. N. Postgate (1992). *Third-Millennium Legal and Administrative Texts in the Iraq Museum, Baghdad.* Winona Lake, IN: Eisenbraums.

Strauss, Steven (2013). "'Welcome' to the Sharing Economy—Also Known as the Collapse of the American Dream." *The Huffington Post,* December 29.

Summers, Lawrence H. (2014). "Lawrence H. Summers on the Economic Challenge of the Future: Jobs." *Wall Street Journal,* July 7. Accessible at http:// www.wsj.com/articles/lawrence-h-summers-on-the-economic-challenge-of-the-future-jobs-1404762501.

Tabarrok, Alex (2003). "Productivity and Unemployment." MarginalRevolution. com. Accessible at http://marginalrevolution.com/marginalrevolution/2003/12/productivity_an.html.

Taub, Liba (2003). *Ancient Meteorology*. London and New York: Routledge.

Taylor, Frederick W. (1911). *Principles of Scientific Management*. New York and London: Harper & Brothers.

Turing, Alan (1939). *Systems of Logic Based on Ordinals*. Dissertation presented to the faculty of Princeton University in candidacy for the degree of Doctor of Philosophy.

Turing, Alan (October 1950). "Computing Machinery and Intelligence." *Mind*, 59(236): 433–60.

Viscato, Giuseppe (2000). *The Power and the Writing: The Early Scribes of Mesopotamia*. Bethesda, MD: CDLPress.

Walker, Francis A. (1887). "The Source of Business Profits." *The Quarterly Journal of Economics*, 1(3): 265–88.

Wilson, Edward O. (2012). *The Social Conquest of Earth*. New York: Liveright.

Whitehead, Alfred North (1911). *An Introduction to Mathematics*. New York: Henry Holt and Company.

Wrangham, Richard (2009). *Catching Fire: How Cooking Made Us Human*. New York: Basic Books.

Winter, Sidney G. (1968). "Toward a Neo-Schumpeterian Theory of the Firm." RAND Working Paper P-3802, RAND.

Wright, Sewell (1932). "The Roles of Mutation, Inbreeding, Crossbreeding and Selection in Evolution." *Proceedings of the Sixth International Congress of Genetics*, 1: 356–66.

Wright, T. P. (1936). "Factors Affecting the Cost of Airplanes." *Journal of the Aeronautical Sciences*, 2: 122–128.

Young, Cristobal (2012). "Losing a Job: The Nonpecuniary Cost of Unemployment in the United States". *Social Forces* 91(2): 609–34.

Young, Nancy K. (2007). *The Great Depression in America*. Westport, CT: Greenwood Publishing Group.

Zink, Katherine D., and Daniel E. Lieberman (2016). "Impact of Meat and Lower Palaeolithic Food Processing Techniques on Chewing in Humans." *Nature*, advance online publication, March 9.

INDEX